Engaged Surrender

THE GEORGE GUND FOUNDATION
IMPRINT IN AFRICAN AMERICAN STUDIES

The George Gund Foundation has endowed
this imprint to advance understanding of
the history, culture, and current issues
of African Americans.

Engaged Surrender

African American Women and Islam

Carolyn Moxley Rouse

UNIVERSITY OF CALIFORNIA PRESS

Berkeley   Los Angeles   London

University of California Press
Berkeley and Los Angeles, California

University of California Press, Ltd.
London, England

© 2004 by the Regents of the University of California

Library of Congress Cataloging-in-Publication Data

Rouse, Carolyn Moxley, 1965–.
    Engaged surrender : African American women and Islam /
Carolyn Moxley Rouse.
        p.   cm.
    Includes bibliographical references and index.
    ISBN 0–520–23794–3 (alk. paper).—
ISBN 0–520–23795–1 (pbk. : alk. paper)
    1. Women in Islam.   2. Muslim women—Social condi-
tions.   3. Muslim women—United States—Social conditions.   4. African American women—Religion.   I. Title.
BP173.4 .R68   2004
305.48'6971073—dc21   2003002462

Manufactured in the United States of America
13   12   11   10   09   08   07   06   05   04
10   9   8   7   6   5   4   3   2   1

For Zora and Yahya

CONTENTS

PREFACE

Almost six months to the day after a group of terrorists attacked the United States by flying planes into the World Trade Center and the Pentagon, I was asked to speak about Islam at a state agency. It had created a "diversity" team responsible for finding creative ways of educating the staff about multicultural issues. The person who invited me had seen me speak about Islam on a local public television show, and in a moment of insanity, I said yes. My television interview had been hard enough, why would I subject myself to the same forms of interrogation? How could I be an "expert" about things I really know nothing about, such as how Americans feel about this tragedy. My expectation was that six months after 9/11 Americans had become more sophisticated about Islam. The explosion of information produced and disseminated was rich, and for a moment the popular press focused on the diversity within the Muslim *ummah* (community). Notably, the press tried to show that Islam does not support violence against civilians, and that at least 99.99 percent of all Muslims want peace.

Accepting the opportunity to talk I thought, naively, that this audience would be interested in learning about a particular group of African American Sunni Muslims. I was hoping this talk would extend further the discussions already extant in the media on the diversity in the Muslim *ummah*. A good month and a half before the event I was given four questions, which I mistakenly did not read until two weeks before my talk. The questions were: "What is Islam, and what are its main teachings? What is the diversity within Islam as far as how Islam is practiced? What is the status of women in each type of Islam? What does Islam teach about violence?" Panic! I am neither an Islamic scholar nor an historian, and from my perspective the first three questions were created to camouflage the fact that what the audience really wanted to know is why Muslims are dangerous and violent people. The fourth simply begs the question that Islam teaches violence at all!

I spent two weeks trying to find the right angle for addressing the questions. I reread all my generalist books by Akbar Ahmed, John Esposito, and Suzanne Haneef. I woke up at three in the morning hoping to find a spark of genius during the stillness of the morning, but after four hours at the typewriter I had written one page that basically read,

> Islam means submission and peace, and Qur'an means the reading or recitation. Islam is monotheistic, and Muslims, like Christians and Jews, believe that they are the Children of Abraham. Muslims believe that 124,000 prophets appeared in every nation before Muhammad: Job, Jacob, David, Moses, etc. . . . Muslims believe not only in the biblical prophets, but in the nonbiblical prophets as well including Luqman from Ethiopia and Hud and Salih in Arabia. Many Muslims I know also include Buddha. Like the other Semitic religions, Islam encourages ethical behavior and *taqwa* (God consciousness) in everyday acts and social interactions. Primary acts of worship are denoted as the pillars of the faith and they include; *shahada* (witness of faith), *salat* (prayer five times a day), *sawm* (fasting), *zakat* (charity), and *hajj* (pilgrimage). About 90 percent of Muslims worldwide are Sunni and 10 percent are Shia. Current estimates on the number of Muslims in the United States range from 1.1 million to six million. African Americans make up about 40 percent of the Muslim population in the United States (Gustav Niebuhr, "Studies Suggest Lower Count for Number of U.S. Muslims," New York Times, October 25, 2001).

While Shia Muslims—primarily in Iran, southern Iraq, and parts of South Asia—follow a religiopolitical leader like an Imam or an Ayatollah, Sunni Muslims interpret their faith for themselves. There are no religious figureheads or divinely inspired teachers. In other words, there are no intermediaries between the believer and Allah. An imam is simply an Islamic scholar well versed in the Qur'an, *tafsir*, or exegesis, Islamic history, Islamic jurisprudence, and the sunnah of the Prophet. Notably, all Sunni Muslims are implored to read the Qur'an and to become familiar with hadith. Muslims can conduct their prayers virtually anywhere and women are not required to attend Friday prayers. Finally, Muslims do not follow imams; in fact, people are encouraged to circulate among the masjids and from week-to-week the imam giving the *khutbah* usually changes. In this respect, the community is somewhat decentralized, and generally women's religious exegesis takes shape outside the masjid in women's homes, where they meet for Islamic study groups, or at women-only events.

I also thought it would be important to discuss how all state systems, Islamic or secular, are structured around notions of morality and ethical social practice.

I arrived at the agency and was warmly received. They eagerly set up the tape of a film I made years ago about an African American Muslim woman who veils. I was expecting a room full of non-Muslims, but notice at least ten people who I suspect are Muslim. I am confused now by the questions. Why doesn't this state agency create a forum during which the Muslim employees could speak about their faith? Very uncertain about what to do, I go up to the podium to deliver my brief introduction and move right into the film hoping that it will generate questions that I can then field.

My ten-minute black-and-white film features Hawaa Akbar, an African American who converted to Shia Islam during the Iranian Revolution. Hawaa was impressed that a Third World nation stood up to the United States, and she credited the religion with giving Iranians the power to reject Western hegemony. This background information is not in the film; instead it shows Hawaa in various contexts, from work to the kitchen to the masjid (mosque), discussing why she veils. She emphasizes that the veil is optional for women, and she describes the support she receives from the Muslim community. It is a rather tame film told from the perspective of one convert. About half way into the film, a woman sitting next to me from Turkey begins yelling in my ear. "You have to tell them that this is not Islam. In Turkey we believe that Islam should be between you and God. This is not right. You are misinforming them. Women don't have to veil!" She yelled for a good thirty seconds.

Shaken, I move back to the podium when the film ends and begin explaining that this is a depiction of one woman and her perspective on Islam and that many Muslims oppose *hijab* (covering) for women and an Islamic state. "For example in Turkey," I say, "Ataturk, the father of modern Turkey, denounced overt displays of faith like *hijab* and separated religion and state." Then I quickly moved to the question and answer session.

To my surprise nobody asked about the film, but there were a number of questions about the definition of *jihad*. *Jihad* means "to struggle," particularly with self-improvement and religious purity. The answer was completely unsatisfying to the non-Muslims, so others kept raising the question. Exasperated, I threw in a "joke" that my husband told me to say as I was expressing my angst about this lecture. He said, "Tell them the only thing more dangerous than Islam is Christianity." I of course laughed. It always strikes me that most Americans are ignorant about how Christianity was used to justify the Spanish Inquisition, slavery, Apartheid, and colonialism. While Westerners imagine the Third World Other as dangerous, Europeans and European Americans have in fact been directly and indirectly responsible for countless genocides and/or the destruction of numerous cultures. So I tell the "joke," which is followed by a silence so still that I thought I actually heard the members of the diversity team think to themselves, "How did we get her?" The comment goes over so badly that I do not even follow it up with an explanation, however eventually I repeat the comment in order to assure the audience that it was meant as a joke, and then I say that the most dangerous thing on this planet is really poverty. Poverty provides its own rationalization for active resistance, religion offers hope.

In the end, I am happy that the Muslims were able to tolerate my mistakes, and that I was able to say what the Muslims perhaps have wanted to say to their colleagues. The event, however, reminds me that I need to clarify—if anyone ever asks me to speak again—that I am an anthropologist. As an anthropologist I enter into conversations about Islam differently from historians, political scientists, or Islamic scholars. I approach this topic from the perspective of Islam's meaning to African American women. How do they develop their particular understanding of Islam? How does that understanding relate to their personal and social history? Unlike the woman from Turkey, I do not evaluate the "accuracy" of their interpretation of Islam.

A member of my dissertation committee once commented that the reason that many African American women cover, or wear *hijab*, is because they are ignorant of the faith. This is not, I believe, a productive way to develop understanding either within or outside the *ummah*. However, I understand that this woman from Turkey and my dissertation committee member are Muslims, and the representation of Islam to their Christian or Jewish colleagues is extremely important. Because there are so few positive representations of Muslims in the United States, every representation is supposed to stand in for the whole.

Being African American, and having studied and worked in film, I understand this well. When Spike Lee's *She's Gotta Have It* (1986) came out, many African Americans were upset that the film did not represent blacks in a particular way. The criticisms stemmed from the fact that there is such a dearth of positive representations of African Americans that tremendous weight is placed on each representation. Muslims are reacting in a similar fashion, but then who can blame them when the media creates terms like "Islamic Terrorist," but do not coin the term "Catholic Terrorist" for describing the Irish Republican Army. Combining the words "Islam" and "Terrorist" creates its own narrative. It says that Islam is not anathema to terrorism, that in fact Islam supports terrorism. That is why I was not asked, "Does Islam teach violence?" I was asked, "What does Islam teach about violence?"

In this book, I try to stay away from either defending or criticizing the faith, although I do not always succeed. Instead, I try to understand how African American female converts make sense of the theology and how their *tafsir* (interpretation) informs their religious practice. The Muslima (Muslim sisters) accept the religiously prescribed gender roles and codes of conduct, believing that liberation emerges out of these disciplinary practices. Ultimately, the social history of black women in the United States contributes substantially to the reason why Muslima view Islam as a faith with the potential to liberate women from racism, sexism, and classism.

ACKNOWLEDGMENTS

Ethnographies are collaborations between anthropologists and subjects, and I am most indebted to the women and men in the Muslim community who patiently explained their faith. Allowing one's moral universe to be held up to scrutiny requires a tremendous amount of courage, and clearly without each contributor's courage this book project would have been impossible.

Among the academic community, I would like to thank my advisor and friend, Janet Hoskins, who was able to appreciate the meaning of soul food. Also, crucial to this project was my intellectual dance partner and unapologetically Marxist advisor Eugene Cooper. In addition, where would I be without my guardian angels Francine Coeytaux and Gelya Frank, who marry theory and practice in their personal and professional lives. Also, I owe a tremendous debt to Amina Wadud, whose 1996 lecture in Los Angeles inspired the book's title, and whose writings inspired understanding.

This project also required the support of institutions, which are comprised, most importantly, of individuals. Therefore, I would like to thank the University of Southern California's Department of Anthropology and Program in Visual Anthropology, particularly Nancy Leutkehaus and Fadwa El-Guindi. I would also like to acknowledge Timothy Asch,

Dru Gladney, Soo-Young Chin, and Walter Williams, who provided intellectual and personal mentorship. I include in my thanks the Haines
Foundation, UCLA's Center for African American Studies, Princeton's
Center for the Study of Religion and Program in African American Studies, and Princeton University for their continuing support of my research
and writing.

This project also benefited greatly from the input of R. Marie Grif-
fith, Marla Frederick, John Jackson, and the work of fabulous photogra-
pher and friend Mieke Kramer. Additional heaps of gratitude and appreciation are reserved for editor and bread breaker Naomi Schneider,
who believed in this project even when, at times, I did not. I also want to
thank the University of California Press crew responsible for the manu-
script's metamorphosis into a book suitable for consumption: Kate
Warne, Matt Stevens, Sierra Filucci, and Jim Clark.

Next I would like to thank a number of teachers and friends who probably are unaware of their impact on my life and scholarship. These
people include sociologist Gene Burns, historian Vincent Harding,
writer Dennis Brutus, filmmaker Fred Wiseman, and historian Adam
Green. Included in this eclectic group are three women who continue to
be my muses: sociologists Sara Curran and Betsy Armstrong and anthropologist Amy Borovoy. These fabulous women provide a safe haven
in which to be intellectually daring. I need to also thank profusely Carol
Zanca, Larry Rosen, Emily Martin, Alan Mann, Rena Lederman, Silvia
Hirsch, Carol Greenhouse, Isabelle Clark-Deces, Jim Boon, John
Borneman, João Biehl, and Akbar Ahmed, who have made it, and continue to make it, a pleasure to go to work.

Ultimately it is my family who has, at a fundamental level, made this
book project happen. I will start with Lorraine, Carl, Forest, and Cecilia.
Each of these incredible individuals could be the subject of a book, so let
me just sum it up by saying how grateful I am to have been born into such
an amazing family. I would also like to acknowledge the newer members
of my family Vivian, Eileen, Ford, Shaheen, and Nidal, who fill my world
with joy and good company.

Last, but not least, I must thank Glenn Eugene Schiltz, who gave my soul new life and whose loyalty and goodness have sustained us. Finally, I must acknowledge Zora Moxley Schiltz-Rouse, my junior assistant during most of my fieldwork, and Elijah "Yahya" Forest Schiltz-Rouse. I dedicate this book to them in the hopes that as they grow they find *iman*.

ONE

Engaged Surrender

In 1991, when I ventured onto the grounds of Masjid Ummah, a mosque in Southern California, I was not new to African American Sunni Islam.[1] In college, I had attempted to understand the "evolution" of the Muslim movement by examining the Nation of Islam's journal *Muhammad Speaks* from the early 1960s through its transformation into the *Muslim Journal*, a Sunni Muslim weekly.

What began my love of and fascination with the African American Sunni Muslim community is what I now see as an important but naive observation. In 1986, while riding on a bus in Chester, Pennsylvania, in ninety-nine degree weather, I observed a woman walking on the sidewalk and wearing dark brown, polyester *hijab* and veil.[2] She had two young children in tow, a boy and a girl, each with the proper, gendered head coverings: a skull cap for the boy and a scarf for the girl. I thought to myself, "Why would a woman in America choose not to be a feminist?" Or "Why would a woman in America choose not to have choices?"

With respect to the first question, in the feminist literature of the 1970s, the psychological, symbolic, and neo-Marxist approaches to the study of gender asked why women are universally oppressed.[3] The assumption of course is that in every society women are considered inferior, an assumption that has been challenged in what is often described as "third wave feminism."[4] At the time I asked these questions, in the mid- and late 1980s, I was unfamiliar with the works of, for example, Chandra Mohanty, bell hooks, and Moraga and Anzaldua, who around the same time were articulating the importance of race, class, and nation in terms of women's experiences with gender. These authors challenged the idea that to be a feminist requires adopting an ideology and political agenda defined mainly by European American women, whose race, class, and education influenced the scope and breadth of their feminist ideals. Indeed, there were numerous reasons poor people of color would choose not to call themselves feminists, but those reasons would only become clear to me well after I asked them on the bus in Chester.

So then, "Why would a woman in America choose not to have choices?" The ideas of choice and rationality are discussed much more frequently within the disciplines of philosophy, psychology, and, because choice and rationality dovetail with ideals of freedom, studies of democracy. While I am poorly equipped to enter into serious dialogue with philosophers and psychologists, I have revisited the anthropological project of cultural relativism and its meaning not simply as a strategy for engaging with our informants, but at the level of unmaking ourselves by challenging our own assumptions. I appreciate the relativist approach, which is not to judge one set of cultural values relative to another; however, it has caused me a great deal of paralysis when trying to address questions about liberation and empowerment. Within a relativist framework, for example, must we agree that a Muslim woman who is physically abused by her husband, but thinks she is liberated, is indeed liberated? In response to my paralysis, I chose to fall back upon the wisdom of a judge who said, "I know illegal pornography when I see it."[5] This approach acknowledges that to make a determination of "decent" or "indecent" is not a science but an art. I adopted this approach when interpreting Muslim women's comments about their own empowerment. Statements like "I'm liberated," or "America is a freedom loving country," can be as exhibitionist as pornography, and the anthropologist must determine the representational values of those personal and political declarations with respect to some referential truth. Freedom always has constraints, and methodologically we must locate the constraints in order to define the freedom, not the other way around.

Since my aborted first attempt in 1986/87 and subsequent resumption in 1991, I have focused my research on Muslim converts on the deconstruction of the theoretical assumptions and biases that informed my initial two questions. After identifying the problems with my initial response, I shifted my focus and began asking, What is feminism? And what choices do women have in America? I decided the best approach toward understanding choices was to abandon the comfort of my secular "Western" worldview in order to relate to a consciousness that often ignores the social, political, and even material environment for intangible rewards. Or are they intangible? They are intangible for people who do not share the same epistemology. For most American women, a Muslim woman's choice to dress in *hijab* is as destructive as suttee or foot binding.[6] But if we only acknowledged one worldview as legitimate, 99 percent of the population could be faulted for ignorance, stupidity, and/or irrationality. Relativists defend, on a theoretical level, cultural choices like hammering off the fingers of Dani girls in New Guinea after a male relative dies. Universalists, however, believe the ideology supporting such acts is indeed problematic. I heard an anthropologist describe the tug-of-war between universalists and relativists as analogous to the American struggle between equality and justice. Put another way, American society has competing social ideals of recognizing others as social and political equals while also believing in universal forms of justice. The universalist part of the American psyche believes in political and moral universals like democracy and social justice while the relativist believes that people must be allowed to be different and to respect those differences as equal. The conflict between these two ideals becomes especially interesting in cases where the Ku Klux Klan wants to march on public property, or when a majority of parents want their children to pray in school. I, like my American counterparts, have the same bifurcated utopian ideal. Therefore, I recognize that my research has been driven in part by the desire to reconcile my belief that these women are my equals in their capacity to make "rational" decisions with my belief that Western feminism and Western freedom are in fact good things.

My interest in understanding "rational" behavior comes from my interest in resistance consciousness and strategies for overcoming oppression. Being African American, I am not unique in my desire to try to understand the puzzle of race and oppression, or in my desire for progressive social change. My initial field notes outline questions and codes that at the time, I believed, would help me determine if African American women who convert to Islam are reproducing their oppression. Questions included: Are you wealthier now than before you converted? What material contributions have you made to the Sunni community? I wanted to know if the Muslim women's religious practices and ideology produced the intended results. Finally, I realized that I was using a modernist sensibility in trying to understand human intentions and action, and my methods could only lead to a determination that my informants were falsely conscious. To accept my methods and data was to accept a universalist social-science approach that takes for granted the idea that people are objective and act rationally, that cultures evolve in a unilinear fashion, and that economic class organizes intentions, actions, identity, and consciousness—a kind of economic reductionism. Ideas of rational praxis are, after all, firmly grounded in history, and the historical production of knowledge, which means even the theories of praxis, most notably Marx's, are tied to powerful epistemologies. I wanted to avoid a teleology that begins and ends with the same determination of what ought to be, a common subtext in political economy theory. Instead, I traced consciousness lineages, if you will, in order to determine not whether the Sunni Muslim resistance consciousness is "rational," in a positivist sense, but how resistance consciousness emanates from and acts upon the American phenomena of racism, sexism, and poverty.[7]

Most expositions on African American Muslims have very limited information on the experiences of women. Paula Giddings challenges Elijah Muhammad's *Message to the Blackman in America*, in which he said, "Allah, himself, has said that we cannot return to our land until we have a thorough knowledge of our own selves. This first step is the control and the protection of our own women."[8] Giddings says:

> Well, that was one way to solve the difficult problem of male-female relationships and assure "Black manhood": revert to nineteenth-century White society's handling of it. However, the irony was lost on many Blacks at the time. C. Eric Lincoln's study *Black Muslims in America* concluded that the organization's most significant achievement was its promotion of men as the dominant force in the family and the mosque.[9]

Barbara Sizemore argues that *Message to the Blackman in America* basically positions women as evil and men as righteous, and therefore it is the religious obligation of black men to "keep women from the streets."[10] Doris Witt argues that Elijah Muhammad associated black women with "filth" and asserts that some of the most well-known male black nationalist leaders of the 1960s and 1970s were misogynists.[11]

There are some exceptions to the overwhelmingly negative expositions on patriarchy in American Muslim movements. In her autobiography *Little X*, Sonsyrea Tate gives readers a much more nuanced portrait of women's roles and perspectives in the Nation of Islam. In *African-American Islam*, Amina Beverly McCloud describes Sunni Islam as empowering to women. Most recently, Robert Dannin describes in ethnographic detail how Muslim women challenge patriarchy in a community in New York. Nevertheless, even the explicit affirmations made by African American Muslim women about their sense of agency are often ignored. Claude Clegg, for example, in his excellent but male-centered history of the Nation of Islam, says about the women:

> The image of virtuous black womanhood presented to the public through Muslim displays of chivalry and propaganda often gave outsiders the impression that female believers actually held a superior

place in the temple. However, the reality of Muslim power arrangements and gender relations confirmed for the insider and the keen
observer that the pedestals on which women were placed had been
constructed by men and could be cast aside when a female believer
needed a good "smack in the face" for challenging the will of her
male counterpart. In future decades, women would continue to play
an ambiguous role in the Nation and would be both the beneficiaries
of glorification and the victims of objectification.[12]

With that comment, Clegg brackets the role of women in the movement,
and moves on to discuss the men, who readers might think *were* the
movement.[13]

In a departure from earlier works, this ethnography describes why
African American women choose to be part of what I loosely define as the
Sunni Muslim movement. Since looking out the window of that bus in
Chester, I have developed an appreciation for the desire for cultural
membership in a community with clear rules of engagement. Using religious exegesis, or religious interpretation (*tafsir*), women open up a
space for themselves within the community. In particular, it is through
the authorizing discourse of Islam that women negotiate and empower
themselves within their community. Far from being "chattel," as Barbara
Sizemore contends, Muslim women are enlisted along with the men in
the creation of an alternative social and moral space. Historically, within
the various African American Muslim communities there have been instances of sexism toward women, but for the most part, women have
rarely, if ever, been systematically discounted as "filth."

ENTRÉE

My first visit to Masjid Ummah was culturally disorienting. While I was
trying to decide which entrance and exit was for women, I was also trying to determine a good entrée into the community.[14] Ultimately that
day, all a priori calculations regarding what to wear and how to introduce
myself seemed meaningless given that the only thing I really had control

over was my desire to get to know the community; a desire that has compelled me to ask American women from the rural Southwest to the urban Northeast the same question, "Why did you convert?" That first day, on a bench just outside the women's entrance, I sat next to an elderly woman. She was wearing a conservative dark blue dress and a white headscarf that was pinned in the back before it was given the freedom to drape over her shoulders. The majority of the other women at Masjid Ummah had dresses cut from colorful African textiles with matching headscarves. While the elderly woman was dressed in clothing reminiscent of that worn by female members of Elijah Muhammad's Nation of Islam, the other women expressed an identity not available to most Muslim converts until the mid-1970s, when it became fashionable to identify as both African and American.[15] The West African clothing is seen to be feminine, modest, and a professional accoutrement. In this clothing the women feel that they can be Muslims, women, African Americans, professionals, and mothers, while at the same time demonstrate support for the local economy of South Central, an area with numerous black-owned clothing stores. In contrast, the elderly woman who occupied the same bench outside Masjid Ummah represented in clothing an identification tied to a particular utopian consciousness.

Having noticed a number of children in school uniforms, I asked the woman where the school office was located. Without putting much thought into methods or self-representation, I decided I would volunteer at the school in order to "give back" to the community from which I was going to extract information for personal gain. In the office the principal, Miriam, asked me what I could teach.[16] Knowing the community's mandate to de-center Europe and Europeans from the canons, I said that I could teach African American history. She dismissed that suggestion saying, "We have a lot of people who can teach African American history." At the time I chastised myself for being so naïve, and in a sense condescending. Clearly, if this is one of their stated mandates, they are finding ways to fulfill it. Miriam proceeded to ask if I could tutor children in math and reading. I was happy to accept the job. Then she asked what continues to be, for me, an extremely difficult question to answer: "Have you taken the *shahada?*" The *shahada* is the "witness of faith" that a person takes in order to convert to Sunni Islam. My unrehearsed reply was that I was taking the job to conduct fieldwork for a class project and to learn more about Islam so that I could decide if I wanted to convert.

In recalling my entrée, I can see that in some respects my research within the Sunni Muslim community has meandered. I initially set out to conduct four months of research for a class, but the experience turned into a job and a long-term relationship with a number of women who frequent one of two masjids. With the exception of my eight-month stint as a teacher, I have been quite marginal within the community. In the years I have studied Sunni Islam I have harbored many different personal views about the faith and the community. I appreciate the rigor involved in being Muslim, the need to be fluent in Arabic, Islamic history, Qur'anic exegesis, and the importance of daily ritual, but the rigor is not for me. My journey, I tell my Muslim sisters, is taking me in other directions that have been shaped in significant ways by the Muslim agenda to seek a non-contradictory social justice that begins and ends at the level of the personal, at the level of the body that is, most importantly, a social body.

Finding the roots of my determination to know and understand why women convert to Sunni Islam would require significant self-exploration. Perhaps the best way to sum it up is to say that I admire the *muhajjabah* (women who wear *hijab*) and who make no apologies for disagreeing with the American mainstream, who are predominantly Christian, and keepers of the American dream of economic and social mobility. After all, how mobile is a black woman in a headscarf? The way Americans presently reward certain physical types, a headscarf has the potential to lower the glass ceiling with respect to job promotion and retention. For African Americans to socially acknowledge their Islamic faith through certain types of dress is like carrying a United States exit visa; it is a sign marking the closure of access to certain social and material rewards. In addition, people confuse Sunni Muslims with converts to the Nation of Islam. The Nation of Islam, a black nationalist movement/religion founded by Elijah Muhammad, is now led by Louis Farrakhan, who has made public anti-Jewish comments. The confusion among the public about the distinction between the two groups often means that African American Sunni Muslims are often presumed to be anti-Jewish.

Ultimately, choosing to adopt a minority faith, and choosing to perform that faith in public spaces, could be considered a form of social suicide.[17] Or maybe not. What if the tenets of Islam, which include economic redistribution and brotherhood, are eventually adopted by the American mainstream? Perhaps there would be a revolution in how social and material rewards are distributed. Or what if through conversion the American mainstream reduced forms of overconsumption, including alcoholism? They might change the number of alcohol-related car fatalities and the frequency of domestic abuse. I use these hypothetical examples to highlight that popular beliefs can have almost as much material force in shaping social relations as ownership of economic capital.[18] Therefore, performing an Islamic identity in the United States, so to speak, may in the long run change social relations. Until these ideas gain popular acceptance, however, what empowerment or agency do female converts have? The women I know who practice their faith struggle daily with biases and/or stereotypes that limit their access to social rewards. Nevertheless, they continue to enter voluntarily into the struggle in order to express their faith. Why? Because for them the rewards include the possibility of a more just community and society, more successful interpersonal relationships including marriage, and, most importantly, the knowledge that one is living according to the will of Allah.

In the daily performance of their beliefs, converts challenge the legitimacy of American assumptions about race, gender, class, family, and community. In the following chapters, I will describe how each of these social issues is filtered through the prism of Islam and inflected with new meaning. Race, for example, is understood as neither a symbol around which the community should unite (many even oppose affirmative action), nor as a meaningless historical, personal, and social fact. In other words, they view race as simultaneously salient and not salient. One finds, therefore, a number of predominantly African American masjids that are in no way exclusively black. These masjids offer greater opportunities for African Americans to assume leadership roles, but at the same time these masjids are racially and ethnically diverse. The community's approach to race is neither reactionary nor exclusionary; it is not what Omi and Winant would call a "racial project."[19] Instead race is constructed according to the Prophet's last sermon during which he says that Allah created different races for the purposes of identification and not oppression.[20] Similarly, the race ethic in the community is based on the utopian ideal of tribal harmony and integration, much like Islamic history portrays Mecca shortly after it fell to the Prophet Muhammad and his followers in 630 C.E. This means, in effect, that for this African American Muslim community, religious praxis is the strategic deployment of alternative approaches to issues including racism, classism, and sexism.

THE SISTERS

My informants were African American women, Muslima who, with the exception of most of the children born into the religion, have had a spiritual, social, political, and personal epiphany. They are members of an African American Sunni Muslim community in Southern California. I explore issues of empowerment and agency from the perspective of women who strive to perfect the practice of their faith through (1) Qur'anic exegesis requiring knowledge of the Qur'an, hadith (words and deeds of the Prophet), Islamic history, Islamic jurisprudence, and Arabic; (2) adherence to the five pillars of Islam; and (3) personal growth through increasing self-awareness. I emphasize that the community is Sunni Muslim, one of the two major branches of Islam, because as I mentioned earlier many people think that most African American Muslims worship with the Nation of Islam and follow Louis Farrakhan.[21] The Muslim community at Masjid Ummah practices "traditional" Islam, which means they believe that the Prophet Muhammad is the last messenger and slave servant to Allah, and that the Qur'an is from Allah as told to the Prophet through the Angel Gabriel.[22] Accordingly, the Sunni Muslim community practices the five pillars of Islam, including: *shahada* (witness of faith); *salat* (five obligatory daily prayers per day); *sawm* (fasting); *zakat* (charity); and *hajj* (pilgrimage to Mecca).

Although no formal surveys have been conducted, most African American Muslim women choose to wear headscarves only in the masjids and during prayer, when it is required. Women who do not to wear *hijab* outside of religious observances struggle against hegemony from a different "war of position" than women who do wear *hijab*.[23] The differences are subtle but important enough that I chose to focus my research on female Muslims who express their faith through dress—the *muhajjabah*. This book explores the lives of several women who through overt displays of their faith use their bodies as sites of resistance. These sisters challenge hegemonic discourse about race, gender, community, and faith at the level of the everyday.

MASJID UMMAH

Sister Clara Muhammad School was a private elementary and junior high school located at Masjid Ummah. I taught math, reading, and eventually video production at the school. The teachers and administrators at Sister Clara Muhammad went beyond the educational basics and encouraged their students to develop a deep appreciation for African American history as well as learn what is required to be a good Muslim— Qur'an, hadith, Arabic, Islamic history, and the rituals of the faith. Given the dismal state of schools in the poorest and most segregated neighborhoods, Sister Clara Muhammad offered families a positive alternative. Positive in the sense that the students had textbooks that were intact, there was no school violence, and all the students were encouraged and expected to excel.

The school/masjid was on an acre of land with a large dirt yard in front. The front space acted at times as a parking lot, and at other times as a market for vendors to sell ethnic clothing, jewelry, perfumes, books, and other items. Bordering the dirt yard was an asphalt parking lot with two large trailers converted into classrooms; a large, portable storage container converted into the school office; and of course the masjid, which was a plain white, one-story stucco building, an odd assortment of functional indoor space.

The masjid was on a north-/southbound street running from the city's downtown into the heart of the poorest and most segregated community. Although the masjid was located in what some people describe as a bad neighborhood, the streets were fairly quiet. Every few nights, however, the sound of a helicopter hinted that either the daytime quiet belied a sinister truth, or that the helicopters were used by the police to intimidate this poor and less powerful community. My conclusion after living in one of these "bad" neighborhoods is that there are multiple truths to which one must attend. This urban community is in one of the most segregated cities in the United States with a tremendous amount of violence and social suffering. While I have no way of knowing how this Southern California community differs qualitatively from other large American cities, many of my informants had plans for "getting out." At the same time that my informants spoke of a need to escape, however, most were investing in new businesses, engaging in long-term projects to improve their communities, and/or deeply enmeshed in extensive social networks built over years. In other words, within the Sunni Muslim community there was significant ambivalence about the city.

The masjid was in a section of town where streets with single family homes ran perpendicular to a street zoned for commerce. The character of this commercial district has changed considerably since 1991. Most notably, large conglomerates like the drugstore chain CVS and the grocery store chain Ralphs have since driven out the mom-and-pop shops. Demographically there is also a shift in the racial/ethnic population from predominantly black to Latino. In contrast, in 1991 the buildings surrounding the masjid included a fried chicken restaurant, a firehouse, and a gas station. Kitty-corner to the masjid was a liquor store parking lot where every day a group of men sat drinking and talking. Further down the street there were several stores selling cheap, imported clothing, accessories, toys, and candy. To the south, on almost every block, stood one or two storefront churches that I imagined received barely enough in donations to meet their monthly rents.

Everyday before classes started, students would gather in the masjid's prayer space and form rows according to age and gender and proceed to sing the "Sister Clara Muhammad" song. Sister Clara Muhammad was the wife of Elijah Muhammad, the founder of the Nation of Islam, and although the parents who attended this masjid were Sunni Muslims, the name of the school honored the first person to institutionalize African American Muslim education. The girls would be dressed in long burgundy jumpers, white blouses, and white headscarves; the boys would be dressed in white dress shirts and dark blue slacks. Following the song and announcements, the younger students would be led to their classrooms just off the largely unadorned prayer space. The older students, fourth through eighth grade, would make their way to two large trailers in the parking lot of the masjid.

Around noon the children and teachers would break from schoolwork and head back to the masjid. The boys would enter the masjid on the north side of the building and the girls would enter the south side of the building, where each performed *wudu*, or ritual cleansing. After performing *wudu*, the boys would take their place in front of the girls, and a male student would perform the *adhan*, or call to prayer. Following the *adhan* they would begin *zuhr* prayer, or early afternoon prayer, led by a male teacher.

I met Imani when I was teaching three of her then seven children at Sister Clara Muhammad. For one semester in 1991, I taught her sons math, and in the summer I taught her oldest son, Hamza, video production. At the time, Imani was living in a one-room apartment next to a junkyard. The room was dark and the children's space was demarcated by several overstuffed chests of drawers. One corner housed the "kitchen," which had a sink and a small stove. Over the stove was a sign reading,

"When life gives you lemons, make lemonade." Imani was investing a tremendous amount of time organizing her children's rap group, which sang Islamicly inspired songs. She would transport all the kids to rehearsals, auditions, and performances. It seemed at the time as though Imani's involvement with her children was going to bring them success.

Imani herself had grown up in poverty in Washington, D.C., and at thirteen years old radically shifted her worldview after listening to a report on the radio about the discovery that red dye number four was a carcinogen. Like most epiphanies, the report confirmed what at some level she already felt, that intellectual and physical "poisons" marred her environment, slowly destroying her body. Freedom, she determined, would come only through knowledge and purification. Eventually as a teenager, Imani became a vegetarian and convinced her mother to adopt the same eating restrictions. Shortly afterward, Imani converted to Islam and by example convinced her mother to do the same. As a Muslim, Imani maintains strict control over her children's diet. Hamza refused my offer of M&Ms, saying, "They cause a disease that you don't get right away, but maybe ten years from now." Clearly, Imani had already explained carcinogens to her young children. Despite destitution, Imani went to a popular and expensive natural food store in an upper-middle class district to buy medicinal herbs that were almost impossible to find in grocery stores in her neighborhood.

The last time I met Imani was at a 1998 *Eid*, or celebration, following Ramadan.[24] Imani drove to the park in an old Suburban truck with eight of her then nine children. The truck was so loaded with stuff there seemed to be no room for the children. The car was as disorderly as the children were orderly. They were all wearing their best matching *Eid* clothes. All the members of the family wore their hair in dreadlocks, and Imani, who used to hide her hair in a tight scarf, had put a loose scarf over her long dreads. Her husband was there. They had separated a few years before, but had since reconciled. When I asked if she plans on having any more children she said, "Allah knows," which is a common response from people who try to live sunnah, or according to the practices of the

Prophet Muhammad. Her husband sold used books, and so they had brought dozens of boxes of used books and videos, many about Islam, to hand out to the children attending the *Eid*. Imani told me that recently they had moved to a remote, and somewhat rural region of Southern California, to a rental property situated on two acres of land; a significant contrast from the one-room space the entire family occupied in South Central. She said the kids had space in which to run around and animals. With the initial picture painted by Imani it seemed as though she had finally found an enclave in which, unfettered, she could live naturally and Islamicly after years of having to contend with the urban artifice of South Central.

I asked if her son Hamza was at the *Eid*. Imani said Hamza was in Juvenile Hall. She said he started hanging around the "wrong crowd," staying out late, and eventually he stopped coming home. I asked if Islam was helping him to rethink his life, and without skipping a beat she and her husband said, "No." This family's struggles are typical of the struggles of many inner-city families, but for those who take a rigorous and less accommodationist approach to living Islamicly, it is surprising that Imani's empowerment was not passed down to her son, or that Imani's sense of her own freedom was rarely revealed through any overt signs of personal agency and empowerment.

Hamza's descent into gang-banging was ethnographically important to me because it brought up so many issues related to my initial fieldwork question: Was conversion empowering or, as my Marxist advisor had said, was it merely false consciousness? Indeed most Americans, Marxist or not, understand Islam to be the opposite of a faith that liberates. In the West, people who know very little about the faith are given permission to condemn it publicly as a theology that promotes violence and oppresses women. Louis Farrakhan, who preaches a nontraditional form of Islam, has done his part to perpetuate these misconceptions. Nevertheless, that does not excuse the fact that even after years of describing my research to my professional colleagues, I discover that they too collapse race and faith, thereby losing the distinction between being in the Nation of Islam and being a Sunni Muslim.

Accompanying this ignorance is another set of misperceptions. Women and men who believe in dividing some domestic labor according to gender are often criticized for re-essentializing gender. Similarly, in scholarly writings, many feminists and womanists collapse Islam with nationalism, and so Muslims are sometimes accused of re-essentializing race.[25] These scholars are correct in positing the Nation of Islam as a nationalist movement, and part of its doctrine was the belief that there is an authentic black male and black female. Slavery, Eurocentrism, and white supremacy, it was thought, made blacks act in ways that Nation members consider detrimental to their economic, political, and personal success: divorce, women working outside the home, homosexuality.[26] The problem is that scholars take these statements at face value and argue that the increasing number of converts to Islam reflects a resurgence of male patriarchy and homophobia, which threatens the potential of black women to liberate themselves and their communities.[27] The problem with accepting the rhetoric of Muslim leaders as fact, is that discourse is not always congruous with deeply held social dispositions and practices. The rhetoric of patriarchy, for example, may be deployed not to make women submissive, but to instill in men a sense of responsibility. So as scholars we need to ask Muslim women if patriarchy is relevant in their daily lives. While popular ideas, such as patriarchy, have material force, ideas by themselves have much less power than cultural practice. With respect to patriarchy, there are often significant disconnects between what men and women say, and what men and women do. Put another way, there is "official" gender ideology, and then there is "practical" gender organization.[28]

For many non-Muslims, clothing, segregated spaces, and prayer rituals define the practice of Islam. In this way, people often view the faith as a performance: the performance of the submission of women to men and the submission of the community to God. The theology that gives rise to these performances, however, is extremely complex, at times contradictory, and always subject to interpretation. One needs to spend very little time in a masjid to recognize that most women are not passive recipients of male authority.

Contrary to the stereotypes, women such as Imani told me repeatedly that Islam had positively and profoundly changed their lives. Conversion for my informants happened in response to police violence against Muslims during the 1965 Watts riots, in sympathy with black nationalist struggles, and in response to incarceration or drug dependency. In other words, conversion was almost always tied to political consciousness, the desire for social change through resistance, and individual empowerment. While informants such as Imani say that Islam has empowered them, my research was driven by a desire to interrogate those claims.

For Imani, it is her struggle for Islamic purity that has been put to the test by her oldest son, who has been seduced by the secular community. Is it possible that her son's choices have been influenced more by the secular world than the parents' religious practice? Imani's rejection of polluted food and ideas seems rational in light of her own experiences growing up in the ghetto, but how those ideas have informed her economic and social choices may simply work poorly for her children in their environment. Sharing beyond what one can afford, and having as many children as Allah decides, represents an orientation to Islam that is not optimal if one wants to improve the next generation's chances for material success. Hamza and his brother Yusef both had significant academic gifts. Unfortunately, the economic deprivation of their neighborhood, and the poor resources in the public schools they attended after the 1993 earthquake, meant that these gifts received very little recognition or nurturance.[29] Even with tremendous parental involvement, there are a number of material impediments to academic success in poor neighborhoods. In this respect, the trajectory of Imani's oldest son is not unfamiliar in this environment, therefore instead of debating whether Islamic conversion represents false consciousness, a more salient discussion would entail asking how Islam empowers some and not others, and in what contexts.

COMMUNITY PRAXIS

The Muslim community has a blueprint for a moral world based upon the Qur'an and the sunnah of the Prophet Muhammad.[30] They attempt to express in every detail of their lives their worship *(ibadah)* of Allah while working to fit under one rubric self, identity, faith, education, economic action, and social and political consciousness, a Herculean task given the contradictions within and between these various personal and social domains. Since I began studying the community, I have shifted my focus away from trying to determine if the women are falsely conscious and toward trying to understand people's desire to create moral worlds. Specifically, I have become interested in how the Muslim community attempts to develop consistent paradigms of moral and religious praxis. My use of the term *praxis* pays homage to Karl Marx.[31] Marx argues that a revolutionary leap is impossible "unless the 'theoretical' criticism of politics is conjoined to the experience of a definite social grouping whose position in society renders them revolutionary."[32] In other words, praxis is the joining of belief with practice, and while I do not use praxis in the Marxist revolutionary sense, the joining of ideology and action is what, I believe, empowers Muslims and gives them agency. The problem is that not everyone agrees about what that praxis should be, and the result is personal ambivalence. This ambivalence, which may be directed at the leadership, the community's Islamic exegesis, or community praxis, aids in shaping, through dialectical and dialogic processes, new theological, political, and personal transformations.[33]

In order to understand Imani's sense of her own agency, it is important to know how she fits into the larger Muslim community. The uniqueness of this study is that it explores a community in which praxis lies somewhere between individual agency and group activism. Individuals shape the community's discourses and political agendas using a particular set of methods of engagement, notably *tafsir,* or religious interpretation. These negotiated political and religious discourses, inspired by individuals and religious texts, continue to lay the groundwork for transformational group action. What the community does in the process of trying to create consensus through Qur'anic exegesis, is to establish the borders of their "community of practice".[34] The ideal community is propagated through *khutbahs*, texts (primary and secondary sources), and study groups. Nevertheless, agreement varies, even with a concerted effort to build consensus, and converts must contend with a community where individuals interpret the edicts of Islam differently. Ultimately, as social realities and community objectives change, so do ideas of social inclusion, membership, and *tafsir.*

There are female converts who read the Qur'an as a feminist text. At the same time there are men in the community who believe that within the Qur'an Allah has given husbands permission to beat their disobeying wives. Both sets of these converts claim to belong to the same faith, but many female converts do not accept that these men have any authority to speak on behalf of the community. These men are viewed as marginal members, and their marginal status is reinforced when the women come together and produce "feminist" Qur'anic exegesis.

What I hope to instill in the reader with these stories of conversion is not the sense that by surrendering to Islam female converts are trying to make one dimensional the otherwise dynamic aspects of their postmodern selves, but that they are engaging in a particular project, if you will, by deciding to be part of a particular community of practice. As members of a community engaged in creating a moral world, they chose to follow certain rules for cultural membership. They do so without necessarily embracing those rules or doctrines as legitimate, but to signify that they are cultural members and therefore have the right to be taken seriously.

In the end, conversion is neither false consciousness nor liberation. Instead the women's choice to engage within this community of practice has the potential to reshape social relationships at the local level. The potential of this movement is that it provides a platform from which men and women can negotiate an agenda for the circulation, "like blood," of wealth in the community; develop methods for community and familial support through exchange and barter; and propagate a moral paradigm for social justice.

Islam speaks to the converts' personal sense of who they are at the same time that it provides a language to transform the personal into the political. In Chapter 6, for example, Zipporah describes how she is an assertive woman and that she believes Islam supports the rights of women to be assertive. Islam is an authorized discourse, a third party through which men and women can negotiate. Islam is their common ground, their moral frame, without which negotiation is impossible. Women's ambivalence toward particular interpretations of the Qur'an usually inspires a formal challenge through engagement with particular texts. These scholarly challenges open a space for the women to insert a critical voice into what constitutes legitimate religious worship beyond the obligatory five pillars of the faith. As such, women are empowered to create a Muslim community where men and women's equality is understood to be a form of worship.

Significantly, African American women who convert have "surrendered" to Islam—but "surrendered" in a way that engages their political consciousness and produces not only a spiritual but a social epiphany. Surrender empowers them to live new lives, even if it is marked by ambivalence toward certain interpretations of Islam—an ambivalence resulting from personal struggles to come to terms with the restrictions as well as the freedoms they have embraced. My study addresses resistance as it emanates from and acts upon the American experiences of racism, sexism, and poverty. But it examines a form of response that may seem paradoxical, since it can be seen as a retreat from the world into religious practices of purity and asceticism. My account stresses the specificity of discourses of resistance, their relation to family life and economic pressures, and it presents an ethnographic portrait of how these women represent their own choices. I argue that African American Islam is a political stance of engaging the world, not only a way of escaping it. I am critical of efforts to explain conversion as either "false consciousness" or simple "empowerment," and argue instead that there is a layered process of identity reformulation that involves dimensions of both ambivalence and empowerment.

SOURCES

Any book on Islam requires an explanation regarding the choice of sources and on the transliteration of language. Let me begin with my choice of Qur'an, which was revised and edited by the Presidency of Islamic Researchers. Both Muslim women on my dissertation committee asked me why I used this Qur'an. They noted problems they had with the translation, particularly the sections on women. They are not alone in challenging the accuracy of the translation; within the preface of the Qur'an, the publishers deny that it is even *the* Qur'an, given that any translation bankrupts some of the meaning and message of Allah. Because of the contentious debates in Islam regarding the validity of sources, I find it necessary to clarify that I am not an Islamic scholar, but merely an anthropologist studying a community of Muslims. Therefore, I use the Qur'an given to me by an imam at my primary field site. I used it because it is from that Qur'an that the community develops a significant portion of its exegesis.

My choice to use sources such as Maulana Muhammad Ali's *The Religion of Islam* (1990), Amina Wadud-Muhsin's *Qur'an and Woman* (1995), and Suzanne Haneef's *What Everyone Should Know About Islam and Muslims* (1985), was determined by their popularity within the community. I believe these authors are popular because their exegesis resonates with the community. For similar reasons, I also derived my transliteration of Arabic to English primarily through Imam Warith Deen Mohammed's *Muslim Journal*. African American Muslims often feel that other Muslims in the United States see them as less knowledgeable about Islam, and I certainly do not want to participate in the reproduction of that consciousness by denigrating their choice of sources.

FIELDWORK

The primary locations for my fieldwork include two masjids where I initiated my contacts with many women and families. The names of the masjids, businesses, and streets have been changed. Also, the names of the people as well as some nonessential facts about their lives have been altered to maintain confidentiality. The frequency of my contact with the community varied from four times a week for more than a year to periods where my only contact was by phone to my closest informants. Ultimately, I collected more than one hundred formal and informal interviews. I also audiotaped or purchased the audio or videotape of more than twenty masjid lectures, attended more than one hundred *Jumahs*, or Friday prayers, and more than thirty women's gatherings.

From the spring of 1991 until the present, I have set out to discover how Islam has been adopted as a method for personal and social transformation in Southern California. Of my twenty-four key informants, five described exploring various religions before becoming Muslim, including Buddhism, Transcendental Meditation, and Evangelical Christianity. Four had been politically active in the radical social movements of the late 1960s and early 1970s. All were dissatisfied with the social, economic, and political position of blacks; but seven were motivated primarily by a desire to change their community. One decided to convert when her son "turned his life around" for the better. Two were personally troubled with drugs and depression.[35] Three were introduced to the religion as children by their parents, and finally two out of three of my white female informants were introduced to Islam by their husbands who are Pakistani or Pakistani-American. Of course there is crossover, for example, one who was born into the faith went on to explore various religions before reentering the faith.

Each chapter in this book attempts to address African American Muslim liberation consciousness and resistance from the position of the actor looking out. Embodying ideology, in particular notions of purity, and grappling with ambivalence are fundamental aspects of resistance that set the stage, so to speak, for collective action and protest.[36] With-out these elements, I believe, everyday forms of resistance are random, lack social significance, and can ultimately be negatively transformative. My ethnographic interest had less to due with the physical maps of the city than the consciousness maps that inform the way the women think about the everyday. The maps these women draw help them to inscribe moral fields around people, places, identity, and family.[37] By drawing these consciousness maps they define borders of safety, productivity, community, friendship, and family. When African American social his-tory, feminism, and Islam share consistent themes of justice, commu-nity, family, and equality, then transformation—in this case surrender to Islam—is possible.

TWO

A Community of Women

Consensus, Borders, and Resistance Praxis

When Alia, an African American convert to Sunni Islam, wakes up the city is relatively still. Outside the early morning is lit by a pervasive orange glow from streetlights reflecting off the dark sky. Her husband, Karim, and child, Tarek, remain in the bed while Alia climbs down the stairs of their poorly furnished and somewhat dilapidated one-bedroom apartment. She gets up to make *suhur*, the meal the family will eat before they make *fajr*, the first prayer of the day. It is the month of Ramadan,[1] and therefore the meal will have to satisfy Karim and Alia until sunset, which is around quarter to six this time of year.[2]

Alia's morning begins with the preparation of cream-of-wheat and eggs. As she cooks, her husband gets up and comes downstairs to join his wife for *suhur*. They eat quickly, leaving the dirty dishes in order to pray before the sun peeks over the horizon. They each take turns in their small downstairs bathroom performing *wudu*, or ritual cleansing, preceding prayer. After *wudu* each pulls out a small prayer rug. Karim stands in front of her facing east and they pray two *rakah*, or prostrations of *Sunnatul-Muakkadah*, or nonobligatory prayer, followed by two *rakah* of *fard*, or obligatory prayer. The second two they perform together because they have read in hadith that praying together brings more blessings.[3] Sunnah prayers are performed individually. Alia and Karim finish before the sun comes up. The night sky by then has become a dark blue, and sounds of cars from the freeway have become more pronounced. They fold their prayer rugs and read 1/30 of the Qur'an, an important daily ritual during Ramadan, before Alia must tend to Tarek, who generally wakes during the reading.

Alia, who used to be a serious athlete, is a thin, dark skinned woman in her late twenties. Her eyes exude eagerness and intelligence, and she has an infectious smile that lights up her large almond-shaped eyes. Her twenty-three month old son Tarek is the product of five years of trying to conceive, and he closely resembles his mother, with dark skin and equally large eyes. Although Alia has one stepchild, she was blessed to give birth to her own child on the Night of Power, an important night toward the end of Ramadan.[4] The night represents the time during the month when the first revelation was told to the Prophet by the Angel Gabriel and is celebrated by gathering and praying throughout the night. The Night of Power is a culmination of a month of tremendous self-control, patience, and devotion to one's faith. For these reasons, the night of Tarek's birth is symbolic of a reward for the parents' devotion to faith and family. Alia informs me that when Tarek wakes in the morning, the first thing he wants is his mother's breast, and Alia is happy she will be able to breastfeed him for the two years idealized in the Qur'an.[5] After breastfeeding Tarek, the typical nonsacred tasks of an American family begin.

· · ·

I met Alia at Masjid Ummah during Friday prayers, or *Jumah*. She and her son sat in the back of the masjid with the other women and young children. Alia stood out because she was one of the few women at *Jumah* wearing a plain black head covering and *jilbab* (dress/robe). The majority of the women dressed in colorful outfits, or African-inspired clothing made from brightly colored, imported fabrics. In this way, Alia was different from the majority of the women because she dressed with a modesty more typical of a conservative Syrian or Lebanese woman. After the *khutbah*, Alia and I exchanged smiles. We engaged one another in small talk about Tarek, who clung to her, and I asked if I could interview her about Islam. Alia accepted my request graciously. At the time, I did not know that she regularly gives *dawah*, all I knew was that she was one of the first people to invite me into her home to conduct fieldwork.[6]

Outside the masjid, Alia's husband arrived to take the two home. Karim and Alia vary the masjids they attend from week to week and include among them masjids that are not predominately African American. This preferred practice is intended to strengthen the community, although it is one that people have a hard time employing because masjids are picked for convenience to work and home, and people also develop a fondness for certain imams. Karim and Alia, however, do rotate masjids and rarely are they even together at the same masjid on any given *Jumah*. So I was able to get a glimpse of her husband as I watched Karim climb into the front seat while Alia and Tarek climbed into the back of their old Audi.

A month after our first meeting, I finally scheduled an interview. Alia's sublet apartment was given to them by Karim's mother, who has rented the space since the 1960s. The area can best be described as a border community both in terms of ethnicity and economic class. It is located between three ethnic neighborhoods; just blocks from their street stand beautiful old craftsman houses, which, at the time, were being purchased by wealthy whites and blacks. Much to the disappointment of those gentrifying the neighborhood, the zoning laws allowed multiple-family dwellings, which meant the area was heavily rented and poor and middle-class families continued to be the majority. As a result of rent control, Alia and Karim paid very little per month, allowing the couple the financial freedom to continue their charitable religious work, including *dawah*, an activity that generates little if any income. Alia was finishing her bachelor of arts in criminology at a local state college, and like her husband had an interest in prison transformations. Karim earned money counseling inmates and lecturing about Islam and incarceration. Alia met Karim during one of his lectures to professors and students of criminology; she then decided to convert.

During the interview we spoke in their kitchen, which was long and narrow. The red linoleum on the floor was old and worn, and the wood cabinets looked as though they have not been refinished or painted since the apartment was built in the 1950s. Hanging on a wall in the kitchen was a large three-by-three foot painting created by Karim during his conversion. The painting depicted a man on a camel with Arabic script over a yellow sky proclaiming, "Allah Akbar," meaning God is greatest. I thought about the Islamic edict against *shirk*, or idol worship.[7] The Qur'an warns, "Among His Signs are the Night and Day, and the Sun and Moon. Prostrate not to the sun and the moon, but prostrate to Allah, Who created them, if it is Him ye wish to serve" (41:37).[8] For many Muslims in the African American community, this verse means that images of humans or animals in painting or sculpture are forbidden in order to protect someone from unwittingly prostrating toward the symbol of a human or animal during prayer. For example, at a weekly "Sister to Sister" meeting at Masjid al-Mustaqim the leaders of the community told recent converts that children must not come to the masjid in clothing depicting animals or people, and that coloring books are forbidden. With such rigid warnings against the practice, I wondered at the time of the interview how Karim, an extremely devout man, understood this edict and rationalized the painting's location in his house. I, however, did not ask for fear he would take it as a criticism of his faith and perhaps remove it.

When I finally had a chance to ask Alia about her decision to convert, she described how she met her husband when he was giving a lecture on Islam at her college in Arizona. She said she knew when he spoke that she wanted to live Islamically, so she left the college and moved back to Southern California to be with him. I asked her how she felt about *hijab*, about sitting in the back seat of the car, and about her domestic responsibilities. She said she had no problem wearing the black scarf, which covered her hair, ears, and neck. She added that her husband would like her to wear the *niqab* (face veil) because he tells her her eyes are so big that she appears to be making eye contact with men even when she is not. While there are a handful of Muslims in the United States who believe the *niqab* is required, Alia believes that the *niqab* falls under the category of personal choice rather than religious obligation. She commented quite strongly that she must practice her faith for Allah and not her husband. About the car, she said she feels safer in the back seat and Tarek prefers sitting next to his mother. About the house, she laughed and said she knows of no married American woman, Muslim or not, who does not clean the house, cook the majority of the meals, and take primary responsibility for the children. "Do you?" she asks. I confessed I did not.

In answering those three questions, Alia articulated some of the primary reasons African American women convert to Sunni Islam: room for personal expression of faith, comfort and safety, and a common sense approach to gender roles. I empathized with Alia's reasoning, but wondered why she did not tie her conversion to a corresponding political transformation, an element often suffused throughout the personal narratives of those who converted from the 1950s to the 1970s. There was no discussion of social justice, redistribution of wealth, or reversing racism and self-hatred. Instead, her conversion story included analyses of Qur'an, hadith, proper eating, proper dress, Arabic classes, prayer rituals, and home schooling. Without an overt political framing of Islam, I wondered, was Alia motivated by a desire to perfect the performance of her faith? And did her singular drive for purity make her more likely to accept interpretations of Islamic doctrine that limited her agency? Put differently, was Alia more likely to disempower herself economically and socially because she privileges religious asceticism over personal empowerment?

The question of choice and empowerment arose for me the day I met Alia at *Jumah*. The *khutbah* at Masjid Ummah was given by an imam who was discussing the beauty of the recent birth of his sixth child. He tied his wife's labor to the respect and blessings women receive as mothers in Islam. As the imam spoke, many women in the masjid acknowledged through "Allah Akbars" and head gestures their agreement with various points in the lecture. A mother of eight children, Marwa, was rocking her youngest in a car seat and nodding enthusiastically. For this wife and mother the *khutbah* affirmed her choice to place her religious beliefs over her material comforts. The Qur'an states, "To Allah belongs the dominion of the heavens and the earth. He creates what He wills. He bestows (children) male or female according to His Will" (42:49). While most American Muslims believe that whether a family chooses to have no children, or many children, Allah is in control of that choice. Others interpret this *ayat* to mean that Muslim couples should not control their fertility. Marwa understands that her role as a wife and mother is to bring as many Muslims into the world as she physically can bare, and she believes that this action will be rewarded by Allah.

In other material ways, Marwa was not rewarded. She continued having more children while the ones already alive struggled. At the time I was teaching math to her oldest son Akbar at Sister Clara Muhammad. Akbar, who was fourteen years old, did not know how to add, and I resorted to giving him a textbook that started with simple addition and subtraction. Despite the simplicity of the math, he was never able to grasp even the basic ideas of greater than and less than, and his parents were unable to give him the attention at home to help him with his studies and disabilities. He was a troubled adolescent who would defend his lack of effort by saying he would never need to graduate from high school because he knew how to survive on meager resources. He explained to me how he could prepare rice and beans, which, he said, is what he eats every night at home. Four years later Marwa told me that Akbar was in prison. She said that when he is released next month, she wanted to give him over to "the brothers" in the Muslim community because she and her husband had done all they could to try to "straighten him out." The road the family had taken was not an easy one, but that *khutbah* on that *Jumah* in February 1991 affirmed for Marwa that her choices were consistent with the teachings of Islam and therefore the right choices.

The examples of Alia and Marwa speak to the current African American Sunni Muslim community as a process-oriented, not outcome-oriented, movement. The women have often rejected mainstream ideals about gender and family, and their newly acquired sense of self and beliefs about the way the universe works, or agency, informs new social practices. Because their faith encourages them to make deliberate choices about what to eat, where to shop, where to invest their money, how to dress, and who to associate with, among other things, I argue that the African American Sunni community is a resistance movement. Generally we define resistance movements by their oppositional goals, whether they are to redistribute wealth, unionize workers, or usher in a socialist revolution. The goals of the pre-1975 Nation of Islam included economic self-sufficiency and a separate black nation. Currently—and this certainly could change—African American Sunni Muslims believe that social and economic justice will be a secondary benefit emerging from the proper practice of the faith. Those who view Islam as both personally and socially liberating generally feel that internalizing the liberation ethic of Islam will naturally precede any substantive material changes within the community.

DEFINING GROUP MEMBERSHIP

Membership to this Sunni community speaks to how the community identifies itself, and to its relationship to the secular or non-Muslim world. It is at this border that, I argue, the interesting work with respect to women and empowerment takes place. Islamic exegesis acts like a screen filtering the secular world. Ideas such as feminism, nationalism, and capitalism are negotiated discursively at this border, and women must find ways to package and transport feminism across this threshold so that their objectives are not perceived as threatening to the community. For Alia, the rhythm of her daily activities from preparing breakfast, to prayer, to breastfeeding, to dress, to career are a deployment of her beliefs about Islam. These deployments are read by other members of the community as signs of her level of engagement with her faith. As a member, Alia is allowed to dispute even the authority of the leadership as long as she follows particular protocols (of course validation of the protocols speaks to issues of power). Alia's rejection of the *niqab*, for example, represents an acceptable type of engagement because her choice is informed by the Qur'an and her selective readings of hadith. In some Muslim communities, membership in the *ummah* is based on kinship or citizenship rather than engagement with Islamic exegesis, or *tafsir*. This is clearly not the case for African American converts who must prove they are Muslims through their knowledge and practice of their faith.

With almost any group, some form of surveillance is used in an effort to police the borders; however, within this community surveillance is fairly informal. There have been exceptions, for example, a *shura*, or council, at al-Mustaqim formally sanctioned a member and banned him for one year from the masjid. The decree was based on a consensus that this man's actions were not permissible in Islam. What happens much more frequently at the local level is that "consensus" about what is and is not permissible is negotiated during each gathering of the community. Islamic *tafsir* circulates at Friday services, Sunday lectures, *Eid*, conferences, and social gatherings where women compare notes on everything from how they feel about men, clothing, hanging family photos on walls, and fingernail polish to whether they should require their adolescents to pray. This attempt to build consensus is related to a desire to "perfect the practice of faith" but is not meant to restrict individuals. Notably, the saying "There is no compulsion in Islam" is an edict with tremendous cachet in the community, and most women believe that each convert has her own faith trajectory. For example, after attending a Friday service, I was putting on my shoes when a woman noticed my nail polish. Mid-sentence, the woman stopped her conversation with a friend and said to me, "I used to wear nail polish. Now I know that it keeps me from doing a thorough *wudu*. But over time, as you learn more about the faith, you'll understand." Within the community, Muslims speak about intentions. Behavior deemed to be un-Islamic is considered acceptable as long as the intentions of the individual are pure. Ultimately, a conscious approach to behavior and personal choice, shaped by a faith in Allah, is the test of community membership.

A clear example of the relationship between consensus building and border creation occurred in October 1995. Early that month word began to spread throughout the Sunni community that African Americans should take the day off in support of Louis Farrakhan's Million Man March. The Sunni Muslim community became divided, and many supporters of the march were chastised by imams who did not want the community to be symbolically or ideologically identified with Louis Farrakhan and his racial projects. In light of the positive media attention following the Million Man March, the imams who denounced congregational support retracted their earlier positions, and in so doing they broadened the borders of their community and redefined appropriate forms of Sunni Muslim praxis. In fact, as a result of the success of the march, two sisters from the community, Zipporah and Nadia, decided to begin visiting the Nation of Islam in order to strengthen the relationship between the Sunni community and the Nation. Nadia started an Islamic study class for women in the Nation, and eventually she publicly atoned for all the years she condemned the Nation before a gathering of three hundred. Importantly, the march opened the door for the reexamination of racialized discourses that since 1975 have generally been considered unacceptable within the Sunni Muslim community.

While the Million Man March was a very public event, when the community has to decide appropriate religious practice, the daily lives of women converts comprise small personal events that require individual decisions on appropriate actions. Personal choices become public debates as individuals share their exegesis, or *tafsir,* with others. These discussions lead to changes in the community's core values, identity, and membership diacritics.[9]

To a large extent, the community encourages individuals to decide for themselves how they are going to practice their faith. The community, after all, is quite marginal and has no institutional authority in the United States outside the walls of the masjid. Membership is voluntary, and because the community needs all the members it can get, the barriers to entry are quite low. The community on the other hand has some standards based on an implicit mandate to develop connections with powerful communities outside and inside the United States by making the practice of their faith compatible with the *ummah*, or the international community of Muslims. The community wants to grow in terms of its understanding and practice of Islam, and wants to be recognized internationally as practitioners of the same faith as Muslims in Indonesia, Asia, Africa, and the Middle East. At the same time, African American Muslims want their religion to be free of the cultural traditions that they believe taint the practice of Islam in countries such as Saudi Arabia. The challenge for the community is to find compatibility between Islamic *tafsir* and feminism, black nationalism, and capitalism, ideological domains with which many converts positively identify. While the community wants to avoid confusing its cultural values with faith, the desire for gender equality, or a radical race-based revolution, or class mobility are ideals that sometimes compete with, or at times are completely incompatible with, the ideological consensus the Muslim leadership is trying to build. In cases where ideological domains compete, Qur'anic exegesis becomes a mediating discourse. Alia's argument, "I must veil for Allah and not my husband," reveals an set of priorities and personal identifications entirely different from, "I'm a feminist who believes women should have careers, and a veil oppresses women by placing them at a disadvantage." Translating her choices using Islamic exegesis speaks to her desire to be part of the Muslim community, to be married to her husband, to participate in spiritual rehabilitation in prison, to raise her son to be part of the Muslim community, to change the way society distributes social rewards, and most importantly to obey, as best she can, Allah. While the limits placed on how Alia can rationalize her choices may seem repressive, paradoxically the potential of this community to reauthor social relations in the inner-city is reliant on the community's engagement with Islamic exegesis. Notably, debates within this community are anchored in such a way as to allow individual expression while also encouraging people with very disparate views to recognize and respect one another as brothers and sisters. It creates a space in which individuals can encourage community reform and authorize social activism.

By focusing on Alia's choice of *hijab*, I have run the risk of reexoticing Muslim dress. I use the example only because it is an accessible symbol of religious faith for people unfamiliar with Islam. *Hijab*, however, is only one of hundreds of obligatory, or recommended, acts of worship articulated in the Qur'an and the sunnah. Ultimately, the only act that is entirely forbidden in the Qur'an is the association of Allah with other Gods; otherwise within Islam (not to be confused with Muslims or Islamic states) there is a great deal of forgiveness even for those who neglect obligatory acts of worship. Given this openness, African American Muslims have to decide for themselves which acts of worship are meaningful to them, and then how to perform those acts without compromising other values.

The high literacy rate among African American Muslims means that many have become lay scholars of Islam, and those individuals feel empowered to authorize, or validate, their religious praxis. But what about the women who are less literate and whose knowledge of Islam comes from imams or husbands whose faith is an expression of their belief in male dominance? Marwa, for example, does not use birth control. There are a number of women in the community who interpret birth control as interference in Allah's plan. While many of them might be extremely literate in Islamic scholarship and are empowered by their faith, there are a handful of women with eight, ten, thirteen children who continue to refuse birth control knowing that their husband's income is not sufficient to properly feed each new arrival. These women are often emotionally overwhelmed, tired, and are forced to depend on the generosity of the wealthier Muslims for gifts of clothing, cash, and food. Women like Marwa sacrifice certain markers of health and well-being in order to fulfill desires for a spiritual life defined by a very literal translation of Qur'an and hadith. Both Marwa and Alia have not only adopted a faith, but have adopted a method for engaging with and expressing that faith. Marwa more readily accepts the limits imposed by her more literal translations of the texts. In doing so she loses some control in deciding the trajectory of her life, but the material conditions that brought her into the faith, including poverty and racism, are equally beyond the borders of her control. While in the past her poverty was merely a sign of her community's oppression, she believes her present poverty has meaning; she is sacrificing material well being in order to bring more Muslims into the world. So are Marwa's actions representative of disempowerment or desire?

For Alia and Marwa, conversion did not happen in a social vacuum. Each had a critical perspective on the social history of their communities, and each believed Islam could successfully house their personal, political, and spiritual selves. Islam for them was understood to be a blueprint for a moral social order that begins at the level of body consciousness and emanates outward. Both feel that disciplining their desires does not lead to disempowerment. Rather, they accept that it is the desire for discipline that is empowering, and the intentionality that comes with God-consciousness that is the first step toward community empowerment. While converts fully accept and embody *taqwa* and *tawhid*, or God-consciousness and the oneness of God, they remain ambivalent toward some doctrine for both personal and political reasons. Some deal with their ambivalence by learning more about Islam in order to reinterpret the primary sources; others choose silence. The ambivalence might be about an issue as innocuous as fingernail polish, or as life-threatening as the dismissal by an imam of a woman's claims of wife abuse. Membership in this Sunni community requires one to have faith in accepted methods of truth verification, or Islamic exegesis, but it does not require one to accept the interpretations of others. As one of my informants noted, while she never doubts her faith she does question what she believes, in which case she relies on the sunnah of the Prophet Muhammad to help resolve her ambivalence.

THREE

Gender Negotiations and Qur'anic Exegesis

One Community's Reading of Islam and Women

In the fall of 1995 at Masjid al-Mustaqim, converts formed a group called "Sister-to-Sister." They met regularly to develop a kind of authoritative community consensus *(ijma)* about their faith. The women used well-established methods for Islamic exegesis, including the use of Qur'an, hadith , and secondary sources written by reputable religious scholars. Each Saturday session was led by a different lay scholar on Islam, and the forum of women educating women gave sisters a chance to share their feminist exegesis with newer converts. In addition, these meetings provided an opportunity to develop some consensus regarding religious interpretations of specific Qur'anic *suras* (divisions of the faith, or chapters) and *ayat* (verses), and if not consensus then healthy debate using valid sunnah (examples of the Prophet) preserved in hadith. This was the women's *khutbah*.

Arriving at the masjid on a Saturday differs markedly from *Jumah* (Friday prayers) when the *adhan* (call to prayer) can be heard coming from the loudspeaker and men and women form a continuous stream arriving for the *khutbah* and *salat* (prayer). Instead, the masjid is fairly deserted, but in keeping with the community's interest and need for security, two brothers open the masjid and patrol outside for the duration of the meeting.

About twenty women came to the first meeting. The woman leading the discussion on *hijab*, Fatima, converted to Sunni Islam in Philadelphia in the 1960s. She is unusual in the sense that she was attracted to Sunni Islam when most African American Muslims were in the Nation of Islam. In the 1960s she and her brothers belonged to a sizable and growing community of African American Sunni Muslims in Philadelphia. She is now married to her second husband and has two daughters in their twenties. She and her husband own a consulting business.

Fatima has a traditional approach to Islam, and proclaims that "Islam is not for everyone." She even encourages people to consider other religions if they are unable to live according to the five pillars, strict dress codes, and etiquette. In the masjid, we all sit barefoot on the dark-green, plush carpet with photocopies of the outline for the day's discussion. Fatima sits surrounded by books, and holds in her hands her lecture. Soft-spoken but very direct, Fatima quietly calls the meeting to order. This is a verbatim transcript of part of this Sister-to-Sister meeting:

NADIA: Assalamu alaikum sisters.[1] Sisters, today our presenter's going to be Sister Fatima. She's going to be talking about Islamic dress. Also, before she starts I would like to please note that last week because there was a disagreement . . . neither person had validation for what they said from the Qur'an or the hadith. Any time you have information you have to validate it with that information.

FATIMA: Now *hijab*[2] is a divine law and guidance based on the Holy Qur'an and the hadith, which are the traditions of the Prophet Muhammad, sallallahu alayhi wa sallam [sws].[3] Now before *sura Al-Ahzab* was revealed, women were not required to observe *hijab*.[4] Now they would cover their hair, but that was not considered *hijab* because, as I stated, it's a total thing. So when the verse was revealed, which by the way was revealed either the fifth or third year of *hijra*, or migration into Medina.⁵ So this was only about five years before Prophet Muhammad, sws, returned to Allah.

We find that a lot of the hadith and stories of believers of the *ummah* of that time were written before *hijab*, so we find a lot of things that we kind of lean on saying, "Well they weren't in *hijab* back then. We don't have to wear *hijab*." That's because a lot of things we read were written before Al-Ahzab was revealed, as we see in *ayat* 33. Would someone like to read that?

HALIMA: *Bismillah ar Rahmanir Rahim* [In the name of Allah, the Beneficent, the Merciful]: "And stay quietly in your houses, and make not a dazzling display, like that of the former Times of Ignorance; and establish regular prayer, and give *zakat* and obey Allah and His Messenger. And Allah only wishes to remove all abomination from you, ye Members of the Family, and to make you pure and spotless" (33:33).

FATIMA: Now this verse a lot of people say was only for the wives of the Prophet, sws, which is true. It was directed to the wives of the Prophet. But as with a lot of revelation in the Qur'an, and with a lot of things that the Prophet Muhammad, sws, did, they started within his family, but they moved out into the *ummah* because it wasn't just for him or his family members. But it's just like within your home, if you expect your children to mimic you, you have to set a good example.

Sisters I'm so nervous. Usually I'm not this nervous; it's the subject matter [laughs]. Because I wasn't sure how to deal with this, and I started so many times and I tore up the paper. I said, "No, they are going to throw me out on Hamilton Boulevard. I know it."

Now of course I had a problem with the *niqab*, which is the face covering, but then when you read I guess it depends on which Qur'an you read, which I had a problem with as

well. I wondered as well, "Why are we getting one interpretation in one Qur'an and another interpretation in another
one?" And this book it really breaks it down to exactly what
Allah meant for us. And I said, "I know I have read this *sura* I
don't know how many times." *Sura An-Nur,* which is another
sura we will be into in a minute, but I just found this to be
mind-blowing. Some people say that you can read a *sura* over
and over again, but when Allah's ready for you to understand
it, you understand it. But then with the help of this book
breaking it down I have to say that the book helped because
it gave you the root words in Arabic, and it broke the meaning down.

The second part of the commandment [*Sura* 33:32] states
that the best way to observe *hijab* is to stay in their homes and
not come out without a valid reason. Now that doesn't mean
that we all have to stay in our house because today we are
working women. There is a valid reason [laughs]. We have to
shop, but just to hang in the street, just to hang? That is my interpretation. I'm not going to put that on anybody else. That's
my interpretation. Just don't hang in the streets. Be out there
on some sort of business [laughs]. I guess that's the reason why
Allah, subhanahu wa taala [swt],[6] has made the man responsible
for us because we shouldn't have to work if we don't want to
work, and they're stronger, they're able to deal with all that, so
let them [laughs]. You know they can do that. And if we were in
a society, in a country where we could stay home . . . okay,
don't go there [laughs]. In sha Allah [God willing].

The result of this meeting was a reaffirmation that wearing *hijab* denotes
one's commitment to faith, thereby situating those who wear *hijab* as core
members of the community. Seven years after the meeting, *hijab* had lost
its significance as a membership diacritic within the community (see the
epilogue).

CRITIQUES OF CHRISTIANITY

Islamic exegesis for African American Muslims usually includes an analysis of the perceived failures of Christianity coupled with Western notions of "freedom." Christianity, they believe, has been used to promote racism and sexism, while Islam, they argue, balances the rights and responsibility of men and women with the need for community cohesion and social justice. While they believe that Islam has greater potential to change social relations, they nevertheless recognize that Islam, like every religion, is a work in progress.

Most Muslims I interviewed believe that Christianity, as practiced in the United States, defines people as created in sin, with impure desires, while Islam has no similar narrative about inherited sin. The following is from an interview with Nadia, a middle-aged convert with four children.

NADIA: We were talking. It may have been with one of my family members. I always try to spend some time doing a Bible/Qur'an study thing, and I said, "So is it true that we're cursed?" I said, "Isn't that what the Bible says we're cursed for all time?"

CAROLYN: You mean the story of Ham?

NADIA: Yes, as black people [the story says we are cursed for all time]. I said, "Now in my religion God is all forgiving, most oft returning, most merciful." I said, "But to think that God would curse a people for all time. I mean they had no other chance, no other this or that. They have to just be here suffering."[7]

For most African American Christians, like Nadia's relatives, the story of Ham is understood to be an allegory. For Muslims, however, the story encapsulates Christianity's role in neutering African Americans in an effort to make them passive to their own oppression. Islam, as interpreted by most sources, deems that everyone has the potential to be spiritually pure, which means that through conversion there is salvation. Past sins—

drug addiction, crime, sex outside of marriage—are forgivable and for-given in Islam.

In addition, the significance of the Muslim ethic of salvation is that even lapses in religious practice and self-control are amenable to correc-tion. No one, in other words, is damned forever unless one dies in a state of impurity. In addition, daily purifying rituals—food and exchange taboos and resource distribution (*zakat* and wages) in particular—act not only on the body, but extend past the borders of the body and in a sense purify the social body. In essence, it is thought that being a moral citizen by controlling one's consumption and behavior has the potential to im-prove social relations. Therefore, the ability to liberate one's community begins and ends with the potential, established within Islam, for spiritual purity; an ethic converts contrast with Christianity and the idea of in-herited sin.

A similar argument to Nadia's is made in a manual entitled *Being Mus-lim: A Rites of Passage Manual for Girls* by Gail Madyun, an African Amer-ican convert to Islam. The manual, written in the genre of an epistolary to a young daughter, begins a discussion on Christianity by describing the present status of blacks in America:

> By now you realize that race is one of the most important attributes our society uses to identify us. You are African-American, black, Negro—whatever term used, you have come to realize whether con-sciously or subconsciously that African-American people have an in-ferior status. We are among the poorest economically and least edu-cated in this country. Individuals in our race may have great respect and high positions of authority, but as a group, we are not respected.[8]

The manual goes on to describe why Madyun converted to Islam:

> One of the reasons we, your parents, are Muslims today is because we refused to be limited by these labels. In your history books and through what we have taught you at home, you know that our ances-tors were Africans. They were forcibly brought to America against their will and were enslaved for four hundred years. Prior to our en-slavement we belonged to highly organized societies with govern-

ment, educational institutions, and most importantly, a religion and value system which supported our development.[9]

Ultimately, Madyun ties the social condition of blacks to Christianity, which, by corollary, means that to escape from oppressive ideology one must escape from Christianity:

> When we were enslaved, we were forced to accept the Christian religion which deified Prophet Jesus [PBUH][10] and portrayed him as the son of God. Moreover, Prophet Jesus [PBUH] was depicted as a blond-haired, blue-eyed European. The logic is if Jesus was the Son of God, created in the image of God, then God must be a European-looking being. What this did was to cut us off from connection with our Creator. . . . We have chosen to raise you as a Muslim because we believe that Al-Islam gives us a proper concept of our Creator and ourselves.[11]

A number of my informants strongly criticize the symbolic deification of a race through the depiction of Jesus as white. Claiming that God, or the Son of God, existed in a human form reflects for Muslims the ways in which the *Prophet* Jesus' message has been appropriated as a tool for oppression. Similarly, while they argue that the Bible has been corrupted by man, the Qur'an, they believe, came directly from God through the Angel Gabriel. With respect to Qur'anic exegesis, this means of course that all Muslims are fundamentalists. The fact that Jesus is identified only as a prophet and that God for Muslims exists in an unknowable form, puts their faith, Muslims believe, at a safe distance from race or gender deification.

Muslims have often reiterated to me that Islam showed them that they were "made in excellence." Through continued immersion in Islamic scholarship, my informants say they have been able to reverse a self-loathing made worse by the church. This emotional trajectory has roots in the Nation of Islam and in the teachings of Elijah Muhammad, who encouraged his followers to rid themselves of their internalized self-hatred. By the late 1960s, the Black Power movement popularized a secular version of what the leader of the Nation had been trying to advance for decades. Expressions like "Black is Beautiful" and songs with lyrics like "Say it loud, I'm black and I'm proud" summarize the intentions of the Black Power movement to instill in blacks a sense of pride. Similarly, intellectuals from Frantz Fanon to Claude Steele to Cornel West argue that the psychological effects of racism have been so devastating to the community that the results manifest in material deprivation, depression, self-destruction, and violent behavior.[12] While it is debatable where structural constraints end and individual agency begins, it is clear that conceptualizations of self-worth have significant repercussions in the lives of individuals. In many ways I believe the Muslim community's most profound corrective has been its grassroots initiative to undo self-hatred.

NADIA: I think that Islam if properly understood could really . . . I mean it would be a motivating factor for African American children especially. The reason I say African American children is because there's something negative that trickles down to all generations of African Americans. There's something, I can't put my finger on it, but something that—and I know that we can use the word *shaitan* [Satan] for lack of a better word—something negative that trickles down through generations that says you can get to a certain point but that's as far as you can go.

But that's not true. And I think Islam validates that. That it's not true. Allah gives everybody potential to go as far as they want to go. All they have to do is make a decision and beg God's help. I mean I don't think things are limited. That's why I think the young boys program is important.

So on the positive side, Islam has let me know that I'm a full individual that is capable. That I have capabilities. That I'm created in excellence and not in sin. That I had the spiritual foundation that Allah has blessed me with and the mental foundation, and then physically, the physical foundation.[13]

"IMAM IN THE HOUSE" AND OTHER MYTHS

Many African American Muslim women believe the Bible has been used to legitimate Western patriarchy. Madyun says to her daughter:

> Another misconception which has hampered our development has been the image woman has received under Christianity as practiced in our society. Even though you were not raised as a Christian, the prevailing concept of what a woman is in our society comes from the Christian doctrine. The Creation myth propagated in the Bible . . . places the blame for the downfall of man on Eve's weakness. It is she who tasted the forbidden fruit which in Christianity condemned man to toil and struggle on Earth. As a further punishment for woman, the Bible says she is also condemned to suffer pain in childbirth because of her "sin". . . . So it is no wonder that we as women have entered the race for human progress at a disadvantage. The earliest images we receive are not nurturing of a positive self-concept both as non-Europeans and as females. But again, with a clear image of who we really are, Allah promises us much more.[14]

Madyun's feminist critique of Christianity was a refrain I heard quite a bit, and notably during events like the Sister-to-Sister meetings gender issues were almost always part of theological discussions. Even during *Jumah* at Masjid al-Mustaqim, the chances were high that an analysis of gender and marriage would be woven into the *khutbah*. Imam Khalil, a prominent and charismatic leader in the community, focused so extensively on marriage and family that my European American friend/informant wanted *my* opinion on why that particular discussion seemed to dominate the services. Her reaction challenged the anthropologist's notion that an informant's voluntary participation represents either knowledge of, acquiescence to, or belief in the implicit and explicit purposes of the event.

In sermons Imam Khalil would often describe his own marriage as wonderful, but not free of struggle.[15] He and his wife had three children who are all active participants in the Muslim community. Although his wife had once worn a head covering, at the time of these observations she only wore one inside the masjid and during religious events. He owned his own business and his wife worked for the city. Unlike most of his congregation, their combined incomes enabled them to own their own home in a middle-class suburb. Imam Khalil wanted the other converts to get married in order to perfect the other half of their religion and to increase their financial and emotional security. Unfortunately, the divorce rate was and continues to be high among people who worship at Masjid al-Mustaqim, so Imam Khalil would often use *Jumah* as an opportunity to counsel the congregation about marriage. In this *khutbah*, Imam Khalil discusses masculinity vs. femininity. This excerpt represents the type of gender negotiations taking place in the Muslim community.

> As we read this verse in the Qur'an and *Sura An-Nisaa* titled, "The Woman," it reads—With the name of Allah most gracious, most merciful [obligatory utterance before reading from the Qur'an]—it says, "Oh humanity reverence your guardian lord who created you from a single person created of like nature his mate and from them scattered like seeds countless men and women. Reverence God through whom ye demand your mutual rights and reverence the wombs that bore you for God ever watches over you. And surely Allah speaks the truth"(4:1).[16]

This *sura* is commonly used by African American Muslims as an example of women's esteem in Islam. The frequency with which this verse was recited throughout my fieldwork indicates to me the importance the community places on representing Islam as a religion that respects women.

> This verse . . . first of all it reminds us in very simple, simple language that Allah created humanity: the human social order from "*nafsin wahidatin*," from a single soul. Then it says from that single soul Allah created the mate. Now not taking the other theological explanations that Allah created the woman from the rib, it's not even saying that nor is it implying that. As a matter of fact, what is excellent about this is Allah has a law in the Qur'an. Allah says he creates

everything in pairs. So Allah [swt] makes it explicitly clear, implicitly clear that Allah began the creation of the human social order from male and female. They represent pairs for each other. And even the word, the Arabic words here, "*zawj*," "*zawjaha*," mean that they're not only pairs, they're not only mates, but they were created in the bond of marriage.

Imam Khalil in this excerpt describes how the Islamic origin myth leaves ambiguous the question of who was created first. According to Imam Khalil's exegesis, Adam and Eve were created out of one living entity (*nafs*) and the mate (*zawj*) was created from the first. Both terms, *nafs* and *zawj*, are gender neutral, meaning one cannot claim gender dominance or superiority based upon the order of creation. Accordingly, in the Qur'an both Adam and Eve are described as having approached the forbidden tree, disobeyed God, and ultimately both were punished equally. For African American Muslim converts, this is one example of how Islam has no gender hierarchy.

> It [the verse] uses *rijal* for the man. So when it talks about man, *rjl* [Arabic root] means masculinity, it means man, it means masculinity, but what it's implying to us is that you are a man because you do what a man should do. You're a man because you act according to the constitution of a man.

> And then when it deals with woman, *nisaa*, it says the woman is female because she does the things belonging to the female world. She does a thing according to her constitution. It says to reverence Allah, to reverence God, but it also says to reverence the womb that bore you. Reverence the womb.

Imam Khalil in this *khutbah* stresses that marriage is a necessity for Muslims and emphasizes that being a man requires acting in accordance with the teachings of Islam. Like most religious leaders, Imam Khalil is familiar with intimate stories of wife abuse, child abuse, criminal activity, unemployment, and adultery within his community. In response, Imam Khalil has made improving relationships a priority by delivering *khut-*

bahs like this one on gender. A feminist reading of this *khutbah* might focus on the seemingly antiquated notion of gender identity, "The woman is female because she does the things belonging to the female world." But I argue that the assumption ignores the context. The lecture is primarily aimed at stopping oppressive male behavior by using the threat of stripping men of their status as men. While the lecture is clearly essentializing gender difference, it is questionable whether these distinctions are to be taken literally, metaphorically, or perhaps even ironically. Even as he tries to assert these constitutional differences, Imam Khalil does not forget to reaffirm Islam's respect and reverence for women. Juxtaposing the controversial statement about gender constitution with the verse "reverence the wombs that bore you," he attempts to transform gender consciousness by arguing that Islam *does* have gender roles, but not to the exclusion of equality and respect. The fact that he must legitimate Islamic gender roles using rhetoric about women's equality indicates that feminism, like Islamic exegesis, is an accepted and therefore authorized discourse within the African American Muslim community.

> Allah has said that the highest regard should be shown to the womb, and this *arham* [mercy] also refers to womb from the standpoint of community, kinship, family relationships, but also . . . the uterus. Allah has commanded us that if you're talking about worshipping Allah, . . . you're not worshipping Allah until you have high regard and reverence for the womb that bore you. This is very important for us because you're saying to yourself as you accept this religion . . . [that] you can't disrespect, you can't mistreat, you can't disregard the wombs that bore you.

In the first half of this *khutbah*, Imam Khalil tries to do two things. First, he outlines the ways in which Adam and Eve are equals in order of creation and degree of sin. He stresses that Eve was not created as a gift to Adam, or from a part of Adam. Eve, in order words, is not symbolically two steps removed from God, but rather Allah created them as a pair of equals. His feminist interpretation of the Islamic story is, of course, set against his own reading of the Christian origin myth, which by inference is sexist ("Not taking the other theological explanations that Allah created the woman from the rib . . ."). Second, set against what Khalil presents as overwhelming proof that Islam is profemale, he begins to outline the more challenging aspects of Muslim gender roles.

> Allah [swt] says [in marriage] a man should be the provider, main-
> tainer, and the protector of the woman. This is his masculinity. And
> the woman has to be what? The woman has to be responsible for the
> property, for the home, and also for rearing the children. And also
> she has to be obedient to the husband. Not obedient in the sense of
> obeying him, but obeying him in accordance with the guidance of
> Allah.

Here Imam Khalil asserts that "obedience" by a wife is conditional on a husband's financial responsibility to his family. The important caveat is that a wife is never required to perform duties beyond those pre-scribed in Islam, a stipulation that opens a space for women to redefine those duties through Qur'anic exegesis. Continuing his *khutbah* Imam Khalil says:

> In the *Sura Luqman* Allah says, "Thy lord has decreed that ye wor-
> ship none but him," and then after that it says you should be kind to
> your parents. And then the next verse says, "And we have enjoined
> on man to be good to his parents." It says, "Travail, upon travail did
> his mother bare him [31:13–14]," and right after that it goes into the
> importance of worshipping the wombs that bore you. Reverence
> Allah, reverence the wombs that bore you. Prophet Muhammad said
> the womb is tied to the throne of Allah. And it says, "With him who
> keeps me united, Allah will keep connection. But whoever severs me,
> Allah will sever connection." And Prophet Muhammad said, "One
> who has severed the ties of relationships will not even enter para-
> dise." Allah Akbar. [Congregation responds, "Allah Akbar."]

It is interesting that Imam Khalil juxtaposes a call for woman and men to submit to gender roles in marriage with a call for children to submit to their parents, particularly their mothers. I interpret Imam Khalil's choice to reaffirm women's place in Islam as a sign that he realizes that by raising the issue of women's "obedience" he is moving into very dangerous territory. The women might be offended and leave the community, and the men might take "obedient to the husband" to mean a wife must obey under all circumstances. Khalil, who is a master rhetorician, recognizes the problematic waters he has entered and so he doubles back to reiterate the responsibility of men to women.

> Prophet Muhammad said that the flee of a man from his family is like that of a slave from his master. He says his prayers and his fast are not accepted until he returns. And then he said the fleeing of a man is like a case where a man is in the family but is neglecting the responsibilities of providing, protecting, and maintaining. It says even though he's present in his life, he's absent. Allah Akbar [Congregation responds, "Allah Akbar"].

When Khalil refers to abandonment he is referring not just to husbands initiating divorce, but to emotional and financial abandonment as well. While politically the right wing seems to get the credit for promoting "family values," in the inner city many progressives would like to see families (absent violence and oppression) remain intact. Progressives recognize that single parenthood is tremendously stressful and a financial hardship, especially for the working poor. Men and children also benefit from being part of a stable nuclear family. The Muslim community believes strongly that gender roles, as outlined in Islam, establish a paradigm for how to create a successful relationship. Khalil embeds new and challenging understandings of gender in feminist exegesis:

> So when you understand the excellence of this, it's putting emphasis on "reverence the womb" [4:1]. Prophet Muhammad even reminded the woman of this. It says, "When a woman becomes pregnant, . . . Allah rewards her, gives the reward as much as he would to someone who goes out for jihad with all its wealth and life." It says, "And then when she delivers her baby, a call would reach her stating all your

sins are forgiven, start a new life again." It says, "Each time she feeds the baby with her milk from her breast, Allah gives her reward equal to that of a freeing of a slave for each feeding." Allah Akbar. [Congregation responds, "Allah Akbar"].

I'm saying this because you can see the excellence that's put on the importance of respect and reverence for the womb. And this is not according to you and our thinking. This is the thinking of Allah. Allah Akbar [Congregation responds, "Allah Akbar"].

And the paradox here is that many non-Muslims view Islam as a man's religion. They say, "That's a man's thing." That's what they think it is. They say that women are oppressed in Islam. They say the women are subservient to the men in Islam. Then they say the women's role is inferior in Islam. And then they say the women look like they're in bondage in Islam. They have no freedom in Islam. And the position of a woman in Islam really to some is perceived to be subhuman.

Much of this paradox is due to the ignorance of Islam because they look at the example in the Middle East. In the Middle East it's a cultural thing. It's not an Islamic, it's a cultural thing. The woman is subservient in many ways. But in the excellence of Islam she doesn't have a subservient role, she has the most excellent of roles. Allah Akbar. [Congregation responds, "Allah Akbar!"].

I have to really relate that because so many times many of our sisters get caught up in that thinking. They think they're . . . in a religion that[oppresses them]. They think there's no equality. But if they only understood how Allah has honored them for everything that they do they would just thank Allah for guiding them to Islam. All the rights that the woman has today; the right to inherit, the right to own property, the right to speak out in public, the right to vote, all of this came from Islam. Allah Akbar. [Congregation responds, "Allah Akbar"].

And Prophet Muhammad [PBUH] even put such an honor on women that they should think about that Prophet Muhammad [PBUH] said that paradise is at the feet of the mother. That Paradise! And then when Prophet Muhammad [PBUH] was asked a question about who deserves the best treatment, the best company, Prophet Muhammad [PBUH] said, "Your mother." They said, "Who next." He said, "Your mother." They said, "Who next." He said, "Your mother." They said, "Well who next?" He said, "Then your father." Allah Akbar. [Congregation responds, "Allah Akbar!!!"]

So the woman in Islam really is treated so special that if she only understood the excellence of her role, her whole attitude would be smiling. She wouldn't worry about being the imam [laughter]. She wouldn't want to be the imam in the house. She wouldn't worry about why she couldn't teach no *khutbah*. See, the attitude will get to them some time; they'll try to take over the imam in the house if you don't watch it. [Congregation responds, "Allah Akbar."] Say look, I'm running this. You got to stand up. Allah Akbar. [Congregation responds, "Allah Akbar"]

What does Imam Khalil mean by "Imam in the house?" What does it mean to the women that they cannot give a *khutbah?* In fact, Khalil is giving credibility to the idea of separate but equal gender roles in the domestic sphere. Why would African American women want such a thing? The women's enthusiastic response seems ironic given that they tend to be extremely pragmatic about gender roles. If a woman needs to divorce, earn an income, protect her family and community, she simply does so. It is within this realm of pragmatism that Islamic gender roles make sense. Many converts want freedom from having to "do it all." They want relief from having to bring in an income and manage all domestic affairs. Many women would like men to have a comparable desire for family stability, and if performing gender is the method to achieve that goal, so be it.

But she is so special in Islam that really she doesn't even have to worry about economic responsibility according to the excellence of this religion. She's free from any financial responsibility according to this religion. She doesn't have to earn a cent. The responsibility goes on the father first. If the father don't show, then the husband. And in an Islamic state if the husband and the father neglect that responsibility it falls on the state—the Islamic state. Allah Akbar.

But this is important because as we look at the excellence of this religion, the example sometimes conflicts. Islam says because of her constitution, because of her makeup, because of the way she is if she is forced to work, if she is forced to provide for her own livelihood, if she's forced to provide for the livelihood of her children, if it takes her out of her role, Islam said it's not good for her. It's not good for the society because . . . when she does this she loses some of her femininity. She loses that capacity for the tenderness and the compassion. And then . . . because she's taken out of her role she takes on a nature, sometimes an attitude that really masculinity increases and femininity decreases. Allah Akbar. [Congregation responds, "Allah Akbar"]

And it says the man, the man's role is providing and protecting. If the man's not able to really make a decent living, then what happens? It says the man suffers now. But he suffers respect. He suffers honor. He suffers dignity. He suffers respect inside of the house. And then he suffers disrespect outside in the society. Allah Akbar.

So you can see how conflicting the Islamic example is because they [America] got a system that makes it very difficult for a man to function in his role. And they got a system here that's designed to take the woman out of her role. Allah Akbar. [Congregation responds, "Allah Akbar"] And this is important for us because Islam knows when she's forced to compete like a man, and believe me, many of our sisters have to go out and work. Because why? The man isn't able to provide the kind of life that's decent by himself because there's not an opportunity in society for many to do it, even when they're educated. So she's forced many times to come outside and work. And most of them would tell you, if they really told you what's in their heart, they don't want to be out there working like that. [Women respond, "Allah Akbar."] They don't need all of that freedom out there. They would rather be home with their little children when they have them. They would rather be home to make sure they have a nice comfortable home. They want a comfortable home though! [Women respond, "Allah Akbar!"] They don't want just a hole home! [Women respond, "Allah Akbar!"]

And Islam, it demands the man to always treat the woman with kindness. That's how special . . . Look Allah said, "Always stay on the footing of kindness." So if you're going to reverence the womb you can't be always irritable, oppressive in the situation. Not the Muslim male, he's got to be kind. He's got to show compassion in the relationship. If the relationship is going to be the upright relationship.

So why do women respond so heartily to the points in Imam Khalil's *khutbah?* Are they acquiescing to patriarchy out of love for Allah? Or desire for order in a difficult situation? Or a need to symbolically identify with a radical social, economic, political, and religious movement? Or to please their husbands? Or to withdraw from the urban mainstream? Or out of ignorance? Why do African American Muslims at al-Mustaqim respond so positively to the Islamic organization of gender? Again, it is important to recognize the desire on the part of women in this community to have successful families. Muslim women argue that if a religious ideology dividing rights and responsibilities strengthens marital bonds, then the division is rational.

Muslim women often want their husbands to abide more, rather than less, closely to their gender roles as defined in Qur'an and sunnah. Nadia is an example of someone who fulfilled her Islamic marital responsibilities and blames the dissolution of her first marriage on her husband's inability to fulfill his obligations. Nadia has four children. She had her first when she was an unmarried teenager; she had the three others with her first husband. At the time of this writing, she is married to her second husband, a Nigerian. She is a teacher and, like all the women I interviewed, very active in the Muslim community. She works out of both economic necessity and because she enjoys teaching, but in the past, during substantial periods in her life, she has been able to take care of her children full-time. For Nadia, Islam is about learning peace—peace with regard to marriage, friendship, community, self, and God. Gender roles help guide a couple, but personalities get in the way of implementing them to the letter. For Nadia, Islam is not about perfection, it is a guide for bringing peace to your life.

CAROLYN: Since your husband is a Muslim chaplain, do you use the Qur'an within your marriage to define roles?

NADIA: My husband uses the Qur'an for every single aspect of his life. He has gone to school for twenty-one years, and all of them were Islamic-related schools. He went to the University of London, which inside had something called the

Muslim College. So I think that's where he did his master's. He went to school in Tripoli. He applies Islam in every aspect. And I have this whole different view about things. And I know I'm a very difficult person to live with as far as mates are concerned; I really am, because I was the youngest of six children. By the time my parents had me, everybody else were almost adults and my great grandparents were still alive. My mom and dad divorced.

I'm [a] difficult [wife] because I'm used to being a single parent. My children's father, he was my first husband when I became Muslim, and I was being taught Islam. My children's father was just coming from the Nation to this part of the faith. And I was studying, and he was reminiscing days of yesteryear [laughs]. So that became really, really a problem for us. We were together close to thirteen years, and the reason I stayed so long was because I thought that's what I was suppose to do. I was supposed to stay. And my husband was . . . he didn't have any idea about Islam.

CAROLYN: What was his interpretation of it?

NADIA: Well he was still living the philosophy of the Nation of Islam. I guess his understanding of the Nation of Islam was being able to have multiple wives without marriage. Secret marriages between him and the person. Not really working—having a real job. He could paint. He was a building contractor.

In Louisiana, I convinced him to go there to live. We lived there for seven years. He made 150 thousand dollars a year because it was the time. Allah blessed us to get there at a time they started building again. And he was the only black contractor in this place. *Al-hamdu lillah* because of my family there, just mentioning my grandparents' names to some of those older white folks opened doors for us. But this man, one day he woke up and said, "You know I'm really tired of going out there in that sun." [laughs] Oh, my God. So he quit. I was overwhelmed. Devastated.

CAROLYN: How did he justify that with his religion?

NADIA: Because he said he didn't want to be bothered with those devils.

CAROLYN: Those white people.

NADIA: Yes, yes. And some of those white people were my relatives [laughs]. But it was just . . . I think the reason I mentioned that was because I'm difficult to live with, because my tolerance became very low. It seemed as though I had given so much time and energy in that relationship that, "okay, it's either going to be this, this, this, or nothing at all." So I was single for maybe four years.

And even when I was married I felt single because I felt the bulk of the responsibility. Everything was on me. Once he decided not to work anymore, I had to go out and be a breadwinner, run the house, take out the children, and see after him pretty much. After I decided that I'm not going to do this ever, ever again, I became somewhat, I think, stubborn. Like I won't even say selfish because I think sometimes we put labels if we want to do something for ourselves, or we think about ourselves, or we're considerate of ourselves and it can be labeled selfish. So I'll just use that for lack of a better word. So I decided that I better start looking out for me, and I better start thinking about me and my children. So we left Louisiana, and I went to Bakersfield. My sister's there; so we moved up there and it was really nice.

Nadia was forced to confront the fact that her personal reality did not correspond with her Islamic exegesis, feminism, or race consciousness. As a result, she acted according to her faith and common sense, and left her husband. Now in her second marriage, Nadia's husband uses Islam as a method for negotiation.

Within the community there is a tension between Islamic ideals and personal realities. Some men in the community are attracted to interpretations of Islam identifying husbands as the protectors of women and rulers of their wives. Women, however, are usually attracted to the man's requirement to provide an income, to woman's rights as stated in the Qur'an, and to the role model of the Prophet and his wives. In a number of marriages the man tries asserting his authority and control without providing the needed financial and emotional support. This is what happened with Ali and his wives (see chapter 8). He tried to assert his rights over his wives without fulfilling his obligations. A significant percentage of African American males who convert to Islam are either poor, undereducated, former inmates, and/or their employment prospects are marginal. While these identifying labels reveal nothing about a male convert's interpretation of gender roles in Islam, the history of black male underemployment is a material reality that causes many Muslim men to be poor financial providers. As such, the dissonance between the ideal and the practical can cause tension. Although women want to reproduce an Islamic family ideal, they are not afraid to end troubled marriages because most of the women are self-sufficient and have extensive social networks.

Marriages rarely end because the woman refuses to fulfill her Islamic obligations. She will take care of domestic chores, willingly seek employment to supplement her family's income, educate her children, dress conservatively, and have sex with her husband when he so desires. But women often find that fulfilling their obligations is no guarantee that their husbands will be good providers, fathers, or husbands. Couples are faced with the fact that black men in the inner city have high unemployment rates while black women have succeeded as single heads of households. They are faced ideologically with the fact that black men want to assert themselves and gain authority within their community while black women hold firmly to the notion of equal rights for women. These material and ideological contradictions impact the community so significantly—in a high divorce rate—that imams like Imam Khalil encourage the community to find solutions through *tafsir*, or exegesis.

EMBODYING FAITH, LOCATING AMBIVALENCE

For Muslims, interpreting the Qur'an is a very creative and empowering enterprise. Islam acts as a third party, as a mediator determining the interests of each party relative to the interests of the family and the community. For American Muslims, the act of interpreting Islam is one of the most significant aspects of the praxis of faith. For African American women, at stake in Qur'anic exegesis is control over readings on gender, family, rights, authority, and obligations. A tradition of Islamic reform, *islah*, began soon after the death of the Prophet Muhammad. Renewing the message of Islam in order to make it relevant is understood by many Muslims to be an extremely important aspect of the faith. The African American community practices *ijtihad*, or reinterpretation of Islam, which requires balancing explicit mandates as revealed in the Qur'an and sunnah. Many conflicts in the Muslim community arise over the policing of the borders between what counts as a reasoned interpretation and what counts as *bida*, or unacceptable innovation. Nadia, for example, describes her first husband's reading of Islam as false, but how can she validate her interpretation? During my fieldwork, various women's *tafsir bil ray*, or exegeses based on opinion or judgment, were challenged. Their responses to the challenges varied from refusing to attend a particular masjid to silence and seeming acquiescence. Therefore, while exegesis has the potential to be extremely empowering for women, the power structures that dictate what counts as valid interpretation turn many women away, not so much from the faith, as from the community.

Shariah, or Islamic jurisprudence, for example, represents an entrenched interpretation of Islam that powerfully limits feminist exegesis. There are four schools of Qur'anic law, and each has a particular political character. The schools of thought include: Hanifi (a liberal school), Maliki (conservative), Shafii (moderate), and Hanbali (orthodox and rigid). Many Islamicists criticize the depiction of *shariah* as immutable and divine, like the Qur'an, when in fact these schools are interpretations of Qur'an and sunnah. The schools were founded by four legal scholars more than one hundred years after the Prophet's death in 632 C.E.[17]

Islamic scholar Muhammad Mujid describes *shariah* as an "approach to Islam" that is shaped by particular social contexts.[18] He argues that there are normative morals, which are timeless, and there are contextual morals, which are ways in which a society is organized in order to maintain the normative codes. *Purdah*, for example, is the practice of confining women to their home except in order to perform very specific tasks.[19] *Purdah*, according to some scholars, was designed to help a woman remain chaste during feudalism, but it was an innovation for a given social context. While the practice, some argue, is now unnecessary, chastity continues to be a normative moral code. Asghar Ali Engineer writes:

> To argue that *purdah* is no longer needed is not to argue that chastity too can be dispensed with. Chastity is the norm while *purdah* was a contextual means to achieve it. A woman can protect her chastity without observing *purdah*. Thus, if our concept of morality is sufficiently dynamic and creative, we will not resist attempts to give *purdah* a new form, discarding the old one and the circumstances permitting doing so without sacrificing the essential norm.[20]

In light of this argument, many Muslims are calling for new *shariah* that consider contemporary understandings of gender and equality.

While Engineer's bifurcated notion of moral standards provides a model for engaging questions of authenticity and faith, I would argue that concepts in Islam, like *hijab*, polygyny, and gender, must be understood as multidimensional rather than two dimensional. Engineer argues that the practice of the faith has essential and normative aspects in opposition to nonessential and contextual aspects, and while I believe Muslims make these categorical distinctions, there are layers of ideological certainty within the normative and contextual categories that overlap or shift over time. While Muslims argue that the Qur'an is normative and immutable, almost every major concept (from slavery to polygyny to *hijab* to usury) is layered in political-historical meaning spanning from the seventh to the twenty-first century.[21] By this I mean that pure, unadulterated Islam is not simply found in the most accurate readings of historical facts, but rather Islam is reread in consideration of all that has occurred since the first revelation. Clearly historical exegesis is informed by contemporary discourses and epistemologies that challenge the idea that methods alone can isolate what constitutes "essential" Islam. Regardless of my skepticism about the existence of religious authenticity, Muslims believe it is in their interest to locate the essential from the nonessential, the normative from the contextual, in order to liberate themselves from false practice.

When it comes to locating authenticity, female converts often confront scripture that seems, on the surface, to cast them as intrinsically dangerous, polluting, and in need of control. Not surprisingly, many women often have difficulty embodying these beliefs either at the level of personal disposition or social practice.[22] Difficulty owning particular beliefs leads to ambivalence, which women attempt to reconcile through a holistic sense-making that combines exegesis, common sense, and pragmatism.[23]

QUR'ANIC EXEGESIS AT THE LOCAL LEVEL

The relationship between belief and ambivalence is expressed clearly in the ways the women discursively navigate particular injunctions in the Qur'an. Seven edicts are frequently discussed in women's gatherings in this community. The edicts any community chooses to focus on are generally relevant to their specific social concerns. Notably these discursive engagements are context driven and therefore vary across Muslim subgroups and across time. The religious proclamations and quasi proclamations are separate from the five pillars of the faith, and some might even argue that these are not what Engineer calls normative moral codes (again codes that are not up for debate, like chastity, charity, or *tawhid*— the oneness of God). These proclamations have been the subject of extensive debate within the community and represent a point of struggle for women who desire to be both fundamentalists and feminists.[24] Therefore, an analysis of how women rationalize these verses leads us to an understanding of which identities and social agendas are prioritized, and in what contexts.

The first proclamation deals with the issue of modesty and *hijab*. For most Americans, *hijab* is a symbol of an antiquated system of gender segregation demonstrating the oppression of women in Islam. In fact, the meaning of *hijab*, which includes demeanor and dress, is far more historically nuanced, leaving it open to multiple readings. S*ura* 24:30–31 demonstrates how women create discursive entrées into gendered proclamations:

> Say to the believing men that they should lower their gaze and guard their modesty; that will make for greater purity for them; And Allah is well acquainted with all that they do. And say to the believing women that they should lower their gaze and guard their modesty; that they should not display their beauty and ornaments except what (ordinarily) appear thereof; that they should draw their veils over their bosoms and not display their beauty except to their husbands, their fathers, their husbands' fathers, their sons, their husbands' sons, their brothers or their brothers' sons, or their sisters' sons, or their women, or their slaves whom their right hands possess, or male attendants free of sexual desires. Or small children who have no carnal knowledge of women. And that they should not strike their feet in order to draw attention to their hidden ornaments. And O ye Believers! Turn ye all together Towards Allah in repentance that ye May be successful. (24:30–31)

Based on this translation, some of my informants argued that *hijab* simply involves covering one's chest and wearing clothing deemed modest by contemporary American standards, for example, a nicely tailored business suit. Other informants privileged an historical reading of the political and social events occurring at the time these *ayat* were revealed. This approach shed light on the intentions behind the injunctions, and for them to stay true to the intentions of Islam was far more important than the specifics of what to wear. Others preferred a hermeneutical reading, and chose to understand *ayat* 24:30–31 in relationship to other *ayat* that mention modesty, including "the verse of the *hijab*," which reads:

> O ye who believe! Enter not the Prophet's houses,—until leave is given you,—for a meal, (and then) not (so early as) to wait for its preparation: but when ye are invited, enter; And when ye have taken your meal, disperse, without seeking familiar talk. Such (behavior) annoys the Prophet: he is ashamed to dismiss you, but God is not ashamed (to tell you) the truth. And when ye ask (his ladies) for anything ye want, ask them from before a curtain[25]: that makes for greater purity for your hearts and for theirs. (33:53)

According to al-Tabari, a companion of the Prophet, *Sura* 33:53 was revealed following the Prophet's wedding to Zaynab Bint Jahsh. According to al-Tabari, who heard it from Anas Ibn Malik, three impolite guests lingered at the Prophet's house after the other guests had left. The Prophet, who was known to be excessively polite to the point of being considered timid, waited until the guests finally left on their own. While drawing a *sitr*, or curtain, between himself and Ibn Malik, the Prophet recited "the verse of the *hijab*."

The verse was revealed after the first Muslim community had already relocated to Medina to avoid persecution in Mecca and during a time when the Muslims were suffering great defeats. The enemies of the Prophet had won an important victory in the Battle of Uhud, during which a march by the Meccans into Medina ended in the slaughtering of seventy men. Every family in Medina was touched by death, and the Prophet feared his followers were growing disheartened. Islamicist Fatima Mernissi argues that the revelation about *hijab* came after the Prophet had grown frustrated with the brutishness of his followers.[26] In particular, some men had discussed which of the Prophet's wives they would marry after he died, and interestingly the end of *Sura* 33:53 reads, "Nor is it right for you that ye should annoy God's Apostle, or that Ye should marry his widow after him at any time. Truly such a thing is in God's sight and enormity."(33:53) So Mernissi argues that *hijab* is a symbolic decree about politeness and order, and she contends:

The concept of the word *hijab* is three-dimensional, and the three dimensions often blend into one another. The first dimension is a visual one: to hide something from sight. The root of the verb *hajaba* means "to hide." The second dimension is spatial: to separate, to mark a border, to establish a threshold. And finally, the third dimension is ethical: it belongs to the realm of the forbidden. So we have not just tangible categories that exist in the reality of the senses—the visual, the spatial—but also an abstract reality in the realm of ideas. A space hidden by a *hijab* is a forbidden space. [27]

Mernissi goes on to describe the etymology of the word in Qur'anic Arabic and then proceeds to try to explicate the meaning from the ways in which the Sufis have used the term. Through an historical and etymological rereading *(ijtihad)* of the requirements of *hijab*, Mernissi ultimately determines that it is not a requirement. Interpreting Islam is a very scholarly and creative process allowing Muslim women the opportunity to find ways to identify more strongly with their faith. Although this does not ensure one against accusations of innovation *(bida)*, it does help women reconcile their ambivalence by validating, for instance, the compatibility between career ambition and faith.

Although the extent of obligatory covering for Muslim women is contested, almost all African American Muslims believe that the strictest prescriptions for veiling and seclusion are directed only at the Prophet's wives, who were under tremendous scrutiny. Except in the masjids, the majority of Muslim women in America do not wear conservative *hijab*, where a woman allows only her face, chin, hands, and feet to show. Interestingly, unlike many immigrant Muslim women, African American women tend to argue in favor of stricter forms of covering outside the masjid. Significantly, for African American women, *hijab* represents the decolonization of the Third World body:

But when you look in the mirror at yourself in the morning and you say I am dressing for the pleasure of Allah you can put on what you need to put on. But if you have another reason, if your intention is different, as the young sister said to me, "But the brothers like for you to have long finger nails. They want you to have your hair a certain way." And that's true they do because they have been infiltrated, it has taken time and time and time in the West since the eighteenth century; their idea of giving women rights was to say, "Do what you want to do, take off your clothes, less is best in the West." That is totally against Islam.[28]

Throughout former Third World colonies, mandated forms of Western dress have, at times, been seen as either an erasure of local culture and history, or as a means to modernity and particular forms of liberation.[29] Leila Ahmed says, "Repeatedly throughout the twentieth century the issue of women and the veil . . . has flared up in one or another Middle Eastern society—and indeed in Muslim societies further afield—and always the debate is charged with other issues—culture and nationalism, "Western" versus "indigenous" or "authentic" values."[30] In the 1970s, for example, progressive women in Egypt and Iran[31] veiled to demonstrate their rejection of Western hegemony when only fifty years earlier their counterparts refused the veil, which was seen as a sign of "backwardness."[32] Either choice represents a struggle to empower societies and individuals emerging from decades of colonialism.[33] Given the significance of *hijab* in former colonies, it is interesting that African American Muslims often feel the same need to decolonize their minds and bodies through modest dress.

Similar to women living in postcolonial states, many African American women also feel the same imposition of Eurocentrism, Western patriarchy, and capitalist markets onto the organization and understanding of women's bodies. Particularly for African American women, *hijab* authors a new female aesthetic in an environment of negative representations of black female beauty:

> The Prophet Muhammad said the only thing that should be showing on a woman is her hands, her face, and possibly her feet. It does not mean you have the right to put some hair out and some hair in. We want to do that because we have bought into a system that says [straight] hair is beautiful. And for the African American woman we

bought into this system that makes us go buy perms, which are temporary. We go and fry it, dye it, lay it to the side, we put everything in it that we can so that we can be someone who we are not. Then Allah told us that we should just put a scarf on. I was really grateful for the scarf.[34]

In addition to "Western" dress being understood as an imposition rather than a choice, Fadwa El-Guindi describes the newer movements that have readopted the veil:

Both veils, the Egyptian feminist and contemporary "Islamic," symbolize emancipation . . . . It is intertwined in a complex way with a Muslim ethic. While Islam puts high value on education, for it is the basis of learning Islamic knowledge and a prerequisite for joining the great tradition, it condemns cross-sex exposure whether by unnecessary or taboo contact or through immodesty in dress and behavior.[35]

The new veiling in Egypt, El-Guindi argues, allows women to participate in higher education through the de-eroticising of coeducational spaces. El-Guindi, therefore, makes the argument that in a context where modesty equalizes the gender playing field, veiling negates sex discrimination and becomes a tool for liberation. Even in the United States, where women can dress immodestly, modest dress is usually a requirement for women in positions of power. In other words, the discourse in the United States about the freedom of expression through dress is an unfulfilled ideal. Particularly in urban settings, *hijab* delineates borders for women in unsafe and crowded spaces:

If you stop and think about it, in American society if a woman cries rape, the first thing the judge and the jury want to know is what was she wearing? And then at the same time, if you try to cover yourself up so that you won't be a spectacle or won't necessarily encourage anybody's negative natures to rise up, you're told there's something wrong with you.[36]

Hijab is the performance of moral character in an attempt to undo racist assumptions about the loose morals of African Americans. The court-room scene Aida begins to paint represents the court of public opinion, and as Robin Kelley writes:

> If racism is essentially a thing of the past, as conservatives and many neoliberals now argue, then the failure of the black poor to lift themselves out of poverty has to be found in their behavior or their culture. In short, the problems facing the vast majority of black folk in today's ghettos lie not with government policy or corporate capitalism, but with the people themselves—our criminally minded youth, our deadbeat daddies, and our welfare-dependent mamas. Indeed, it is precisely the prevalence of these kinds of images that allow writers such as Charles Murray and Dinesh D'Souza to be taken seriously in spite of deep and obvious flaws in their scholarship. Stereotypes and sweeping generalizations stand in for serious analysis and complexity. The dozens stand in for fair and impartial intellectual engagement.[37]

At an important level, *hijab* symbolically engages converts in these urban culture wars that depict African Americans as dysfunctional, pathological, and intellectually moronic. *Hijab* designates commitment to family, spirituality, and community—the ideal core American values—at the same time that it contests racism, gender oppression, Eurocentrism, and inequality. At times *hijab* has been used by some men to control women, particularly their wives. Modernist Muslim feminists would argue, however, that there is nothing in the Qur'an, or examples within the Prophet's lifetime, to justify the seclusion, political disempowerment, and social isolation of women. African American converts are familiar with the appropriation of Islam to serve the interests of men when it comes to issues of gender separation and the rights of women. Generally, however, in the African American community, the symbol of *hijab* connects with identity struggles that exist beyond the borders of faith.

Hijab, interestingly enough, is just beginning to be seriously challenged in the African American Muslim community. The reasons are largely historical. Elijah Muhammad instituted a strict dress code for both men and women, so dress became a symbol of character and unity in the inner city. Many still hold onto this desire for identification and use dress as a symbol of consciousness purity:

> Our Islam is out front. We cannot say we are Muslims when we come to the masjid, and when we step outside we're not known as Muslims. When we cover, when we walk down the street, everyone knows that we're Muslims. As I said before, the *hijab* is not only the external part of what you wear, it is what is internal. It is a behavior. It is what Allah has given us in our nature, in our character, and we have the Prophet and his wives as an example of how we ought to carry ourselves. Whether we are in *hijab* or not we are still to have the same demeanor. However the responsibility is two fold, three fold when we are in *hijab*.[38]

Another difficult verse for many converts explains, "If you fear that you will not deal justly with the orphans, marry women of your choice, two, three, or four. But if you will not be able to do justly (with them), then only one" (4:3). Later the Qur'an states, "You are never able to be fair and just between women even if that is your ardent desire" (4:129). Therefore, monogamy is preferred, and some Muslim scholars believe a legal ban on polygyny is permissible. The idea that men can have more than one spouse bothers many non-Muslims, but African American Muslim women, who would personally refuse to participate in a polygynous marriage, do not view it as threatening:

> AFAF: You know in Islam you make a contract before you're married. You're supposed to sit down and make a contract that's legal and binding like, "We're brother so-and-so . . . sister so-and-so . . . we're getting married." And state your terms in the contract, so that's what a lot of them, if they're

doing it right, that's what they're doing. I've heard that
some of them don't even bother to even do that.

CAROLYN: What do you think about it?

AFAF: Well, I'm like this, I know what the Qur'an says, and I understand why it was allowed because men at that time
were having five hundred, six hundred wives, and you
know they marry one a day and throw her aside and next
day they're on to somebody else. There are some women
who can go for it, and some men who go for it. Myself,
personally, when I get married I want it to be me and my
husband.

If it gets to the point he feels he needs somebody else,
it's time for me and him to go our separate way. Because in
this country the black man especially cannot take care of
one woman financially. How can he take care of two? Because it says if he's going to marry me, and I'm used to living in a certain kind of house and he marries someone else,
he's got to have a certain kind of house for her. If I wear
fine clothes, he got to put fine clothes on her and fine food
in my stomach, you know. So how can the average black
man afford all that? And she's not supposed to be over here
on welfare like a lot of them are. That's not right. She's taking care of him.

I don't really see the need for it unless maybe okay . . .
now I know a situation where a brother and his wife have
been together for about thirty-some years and he loves her
dearly, but she never bore him children. He wanted children so he did take on a second wife and they did have a
baby about a year or so ago. But I understand he takes care
of both his families very well you know. And the wife, she
understood. She just said okay, that's what she wanted to
do, and everybody seems to be happy.[39]

Islam requires the drafting of a marriage contract prior to legalizing the union, and this contract can specify that polygyny is unacceptable. Therefore, Muslim women view polygyny as the choice of both the man and the woman, and if a husband breaks a contract forbidding polygyny, a woman has a legitimate reason for divorce. Other rationalizations for the practice date to the seventh century, when there were many war widows who were poor and alone, which to my informants means the decree was pragmatic rather than oppressive. In inner-city America, where a high percentage of black men are, or have been, incarcerated and the homicide rate among young men is high, some Muslims feel that the current gender imbalance similarly justifies polygyny. Finally, others argue that polygyny prevents men from committing adultery, or put more cynically by a number of Muslim women, in a polygynous marriage at least the wife knows whom her husband is fooling around with. Most Muslims argue against polygyny and view it, except in rare instances, as oppressive to women. Men who have cowives are judged by how well they follow the edict to treat the wives equally and provide for them financially.

One of the most difficult verses for African American women is:

> Men are the protectors and maintainers of women because Allah has given the one more (strength) than the other, and because they support them from their means. Therefore the righteous women are devoutly obedient, and guard in (the husband's) absence what Allah would have them guard. As to those women on whose part ye fear disloyalty and ill-conduct, admonish them (first), (next), refuse to share their beds, (and last) beat them (lightly—*dharaba*). But if they return to obedience, seek not against them means (of annoyance): For Allah is Most High, Great (above you all). (4: 34)

Clearly this verse could be used, and has been used, by Muslim men to justify beating their wives. The problem, Muslim women say, is the verse is poorly translated and misapplied. According to Islamicist Amina Wadud, *dharaba* can be translated to "strike with a feather." In addition, the *ayat* describes first admonishing the wife, then refusing to sleep with her, and then if these two actions are ineffective, some women argue, the next step should be divorce, not *dharaba*. The Prophet, for example, was repudiated by three wives before these marriages were consummated. In the case of his marriage to Asma Bint al-Numan, when the Prophet approached her she uttered, "I take refuge in Allah from thee." The Prophet followed these utterances with the proclamation, "You are granted such a protection," which he repeated three times.[40] The gentleness with which the Prophet dealt with this rejection on his wedding night underscores that he did not practice physical punishment in marital disputes. In one hadith, the Prophet Muhammad is reported to have said, "The best of you is he who treats his wife best."[41]

Daa'iyah Muhammad Taha, an inspirational African American Muslim writer and speaker until her death in the late 1990s, wrote in her reference guide, "Women in Al-Qur'aan":

The enemies of Al-Islam and the weak and ignorant among us would have one to think that this *ayat* is not only a sanction but an encouragement for men to beat women almost at will. Unfortunately, the cruel treatment of women has existed throughout history. Praise be to Allah (swt), Al-Qur'aan provides not only for the correction of all evil behaviors towards women, but provides women with Divine protection in the form of Qur'aanic ordinances demanding their kind treatment, maintenance, spiritual, intellectual, and economic freedom, as well as other important human rights.[42]

Ultimately, she redirects her argument to one of defining the spirit of the Prophet's message and understanding it against the enormity of his task:

Historically speaking, this *ayat* was revealed in Medina where the Prophet (swt) faced the awesome task of establishing the first Islamic State . . . . In the midst of this struggle, Allah (swt) sent revelations concerning women that demanded sweeping changes in the attitudes of men towards them. Women could no longer be legally sold, prostituted, inherited, married against their will, divorced frivolously, cheated on, slandered, raped, nor could the live burial of their daughters continue. Moreover, the revelation recognized their status as full human beings having the same souls as men, having the right to ownership, education, protection, maintenance, expression and respect.[43]

In this respect, Taha's approach to Qur'anic exegesis parallels that of modernist Muslim feminists. She argues that context has relevance to the ways in which the message was revealed, and that in order to interpret the Qur'an one must look at the general message of gender equality and respect. Also, her etymological approach, like Mernissi's, has been adopted by many converts who discover in translation the hopeful connotations and denotations of the Arabic spoken during the Prophet's lifetime. What is at stake in this linguistic approach is retranslating *dharaba*, or more concretely, problematizing an edict that might allow for men to beat their wives. This approach is one of the many creative ways in which scholars are trying to reappropriate Islam for the needs of contemporary women.

In *ayat* 4:34 men are also cast as the protectors and maintainers of women, and they are preferred. Amina Wadud argues that preference is given based on two conditions that must be met: first, the husband must have the means for providing; and second, he must provide for his wife and children. If both conditions are met, then the husband has certain rights over women, one of them being to lightly beat, or *dharaba*, a woman who disobeys. Zipporah interprets this *ayat* as follows:

> I think there are women like myself who see that *[ayat]* as subject to translation and interpretation. We think that men primarily have been the translators of and interpreters of [Islam]. And we see that [Islam] has not [always] been properly translated. That's the kind of thing that we [have] difficulty accepting, although we all say, "We accept what Allah said." But I think we interpret. I think Allah asks us to be gentle. So when you use your intellect it tells you that it's not right to strike another person. Hitting a Muslim can get you the hell fire. So you know what I mean. There are things in the Qur'an that don't support *[dharaba]*.
>
> Another thing about the Qur'an is you have to look at when things were revealed and why they were revealed at the time, and see

if they were updated. I have one of those Qur'ans that has why a revelation came. Unless you are a good researcher and really understand the Arabic, it's hard to really be able to link it directly and say "okay this is overruled by this or this was a kind of amendment to this statement." It's the same thing that happens with the *ayat* that it's permitted to have more than one wife. Everyone quotes that. Every man I know quotes that *ayat*, but the thing they always leave off of that is "but one is best if you but knew."

We always have to put things into context and use our intellect. My relationship with Allah is clear and precise. My relationship with people outside may not be quite as clear and precise. People may not quite understand why I do what I do, and I finally got to the point where that is not as important as it was when I first became a Muslim.

I don't question as much, like I don't question that Allah wrote this. I have this thing about putting the *baraqat*, the blessings, in the bank because I'm not a perfect person and so maybe that's the sin that I have. If that's all I have to worry about, that I didn't quite get that particular point, or I didn't accept that that was appropriate for my husband to do, I think I'm okay. Because I think there are a lot of bigger, much more important, issues that we need to be focused on, and that is small. It only becomes a big issue when someone takes advantage of that situation and tries to use that as an excuse for domestic abuse. And that's unacceptable because you have to be able to see the other parts. There are a few *ayat* that are gender based, most of them are not, they are written to apply to everybody.[44]

Aida, a physician in the community, interprets *ayat* 4:34 as such:

AIDA: I have to be honest. I have always had trouble with the fact that that *ayat* is there, but I think it's saying, "Let's be realistic." Allah knows how human beings act, how men act. It tells us in the Qur'an that men are superior in strength to women. Allah knows human nature and realizes that the male species has oftentimes abused the physical power and strength they were given. Instead of using it to protect the weaker, as they are commanded to do in the Qur'an, they have used it to abuse the weaker. Men do it to other men, and they do it to children, and they do it to women. Allah knew, "If this is in man's nature, and they were going to do this, then I need to put some serious restraints there."

CAROLYN: And how does a woman decide if her husband's demand is or isn't within the bounds of Islam? How does she communicate that to her husband?

AIDA: She should communicate that through the Qur'an and hadith. She should say [using a high-pitched voice as she embodies a Muslim sister consulting with her husband], "Excuse me brother, or honey, sweetheart," whatever you want to call him. "Knucklehead," . . . whatever [laughs]. . . . "But in *sura* so-and-so the Qur'an says this. . . ." And read the passage. "And that's further backed up by hadith, where Prophet Muhammad [sws] did this, and said this under this circumstance. Therefore, we need to get some further advice if you really think I need to stop doing this or stop saying that," or whatever the action is she's doing that the man feels necessitates him taking all these steps. The Qur'an makes it mandatory. First, you need to talk to her about it. And if you take the literal translation of the Qur'an, it's basically implying that you fear that your wife is out having an affair. That's really what it's talking about. It doesn't mean the dishes weren't cleared, or the food wasn't seasoned well enough, or I told you to be back at five and you were back at 5:30. It's very clear-cut that this step *[dharaba]* is only permissible if you think your wife is trying to have illicit relationships.

And if you stop and think about it, right here today in quote-unquote "civilized societies" there are laws on the books. I think in Argentina or Chile, it's legal for a man to kill his wife if she has an affair. It's legal I think in Chile or Argentina, may Allah forgive me if I've got the countries wrong, for a man to kill his mistress if she's caught having an affair.[45] Because that's an insult to his pride. That's his most prized possession, and if his prized possession goes out and has an affair, he pretty much has a right to go crazy. And he needs to do it right away. He can't wait a month. He's got to do it as soon as he finds out about it so that he can say, "It was in a fit of rage. I was emotionally out of control because of my wife. . . . Blah, blah, blah."

So I believe that the Qur'an is basically saying that you can't just go kill your wife because you think she's having an affair. If you think she's doing something morally inappropriate, you first have to sit and talk to her about it. Then if you really sincerely feel that the problem is still going on, then you've got to separate her from your bed. Refuse to sleep with her. Then if she keeps fooling around, then it says, and only then, does it say that you can touch her lightly, and it compares it to the thing they used to hit a camel. You have to remember [during the Prophet's life-time] camels were extremely prized animals in Arabian culture. They didn't beat their camels. They took better care of their camels than they did their families, as a rule, because you can't get across the desert on your feet. So to use the word that means the thing they used to let the camel know, "Come on let's move along," a little whip. To me that's saying if you're going to do this, you are going to have to do this in a restrained way after lots of thinking about it and giving time for tempers to cool off. That's my interpretation of it.

Then the hadith further backs it up. Number one, the Prophet Muhammad [sws] never in his life hit a single woman, and it's well documented that he had lots of problems from his multiple wives. At one point he divorced them all because they were problematic. People go around

saying [using a low-pitched voice], "Oh the wives of the
Prophet. . . ." You can't deify them. You can't canonize
them. They weren't saints. They were human beings like
you and I. But he never hit a single one of them. You cannot justify beating your wife if you say, "I'm a Sunni Muslim, and I'm following the example of the Prophet Muhammad [sws]." You've got people going around doing much
more minor things saying [using a low-pitched voice], "I
have to do this because it's sunnah, because the Prophet
Muhammad [sws] did it." So if that's your belief then be
consistent. It's well documented that the Prophet Muhammad never even slapped his wives. He just never hit them
period. You need to really, really have a good reason if you
even think about touching your wife other than out of love
and compassion and tenderness.[46]

Aida's pragmatic approach to domestic violence is built on presump-
tions about male aggression, but her reliance on traditional notions of
masculinity and femininity is rather unconvincing even for her. Remember, Aida began her explanation by saying that she wished that the
ayat did not exist, and while she argues the merits of redirecting a husband's aggression by forcing him to submit to these steps, she also argues that the second step, beds apart, means divorce, which negates the
last step.

Aida makes sure to express her ambivalence to the *ayat* but not to the
faith by ultimately reaffirming the example of the Prophet Muhammad.
The Prophet never physically punished his wives, and Aida stresses that
orthopraxy requires following the sunnah of the Prophet. Aida's use of
the everyday ethical practices of the Prophet as a source of family law
is an accepted source of *tafsir*. Significantly, the tension between the *ayat*
and the Prophet's practices opens a space for a feminist rereading, but
it also opens a space for men to commit acts of domestic violence. In this
instance, it is important to note that a hermeneutical reading of Islam

only is not generally a primary source for feminist exegesis. Notably, feminism for this community exists a priori to the community's *ijtihad*. Without the multiple cultural and ideological borders that juxtapose the Muslim community and force a continual rereading of the Qur'an and sunnah, *ayat* such as 4:34 could be extremely dangerous to women.

Women have problems with another *ayat*:

> Women who are divorced shall wait, keeping themselves apart, three (monthly) courses. And it is not lawful for them that they conceal that which Allah has created in their wombs if they believe in Allah and the Last Day. And their husbands would do better to take them back in that case if they desire a reconciliation. And the rights due to the women are similar to the rights against them (or responsibilities they owe), with regard to what is equitable, and men have a degree *(darajah)* above. Allah is Mighty, Wise. (2: 228)[47]

Some scholars believe that this verse indicates man's general superiority over woman. Others, like Sayyid Qutb, a famous traditionalist Islamic scholar, applies the verse to marriage, saying men are given preference over women because the man is required to provide materially for the family.[48] Therefore, within the family men have a degree above the female. Amina Wadud argues that the passage should be applied generally. She agrees with Qutb on the functional aspects of these assigned roles both within marriage and for society as a whole. Wadud's primary argument for the justice of this verse, however, is that the Qur'an was revealed to destroy oppression. She reasons that since women are given the most important role, overseeing the continuation of human existence, then men must be given an equally important role. Therefore, Islam provides men with a comparable role in terms of responsibility and privilege, which is the material maintenance and overseeing of his family. Similarly, men are given twice the inheritance of women due to their responsibility to provide for the family. Wadud describes the relationship between men and women in marriage and how the rights and responsibilities are balanced in order that neither is oppressed:

This ideal scenario establishes an equitable and mutually dependent relationship. However, it does not allow for many of today's realities. What happens in societies experiencing a population overload, such as China and India? What happens in capitalistic societies like America, where a single income is no longer sufficient to maintain a reasonably comfortable life-style? What happens when a woman is barren? Does she still deserve *quiwamah* (responsibility) like other women? What happens to the balance of responsibility when the man cannot provide materially, as was often the case during slavery and post-slavery US?

All of these issues cannot be resolved if we look narrowly at verse 4:34. Therefore, the Qur'an must eternally be reviewed with regard to human exchange and mutual responsibility between males and females. This verse establishes an ideal obligation for men with regard to women to create a balanced and shared society. This responsibility is neither biological nor inherent, but it is valuable.[49]

The exegesis of Zipporah, Aida, and Wadud illustrates several points. The first is that African American Muslims rely heavily on the Qur'an to form their religious identity. A convert's beliefs may start because of an identification with African American nationalism, socialism, or interest in community uplift. Ultimately, however, the majority come to rely on the Qur'an to shape their identity and consciousness.

The second point is that African American Muslim consciousness is informed by a strong belief in the equality of men and women. Most notably, some of my female informants expressed that they are uneasy with some hadith, or the sayings of the Prophet Muhammad, because sometimes they seem misogynistic. One female informant said that "the religion is easy as long as you stay away from the hadith," by which she meant that for her many hadith contradict her feminist exegesis of the Qur'an. Hadith were passed orally after the death of the Prophet in 632 before being written down in the ninth and tenth centuries. The validity of certain hadith were determined by what John Esposito refers to as the "science of tradition criticism."[50] This science identifies the credibility of the lineage between the narrator of the hadith and the Prophet

Muhammad. Thus, some hadith are considered to be more valid than others, which means Muslims must be cautious in deciding which hadith to use as a religious guide. The cautious approach of many African American Muslim women to hadith is based in part on their belief that what Mir-Hosseini calls the "essence of divine justice," and what the African American community calls the spirit of Islam, is clearer in the Qur'an.[51]

A third point is that most African American Muslim women do not feel threatened by the absence of certain rights. Wadud interprets the Qur'an from the position that it is written in the best interests of men and women. Therefore, the phrase "men have a degree above" does not strike Wadud as negating the power of women. Instead, she understands it in the entire context of the religion, where all people have been told to "cherish the wombs that bore you," and that "Paradise lies at the feet of the mother." There is no equivalent assertion in the Qur'an that men are due the same reverence, but men do have "a degree above" when it comes to marriage and inheritance. Ultimately, converts see the rights and obligations of men balanced with the rights and obligations of women.

The fourth point is that the prescriptions in Islam regarding family are understood as an ideal. For example, it is not unlawful to live as a single mother. There is room for regional differences, and African American Muslims are determined to develop an indigenous Islam. When Wadud lists the different scenarios in which the religion can work, the importance of this should not be downplayed. Generally, African American converts believe Islam is adaptable to any social system.

Other verses in the Qur'an are Islamicly relevant, but for cultural reasons they have less impact on the lives of African American Muslims. The first states that women inherit half that of their brothers: "Allah (thus) directs you as regard your children's inheritance: to the male, a portion equal to that of two females: if only daughters, two or more, their share is two-thirds of the inheritance; if only one, her share is a half." (4:11) This typically is not a concern for African American converts, of whom most come from Christian families that do not abide by these rules of inheritance. Also, many families have little or no wealth to distribute. By contrast, there is a significant number of immigrant Muslim women who have to fight their families over fair distribution of familial wealth. The issue is prominent in their discourse over women's rights. While my informants are generally not battling families over equitable distribution of their inheritance, they must come to terms with this institutionalized gender preference. Many understand this inequality as necessary, given a man's financial obligations to his family and a woman's right to financial support from her husband.

Another set of Islamic laws are those concerning divorce, including the most controversial in which a man divorces his wife by simply proclaiming "I divorce you" three times in a public space. I have never heard about, nor witnessed, such actions in the American Muslim community, and divorce by Muslims is almost identical to their Christian and secular counterparts. While these laws are rarely, if ever applied, women recognize their destructive potential. The feminist response to this *ayat* is the circulation of the hadith, "PBUH: Of all the lawful acts the most detestable to Allah is divorce."[52] This hadith was reiterated in numerous Friday lectures and interviews, and the power of this counter discourse is that it turns male privilege into a privilege to displease Allah.

The final edict has to do with legal witnessing, in which a woman's observations are held to be less credible than a man's. In Masjid al-Mustaqim, rules regarding witnessing could be used to deal with issues of domestic violence, violence against women in general, or adultery. It is unclear to me if the community will institutionalize these practices, but I predict that as the community grows in terms of the practice of their faith, these last three proclamations will eventually be sites of significant contestation and reinscription.

ENGAGED SURRENDER IN EXEGESIS

Membership in this community means channeling ambivalence in ways that do not undermine the core values of the community. The mission to strengthen families and promote economic self-sufficiency is understood to require at least some consensus about faith and practice. Indeed, much of the community's discourse attempts to define the extent of required submission and surrender in order for the community to thrive. Having grown up in a society that promotes individualism, most of the women hope that surrendering does not come at the expense of personal agency, a concern that motivates a scholarly engagement with Islamic exegesis.

For any sane believer there is an act of engagement in the ever changing objectification of self and other, and the insertion of religious ideology and the sacred into that self-construct. For Muslims, engagement is a process where commonsense informs religious consciousness, which in turn informs one's sense of reality and objectivity. Although Muslims feel they must surrender to God and the revelations in the Qur'an, they actively engage in making Islam representative of what they know to be "objective." Most converts think, for example, that women are equal to men, and sexist translations of Qur'an and hadith will, most likely, not change that fundamental, embodied sense of self. So Muslims understand their religious transformation to be from alienation to reappropriation of "knowing as knowing, thinking as thinking," and like Marx they recognize that mystification accompanies capitalist systems of inequality.[53]

Marx, who viewed religion as a byproduct of an alienated consciousness, would loathe the comparison, but most anthropologists view religion as a "meaning system," functioning culturally as a starting point for communication. Like any language, religion simply imparts different lexical meanings on various signs. For Muslim converts, the community had been formed around a group of people who felt that they had lost a part of themselves by surrendering to the racist and sexist symbolic lexicon of American culture. For them, Islam, particularly the community of African American Muslims, breathed new life into stale and oppressive social structures, rhetoric, and political discourse. Sunni Islam and the Nation of Islam contextualized everything from food to gender to family to sex in ways that made sense to the convert, and as a result the Muslim community became a place where converts felt safe to transform their consciousness without feeling threatened by self-hate or prejudice.

The African American Sunni community is not a revolutionary movement in the sense of demanding sweeping economic or political reforms. Their efforts extend in the direction of articulating an empowering social narrative that repositions the meaning of race, class, and gender. The women share in the authorship of this new narrative using Islamic exegesis to substantiate the values they believe the community should promote, including feminism. Feminist exegesis transmitted orally at women's gatherings will, if found to be valid, begin to circulate in the community and will become the community's *tafsir*. The women do not create an African American women's interpretation of Islam, rather women isolate from the sunnah or from the *tafsir* of Islamic scholars interpretations that makes sense given their particular social reality. They then emphasize this *tafsir* through oral repetition in groups, such as sister to sister. Often ideas discussed in women's meetings made their way into an imam's *khutpah*, demonstrating the potential of the women's exegesis to shape the community's moral discourses.

FOUR

Historical Discourses

Close to noon, a few parents start arriving at Sister Clara Muhammad School. Zahrah, a mother and one of the few women in the community who wears *purdah*, arrives for prayer.[1] Presently four of her children go to the combination elementary/junior high school and another, already in high school, comes to the school in the afternoon for Arabic lessons. Also accompanying Zahrah for prayers are her two toddlers, one and three years old. Although classes continue until two o'clock, Zahrah comes to be with her children and with the sisters working at the school. Today is special because after school there will be a barbecue featuring Islamically sanctioned (*halal*) foods, a market, and games for the children.[2]

All of Zahrah's children are excellent students, not solely because of their academic gifts, but also because of their enthusiasm and gentleness. With seven children, and one on the way, Zahrah confesses to having no secrets, but one can imagine her children simply mirror Zahrah's gentleness, intelligence, generosity, control, and devotion. Zahrah grew up in the South and moved to California with her husband, Jamal, who was in the military. As teenagers they were looking for something spiritual, and they found Islam. Not moved by the Nation of Islam's racial politics and religious doctrine, they discovered Sunni Islam and chose to convert.

Jamal has three jobs, one of which is at Salaam Books on Douglas

Boulevard. Salaam Books acts as a distributor of incense, perfumes, books, and "ethnic" objects for African American Muslim street vendors. Often the activity in the shop includes men funneling oils from large containers into small jars that will eventually be sold individually. In this section of Douglas Boulevard, small black-owned stores dominate the area. During the 1992 civil unrest, many businesses on the street hung hastily written "Black Owned" signs in their windows in order to be spared from looting and destruction. The consciousness involved in the act of sparing black-owned businesses during the unrest connects the block to more than a century of black self-determination movements first institutionalized toward the end of slavery and recast in multiple, more radical forms throughout the twentieth century. The goal of encouraging entrepreneurship and economic self-sufficiency in the late twentieth century is tied to an increasing awareness that changes in material structures are more powerful than idealism; an ideological lineage connected in no small way to the Nation of Islam.

Not surprisingly, the encroachment of urban postindustrialism is taking its toll on this business district, and as a result the mom-and-pop shops selling ethnic wares, natural foods, trendy clothing, and music must compete with the growing intrusion of large malls and minimalls containing chains like Payless ShoeSource, Pep Boys, and The Gap. Therefore, despite Zahrah and her husband's disinterest in the political aspects of the Nation of Islam, they are intricately tied to the dream of self-sufficiency started before Reconstruction, Afrocentricly reframed by numerous charismatic movements, and institutionalized in some cities by radical urban organizations including the Nation of Islam.

From the location of the masjid, to the name of the school, to the clothing worn by the children, to the choice to eat Islamically sanctioned, or halal, foods, Zahrah's personal story emerges less from the creative choices of individuals than from historical and ideological lineages. The events and descriptions in the story are very much a product of a rich social history that begins with a place, an institution (racism and segregation), a community response (nationalism), and a personal response (conversion, purity, and gender). The history of the Muslim community in America is a history of consciousness. It is about the struggle to alter the perception blacks have about themselves and society in order for the African American community to become politically effective, economically empowered, and to attain what bell hooks describes as "self-recovery."[3]

. . .

The roots of the modern Muslim movements can be traced to post–Civil War black migration and urbanization, a disappointing time for blacks, who during Reconstruction expected full integration into American institutions.[4] The black community was poised to work for the social and economic rewards most whites were receiving from a democratic, capitalist system; many educated blacks expected the rewards would be swift. Some were quickly integrated into white Southern society, like Blanche Bruce who, during Reconstruction, became a United States senator for the state of Mississippi (1875–81). As readers of American history know, expectations were dashed as white militia and vigilante groups formed to oppose integration. With the growing violence, many blacks retreated from the goal of working side-by-side whites and instead continued to develop a now freed, separate community that paralleled the values, organization, and hopes of their white counterparts. There were white Christian churches, there were black Christian churches; there were white schools, there were black schools; there was white entrepreneurship, there was black entrepreneurship. Most blacks believed that participation in this segregated, black civil society was not only a moral obligation, but might lead to redemption, salvation, and perhaps some earthly financial success. While blacks accommodated to white middle-class models of morality and respectability, they received very little in the way of compensation, such as decent schools and infrastructure, equal legal protections, or the supposed benefits of a participatory democracy. Out of this functional/dysfunctional social system emerged many black religious and radical movements.

Vincent Harding chronicles the black struggle against slavery and racism, focusing specifically on what inspired blacks to resist in the face of overwhelming odds. He asks, What is the hope that springs eternal? What gives a life of poverty, degradation, violence, and deep sorrow meaning? Harding argues that African American religions and political activism have been deeply interconnected since slavery, with theology being used to inspire a desire for change vis-à-vis struggle:

> Without the search for meaning, the quest for vision, there can be
> no authentic movement toward liberation, no true identity or radical
> integration for an individual or a people. Above all, where there is no
> vision we lose the sense of our great power to transcend history and
> create a new future for ourselves with others, and we perish utterly
> in hopelessness, mutual terror, and despair.[5]

The quest for transcendence was a feature of both the Christian and Muslim theologies, and worldly issues of racism were often interwoven into millenarian themes of redemption. Fighting racism, in turn, became a practice of faith.

Gayraud S. Wilmore defines three consistent themes in African American resistance movements: "(1) the quest for independence from white control; (2) the revalorization of the image of Africa; and (3) the acceptance of protest and agitation as theological prerequisites for black liberation of all oppressed peoples."[6] An important quasi-religious, radical movement that had all the features described by Wilmore was the Marcus Garvey movement, an important predecessor to the Nation of Islam. Marcus Garvey founded the United Negro Improvement Association (UNIA) and African Communities League in 1914 in an effort to unite the Pan-African community. In 1916, Garvey established a division of the UNIA in New York City and, although unconfirmed, Garvey's publication *Negro World* claimed membership of two million, making it the largest organization of blacks in United States history.[7] Garvey's message was one of social and economic empowerment, resistance, racial separatism, return to Africa, and religious devotion. He praised the Pan-

African community for its sacrificial loyalty to its "host" nations while also criticizing the African Diaspora:

> Our Negro here hates to see the other Negro succeed and for that he will pull him down every time he attempts to climb and defame him. The Negro here will not help one another, and they have no sympathy with one another. . . . We have no social order of our own, we have to flatter ourselves into white and coloured society to our own disgrace and discomforture, because we are never truly appreciated. Among us we have an excess of crimes and prison houses, alm houses, and mad houses.[8]

Later in a campaign speech made in Philadelphia, Garvey said, "The so-called big Negroes are the ones who have kept back the race. Some of them are doctors and lawyers and other professionals. . . . Those are the people who have done nothing to help the race because they sell out the race."[9] While Garvey did not discount whites as devils, he believed in the purity of both races, excoriating them for their treatment of blacks.[10] Garvey tapped into a profound love/hate ambivalence toward whites and self, an ambivalence that was reflected in the religious praxis of the Nation of Islam.

Many Islamic movements in America were founded around the same time Marcus Garvey was leading the UNIA. Early movements included the Moorish Science Temple (1913), Ahmadiyyah Movement in Islam (1921), Universal Islamic Society (1926), First Muslim Mosque of Pittsburgh (1928), Islamic Brotherhood (1929), Nation of Islam (1930), Addeynu Allahe Universal Arabic Association (1930s), African American Mosque (1933), Islamic Mission Society (1939), State Street Mosque (1929), and Fahamme Temple of Islam and Culture (1930s).[11] Additionally, a number of Sunni mosques were established around the same time in cities throughout the United States.[12] The conflict for many African Americans in all these movements was the issue of whether they should identify more closely with their local community, or whether they should identify with the African or Islamic Diaspora. With respect to the Islamic communities, Aminah Beverly McCloud in *African-American Islam* describes these competing principles as *asabiya* versus *ummah:*

> If a Muslim community pursues nation-building *(asabiya)* and commits all resources (intellectual, spiritual, and physical) it necessarily is marginalized in the larger Muslim world. If a Muslim community sees itself solely as a portion of the world community of belief *(ummah)* and commits its resources there, it forgoes the individual accountability and responsibility to struggle against injustice in its own locale.[13]

A few Islamic movements committed themselves to *ummah*, including Ahmadiyyah Movement in Islam, Universal Islamic Society, and First Muslim Mosque of Pittsburgh. Most movements, however, pursued nation-building, *asabiya*, the largest of which were the Moorish Science Temple, Islamic Brotherhood, and the Nation of Islam. The importance of this distinction continues and again is rooted in ambivalence between, on the one hand, desiring the political power that results from engaging in local struggles, and on the other hand, desiring international legitimacy and religious authenticity.

In the "transition" from the Nation of Islam to Sunni Islam, the community has struggled to identify the appropriate balance between *asabiya* and *ummah*. Driving the transition from Nation of Islam to Sunni Islam has been a desire to resolve these tensions.[14] While the approaches and goals of *asabiya* and *ummah* may at times overlap, privileging local concerns can often directly contradict the ideals of religious universalism. Valorizing African history to instill racial pride, for example, de-centers Islamic history.

The Nation of Islam's transition to Sunni Islam represents only one of an array of historical trajectories for Islam within the African American community. While the Nation of Islam has a complicated and at times offensive history, it was at one time the largest Islamic movement, and certainly the most significant in authoring a race and empowerment counterdiscourse during the Civil Rights movement. Rather dismissive of the Nation of Islam's place within the growing "orthodox" Muslim communities, Dannin in his ethnography characterizes Nation followers as practitioners of "a combination of popular mysticism and authoritarian control, lacking an essential connection to Arab-Islamic pedagogy and the Quran."[15] He also describes it as "an unfettered development of the lodge, a secret society unchained, bursting into the street with the political beat of separatist-nationalism."[16] Nation of Islam discourse is much more connected to past racial struggles, and therefore the philosophy is more politically informed than it is mystical. In addition, while Dannin rejects the idea that the Nation was in any way a spiritual movement, I argue that the dialogic critique of Christianity was tied to a politically informed spiritual reawakening. Conversion meant purification from the pollution of white supremacy and Eurocentrism and for the reclamation of an authentic social and spiritual identity. Although less significant, the identification of mainstream ideology with pollution and oppression remains a part of the Sunni community's ethic.

THE NATION OF ISLAM

Elijah Muhammad, formerly Elijah Pool, assumed the Nation's leadership after the founder, Wallace D. Fard, disappeared from Detroit in 1934.[17] Elijah Muhammad claimed that God came to Earth as Fard to bring the "so-called Negro" out of his bondage in North America.[18] Blacks, according to Elijah, were destined to reinherit the earth after overthrowing whites—devils bred by an evil scientist. This theology was taken literally by some followers who, in an attempt to unburden themselves of their own self-hatred, turned racial essentialism on its head; now whites embodied evil. Others accepted this origin myth as a metaphor symbolizing the behavior of whites toward blacks during slavery, Reconstruction, and post-Reconstruction. Either interpretation supported Elijah Muhammad's goal of promoting a racially charged agenda for black revitalization through racial separatism.

The message struck a cord with many poor, urban blacks; and eventually Elijah Muhammad moved Nation headquarters from Detroit to Chicago's South Side where the movement attracted thousands of recent migrants.[19] The reason the Nation of Islam initially attracted urban blacks has largely to do with the history of black migration. During the first wave of the Great Migration beginning around 1916 and continuing until 1919, blacks moved north in order to increase their political and economic opportunities and to escape racial violence. Like his followers, Elijah Muhammad and his wife Clara were part of the Great Migration. The couple chose to abandon Macon, Georgia, for Detroit, Michigan, in April 1923, about nine months after the Ku Klux Klan staged an intimidating and brutal lynching near their home.[20] Elijah Muhammad, like most of his followers, had been raised on a southern farm and had witnessed horrific acts of racism. For many black Southerners, the Northeast and Midwest became symbols of freedom. What they found after migrating, unfortunately, was racism and exploitation in a new form. Nicholas Lemann lists several ways in which Chicago's South Side mirrored the racist South:

> The neighborhoods became poorer and denser, and the black middle class became discontented and tried to get away from the slums by expanding the black belt southward into previous white neighborhoods—a difficult process, because nearly all the white neighborhoods were segregated by fiercely maintained custom and in many cases, also by force of law, through "restrictive covenants" that barred blacks from buying houses and were then perfectly legal.[21]

In addition, there existed violent white supremacist organizations that were as powerful as those in the South.[22] In terms of physical protection and jobs:

> Law enforcement was casual because the Chicago police didn't consider black-on-black crime to be a problem worth solving. Black people were regularly charged more rent and paid lower wages than white people, and they were barred entirely from many good jobs. . . .

What made the South Side look so good to . . . most of the other migrants moving there, was the comparison to the South: money and dignity were indisputably in greater supply in Chicago than in the Delta.[23]

While the black church was well adapted to handle the economic, political, and social realities of small southern cities, the message and social expectations of the church were not always well suited to the black experience in the North.[24] Middle-class Christian churches sometimes put the burden for the condition of the African American community on individual behavior rather than on structural impediments. This was a difficult message for blacks, who were being confronted with continued institutionalized racism sui generis of their work ethic or moral character. Clearly not all Christian churches did a poor job of adapting their message to the social and economic conditions in the North. Indeed, many migrants stayed with the church. Nevertheless, there was a constituency of blacks who were beginning to believe that the only thing that was keeping them down was their compliance with a system designed to keep them down.

The Christian church in the early part of the twentieth century played a role in determining the contradictory space Islam continues to occupy in contemporary urban America. The philosophy of the Nation of Islam asserted that American Christian theology contributed to the reproduction of a hegemonic discourse on race, class, and gender. George Rawick says, "In the nineteenth century there was a strong attempt by whites to use religion as a form of social control."[25] Masters attempted to quell resistance by teaching their slaves that unequal social relations between blacks and whites was part of God's plan. Slaves were able to disentangled Christianity and white supremacy, and as Rawick argues, "While religion certainly may at times be an opiate, the religion of the oppressed usually gives them the sustenance necessary for developing a resistance to their own oppression."[26]

Regardless of the church's role in fighting racism, from the perspective of Nation followers, accepting Christian theology was tantamount to acquiescing to racism and Eurocentrism. While the Nation, perhaps wrongly, promoted the idea that Christianity was an opiate of the black masses, the Christian church instantiated moral paradigms established by European Americans. In particular, many black Christians in the early decades of the twentieth century could not appreciate the connection between race and class. In fact, W. E. B. Du Bois experienced tremendous resistance when he tried to introduce issues of class at the National Association for the Advancement of Colored People (NAACP). Du Bois wanted the NAACP to prioritize the strengthening of black civil society over racial integration. From Du Bois's perspective, the bourgeoisie within the NAACP problematically distanced themselves from the black working class. The organization feared that any ideological connection with working-class issues would symbolically identify them with lax morality and behavior that might make the goal of integration impossible. In *Dusk of Dawn,* Du Bois recounts his choice to leave the NAACP and *The Crisis,* the organization's journal founded in 1910, after concluding that universal democracy is the key toward eliminating caste:

> No sooner had I come to this conclusion than I soon saw that I was out of touch with my organization and that the question of leaving it was only a matter of time. This was not an easy decision; to give up *The Crisis* was like giving up a child; to leave the National Association was leaving the friends of a quarter of a century. But on the other hand, staying meant silence. . . . I knew something of the seething world. I could seek through my editorship of *The Crisis* slowly but certainly to change the ideology of the NAACP and of the Negro race into a racial program for economic salvation. . . . The Association seemed to me not only unwilling to move toward the left in its program but even stepped decidedly right. . . . [I]t was most difficult for me to understand that the younger and more prosperous Negro professional men, merchants, and investors were clinging to the older ideas of property, ownership and profits even more firmly than the whites. [27]

Du Bois's advocacy for the empowerment of the lower economic classes was out of step with the agenda of the black Christian bourgeoisie.

Complicating the question of the role of the Christian church in reproducing the oppression of the black working class, Evelyn Higginbotham says that while the conservative accommodationist position of the Baptist Convention speaks against the model of the church as an antithesis to race and class-based oppression, the church, she argues, was a public space where symbols, meanings, political tensions, and multiple discourses were articulated, contested, and sometimes resolved in a dialogic process of engagement. Arguing that the church realm afforded blacks a sphere in which to define self and family and spur political activism, Higginbotham makes the case that Baptist church activities and associations in the early twentieth century represent everyday forms of resistance.[28]

Higginbotham contends that the women in the Baptist Convention brought dignity and legitimacy to the black community through the establishment of many black colleges and universities. Ultimately, the institutionalization of a black elite had the effect of distributing cultural, educational, and economic capital within the black community. In that sense, even though the women had internalized white-supremacist rhetoric about black working-class moral degeneracy and had accepted sexist Baptist theology and secondary leadership positions, they created a public space within the church that contested hegemony.

It is clear from Higginbotham's account that many active Baptist women were able to become economically and politically successful within the limits established by institutional racism, particularly Jim Crow. By tying economic, political, and personal rewards to individualism and capitalism, the women embodied and enacted an identity that did not reproduce their own oppression, but reproduced the oppression of a large class of blacks. Instead of creating a discourse that challenged the ideology and structures that supported an unequal distribution of resources, Baptist women invoked culturally defined paradigms of merit ("the talented tenth"—ironically a concept developed by Du Bois) as a method for determining access to economic, cultural, and educational capital. In opposition, the Nation—in a desire to reach out to all African Americans poor and rich, talented and not-so-talented, law abiders and law breakers—strongly opposed using the moral yardsticks created by a system that they defined as morally broken.

The yardsticks created within the Nation were not, however, egalitarian, and according to historian Adam Green, "the relentless attacks on 'bourgeois negroes' inverted elitist logics more than they did away with them."[29] The Nation had its own methods for bequeathing elite status on individuals, and those individuals were rewarded financially. Thus, the Nation's verbal attacks on the black middle class had less to do with the actual wealth of the middle class than with the fact that the black middle class sought status and financial security through assimilation. In the middle of the twentieth century, black assimilation often meant fetishizing lighter skin and European culture, and generally rejecting all things African American. Black people interested in assimilation were accused by the Nation of being complicit in the reproduction of racism and classism.

While the Nation publicly emphasized these asymmetries, the Baptist Convention and the Nation of Islam shared an uncertainty about the best counteroffensive to racism: community uplift en masse or the concentration of wealth into the hands of an elite group of blacks who might then redistribute wealth within the African American community. Since Reconstruction, many contentious debates within the African American community have been about defining the hierarchy among issues of class, race, and, less explicit but always present, gender. Many black organizations, such as the Baptist Convention, blamed the lowest economic classes for reproducing the community's oppression. Lapses in moral behavior, laziness, degeneracy—the language of white supremacy—were understood to be limiting the community's moral capital. The repackaging of white-supremacist discourse to address what Gunnar Myrdal characterized as the "Negro Problem" spoke to the community's uncertainty about the entities responsible for continued institutional racism.[30] Apropos to the late nineteenth and early twentieth century, the Baptist Convention subscribed, at least at some level, to what Max Weber described as the Protestant work ethic, which collapses individual wealth with Divine salvation.

While the Nation leadership was clearly corrupt (one could characterize some of their actions as stealing pennies from the poor), it did encourage its members to look beyond a person's education, social status, and even past deeds. The moral message was that fundamentally black people were equally deserving of salvation. Returning to the question of Islam and how it differed from black Christianity, the answer lies less in Nation praxis than in the Nation's attention to what one imam in the community described as "the psychological effects of slavery." Maimouna, a convert who started out in the Nation of Islam before transitioning to Sunni Islam, articulated the power of this psychological intervention:

> If you're only submitting to Allah you really can't be a slave to anybody else. So that wipes out a whole range of oppressions that would afflict people: Gender issues, age issues, race issues. [These were] a burden for me 'cause I always wanted to feel, "Okay, I'm a woman, I'm African American, I have all these negative things, and society is saying you're second class." But you know in all these efforts I always wanted to feel, "No, I'm a winner. I'm with a group that wins." I wanted to see some achievement. So Islam came along and it says none of that matters because Allah has already given you your identity, and you can go anywhere in the whole world, and it's only your own attitude that would restrict you. And I began to see that, and I began to say, "Hey African Americans could achieve if we lost this slavery mentality. . . ." You know it's ingrained, it's in our skin, it's in our genes that we're Negroes, we're niggers, we're not the full human beings that we should be.[31]

This part of the Nation's ideological history, this message of basic equality among all humans, is also a significant part of Sunni Muslim consciousness. One could argue that this ethic is learned after one converts to Islam. However, many believers are attracted to Islam because they believe that it validates their ideal of a classless brotherhood. It is a social space in which one is not deemed to be in God's good graces based simply upon their economic status.[32]

In 1942 Elijah Muhammad was sentenced to five years in prison for violating draft laws. Nation followers refused to be drafted for World War II, a war they believed was the inevitable outcome of centuries of European expansion and destruction. During a one-day trial on October 5, 1942, thirty-eight Muslims defiantly pled guilty to charges of draft evasion, and most were sentenced to three years in prison. In the case of three defendants, including Elijah Muhammad, J. Edgar Hoover's Federal Bureau of Investigation (FBI) was able to increase the charges to sedition. The FBI set as its goal the imprisonment of all black nationalist leaders during World War II based on the rationale that movements die without their leaders.[33] Equally determined to see the organization survive was Elijah Muhammad's wife Clara, who continued the Nation's educational mission throughout her husband's imprisonment. Until his release in 1946, Elijah Muhammad communicated through his wife to his small flock of thirty-five followers at Temple No. 1 in Detroit.

The federal correctional institution (FCI) in Milan, Michigan, where Muhammad was housed was relatively self-sufficient, with a three-hundred acre farm that produced food for prisoner and staff consumption. It was a wonderful example of a cooperative, and one could argue, ironically, that Elijah Muhammad's experiences in prison shaped his utopian vision of a self-sufficient black nation. Elijah Muhammad saw the benefits of an agrarian collective in which raw materials were produced, manufactured, and eventually sold. Even before his release, Elijah Muhammad encouraged his small group of followers at Temple No.1 in Detroit to purchase cattle and a 140-acre farm in White Cloud, Michigan. Only a year after his release in 1947 Temple No. 2 in Chicago owned and operated a grocery story, restaurant, and bakery on South Wentworth Avenue. With as few as four hundred members nationwide,

Elijah Muhammad demonstrated the potential of black economic self-sufficiency to redefine race relations.[34] Now it was only a matter of spreading the power of his message to the black community, which Elijah Muhammad realized in prison could be accomplished through radio and print journalism.

In 1948, while serving a seventy-seven-month prison sentence for larceny in Norfolk Prison Colony, Malcolm Little's brother Reginald introduced him to the teachings of Elijah Muhammad. In his autobiography, Malcolm X describes how his epiphany was inspired by the idea that the white man was the devil. Changing the traditional structural binary to "black/good, white/evil" allowed Malcolm, for the first time, to make sense of his past experiences. His epiphany motivated a deep engagement with philosophical and historical texts in an attempt to understand the epistemological roots of white supremacy. Deeply engaged in a project to understand the tragedies of his past and to take control of his future, Malcolm enlisted the aid of Elijah Muhammad. Through regular correspondence with Elijah Muhammad while in prison, the leader's message of black redemption and salvation healed Malcolm, who had been tragically scarred by racism. Eventually Malcolm, who earned his X in prison, emerged a passionate and articulate champion of Elijah Muhammad. After his release in 1952, and subsequent integration into the Nation's hierarchy, Malcolm's effectiveness as a spokesperson represented itself in a phenomenal increase in membership.[35]

By the sheer force of his passion, charisma, and intelligence, Malcolm X became the number-two man, and recognized number-one spokesman, for the Nation of Islam in the 1950s. His ability to deconstruct the faulty logic of American race and class paradigms began to penetrate mainstream black consciousness. While membership in the Nation of Islam probably never surpassed twenty thousand at its height in the early 1960s, Malcolm X was able to create tremendous sympathy for the Nation among non-Muslim African Americans.[36]

Clegg hypothesizes that the first problems Malcolm had with the Nation's doctrine occurred on his trip to the Middle East in 1959. During the trip Malcolm was hosted by a number of high-ranking officials, but to his grave disappointment he discovered that Saudi Arabians could legally enslave black Africans. The revelation that the Muslim/good and Christian/bad dichotomy was simplistic and wrong supplied one of a series of blows to Malcolm's tremendous loyalty.

One of my informants argues that the shift from Nation of Islam to Sunni Islam really began in the 1950s when some members were introduced to the Qur'an. This informant said that the inability to reconcile the teachings of race separatism and white devilry with Islam provoked introspection and dissension on the part of Malcolm and two of Elijah Muhammad's sons, Akbar and Wallace. Wallace, for example, had converted to Sunni Islam in 1961, and was estranged from the Nation for years for his public challenge to his father's teachings.[37]

Malcolm's dissension was fairly covert until the early 1960s when his messages to the media grew increasingly at odds with the Nation of Islam's political agenda. The most famous example of this growing division was when Malcolm X equated President Kennedy's assassination in 1963 to chickens coming home to roost. His impolitic media sound bite came while Americans were still mourning the president and represented, at some level, an overt challenge to Elijah Muhammad, who felt that President Kennedy was in many ways an ally to black Americans. For punishment, Muhammad immediately silenced Malcolm X for ninety days.[38] Malcolm X, nevertheless, continued to garner attention for his provocative and controversial opinions, and the media attention corresponded with his growing popularity. The seeds of the split between Muhammad and Malcolm were sown over a number of years, resulting from a clash of egos, power, and a growing divide between their religious and political convictions. He admitted in a radio interview in 1963 that in order to demonstrate loyalty, "Many of my own views that I had from personal experience I kept to myself."[39] Most significantly, Malcolm began to separate his religious faith from his radical nationalist politics.

Malcolm X, who had also lost tremendous respect for Elijah Muhammad for a number of the leader's indiscretions with money and women, revealed to his followers that Muhammad could not claim to be both a believer in Islam and a Messenger of Allah. In the face of embarrassing and heretical criticism, the Nation of Islam decided in its journal, *Muhammad Speaks*, to attack its most powerful detractor. In 1964, with newly gained independence from the Nation and with the establishment of his own mosque in Harlem, Muslim Mosque, Inc., Malcolm X began teaching that racial essentialism was antithetical to orthodox Islam and that racism was a problem throughout the African Diaspora. He asserted that race was spiritually irrelevant, but politically relevant, which was a complicated message for people who still saw the world in black and white. Malcolm X, now El-Hajj Malik El-Shabazz, continued to be vilified in the Nation's journal as an Uncle Tom until his assassination in 1965. El-Shabazz's death forced the Nation of Islam into a crossroads. In response to the potential threat of organization decay, the Nation's leadership focused attention away from the divisive issue of Sunni Islam versus the Nation of Islam and toward the good works of the Nation. The organization even participated in a well-publicized meeting between Martin Luther King Jr. and Elijah Muhammad in 1966 in what could be interpreted as an effort to build bridges with more mainstream blacks. The Nation of Islam's journal, from the mid-1960s through the early 1970s, made it clear that Elijah Muhammad and his ministers, perhaps in an effort to redirect attention away from the scandals plaguing the Nation, chose to publicize the tangible results of their economic programs. This meant that *Muhammad Speaks* pulled away slightly from the radical, race-based message of empowerment and moved toward race consciousness and community uplift.[40] Muhammad continued to vilify Martin Luther King Jr., Malcolm X, Jesse Jackson, and other Christian leaders as hypocrites and enemies, but with far less frequency and viciousness.[41]

The Nation of Islam began a process of bifurcation in 1977 just two years after Elijah Muhammad's son, Warith D. Mohammed (formerly Wallace D. Muhammad), inherited the leadership and began to transition the Nation followers to Sunni Islam.[42] W. D. Mohammed changed the name of the organization to the World Community of Islam in the West (WCIW), and under his leadership the goal of creating an economically independent and viable community was subsumed under the goal of perfecting the practice of Islam. W. D. Mohammed encouraged the Sunni community to strive to assimilate Islam into traditional American social, political, and economic life. Opposing this ideological shift, Louis Farrakhan, along with a group of disaffected members of Mohammed's WCIW, splintered off and in 1978 reinstituted Elijah Muhammad's teachings and called their group, not surprisingly, the Nation of Islam.

THE NATION VERSUS THE INDIVIDUAL: THE CHANGING SOCIAL AGENDA

Regardless of the problems in the Nation of Islam, Elijah Muhammad's promotion of African American race consciousness and nationalism was a creative response to the political and social conditions of blacks prior to the 1970s. Race consciousness is a poorly understood political philosophy and often equated with reverse racism. Gary Peller points out that this is a false comparison. White supremacy, he contends, defines blacks as having essential characteristics that are fundamentally different from whites, while African American race consciousness does not make a biological or spiritual distinction between blacks and whites. While it can be argued that integration has diminished overt racism and improved the lives of middle-class blacks, Peller says, "Integration has been pursued to the exclusion of a commitment to the vitality of the black community as a whole and to the economic and cultural health of black neighborhoods, schools, economic enterprises, and individuals."[43] Peller asserts that the premise of integration is that white civil society is an improvement over black civil society, and therefore black people need exposure to white institutions and cultural practices. Peller imagines what might have happened if American social reforms had been modeled on race-conscious community revitalization:

African-Americans in virtually every urban center would not be con-
centrated in disintegrating housing, would not be sending their children to learn a nationally prescribed curriculum in underfunded,
overcrowded schools and to play in parks and on streets alongside
drug dealers and gang warriors, and would not be working at the
bottom of the economic hierarchy (if they are lucky enough to have a
job at all).[44]

In this remarkable utopian assertion, Peller opens the door for envision-
ing the potential material outcomes of race consciousness. Additionally,
his assertion hints at the idea that integration is not necessarily liberating, or, put another way, integration can be disempowering, a conclusion
Du Bois made before resigning from the NAACP and *The Crisis*.

The Nation of Islam inspired and validated race consciousness, and
the material manifestations were tangible. By the time Elijah Muhammad died in 1975, the Nation had forty-six million dollars in assets and
an equally impressive debt of 4.6 million dollars.[45] In order to pay off the
debt, W. D. Mohammed began to dismantle the fairly extensive business
enterprise. While the dismantling was a prudent decision given the disputes over money that followed Elijah Muhammad's death, it is important to acknowledge that the Nation had a program to redistribute
wealth and change essential elements of production that, for its time, was
extremely progressive. The Nation's agenda to redefine relationships of
power within a short period of time was, for a group interested in social
change, an important liberation consciousness. Through cooperative
economics, the community in Chicago built a city within a city by the
1970s. In addition, the Nation inspired race pride in children, who as
adults continue to distinguish themselves from African Americans who
have internalized black self-hatred.[46]

Unfortunately the Nation, before the transition, was not an organization free from repression. Before 1975, member praxis was uneven at
best and oppressive at worst. A good percentage of the doctrine of the
Nation was highly problematic and anything but liberating. Therefore,
perhaps it is fitting to distinguish race consciousness from black nation-

alism by quoting Wahneema Lubiano, who speaks of the dangers of black nationalism in a discussion of the Million Man March:

> If the Nation of Islam—with its call for "policing" the black community, its instantiation of black male leadership and responsibility, its marginalization of black women, its aesthetics of precision group control, rituals of self-effacement in the presence of strong, charismatic leadership, and moral asceticism, its centering of black male bonding at the expense of gender and sexual orientation inclusiveness—is the answer, what on earth is the question?[47]

Peller's vision of community solidarity, which is not unlike the Nation's utopian goals, contrasts sharply with Lubiano's image of individual oppression born of a rigid nationalist agenda. Perhaps Peller and Lubiano agree that the practice of nationalism and the ideals of race consciousness are different, but Peller's vision would undoubtedly require sacrifices to individualism and the continued use of race as a necessary category for defining group membership.

The inability to marry utopian ideals to institutional pragmatics causes much consternation within the African American community, particularly by making African Americans feel as though they have to prioritize one identity—race, gender, or class—over others. The hierarchy is, of course, artificial, which is why there is so much confusion about which identity diacritic is more crucial and potentially liberating. About this choice, Stuart Hall says;

> Either one "privileges" the underlying class relationships, emphasizing that all ethnically and racially differentiated labour forces are subject to the same exploitative relationships within capital; or one emphasizes the centrality of ethnic and racial categories and divisions at the expense of the fundamental class structuring of society. Though these two extremes appear to be the polar opposites of one another, in fact, they are inverse mirror-images of each other, in the sense that, both feel required to produce a single and exclusive determining principle of articulation—class or race.[48]

Many Sunni Muslims believe that instead of privileging racial/ethnic, gender, or class identity, their faith is the umbrella under which all their identities can be expressed without coming into conflict. At the women's entrance to Masjid al-Mustaqim there were always several copies of the Prophet Muhammad's last sermon, and the continual availability of the sermon is no accident. The sermon resonates so powerfully with this community that it is used to represent the essence of the faith to both new and old converts.

About wealth and inequality, the Prophet is reported to have said:

> Allah has forbidden you to take usury (interest), therefore all interest obligation shall henceforth be waived. Your capital, however, is yours to keep. You will neither inflict nor suffer inequality.

About gender the Prophet said:

> O People, it is true that you have certain rights with regard to your women, but they also have rights over you. Remember that you have taken them as your wives only under Allah's trust and with His permission. If they abide by your right then to them belongs the right to be fed and clothed in kindness. Do treat your women well and be kind to them for they are your partners and committed helpers.

Regarding race the Prophet said:

> All Mankind is from Adam and Eve, an Arab has no superiority over a non-Arab nor a non-Arab has any superiority over an Arab; also a white has no superiority over black nor a black has any superiority over white except by piety and good action. Learn that every Muslim is a brother to every Muslim and that the Muslims constitute one brotherhood.[49]

The issues of economic redistribution, gender, and tribe are elaborated much more fully in the Qur'an, nevertheless converts find comfort in how the Prophet clarifies social relations in this sermon. Sunni Muslims are not black nationalists; in fact many do not believe in affirmative action, yet they attend a predominantly African American masjid. Race for them denotes a common history and culture, but it is not used to construct a social agenda other than community uplift, which in segregated urban America is relevant to race. The community, in other words, recognizes that race is salient and not salient at the same time. Muslim converts believe that within the faith gender is used to assign roles, not hierarchy, for the purposes of social and family harmony. Finally, Muslims do not renounce capitalism, but insist on redistribution. African Americans characterize their economic ideal as an incentive-based socialism. That means that they do not object to wealth as long as the wealthy understand that they are required to circulate capital to sustain the community, similar to the way blood sustains the body.

PRAXIS: FROM NATION TO SUNNI ISLAM

Maimouna, in her early forties and a recently divorced mother of three, joined the Nation shortly before Elijah Muhammad died. A Stanford and Berkeley graduate, Maimouna grew up in an upper middle-class family in Southern California. After moving back home, she went to work for her father's successful law firm, which she has headed since his death. Maimouna was attracted to the Nation of Islam's revolutionary discourse that she felt mirrored the ideals taught to her by her father. Maimouna describes her ideological evolution in the years following Elijah Muhammad's death:

> I met my husband after I joined the Nation. So we married at the end of seventy-five. My husband was very active and a business manager in the Nation. Fortunately we both made the transition because for a lot of couples that didn't happen. You know one wanted to stay with the old way and some were ready to go with W. D. Mohammed. [At the time] it began to click to me that there was this spiritual side. I think that goes to your question about the focus for the community

because the Nation is perceived as being in the forefront in terms of a social movement, and Sunni Islam is not. For a person like me, who came in [during] the social movement days, how do you resolve that conflict?

Well, I had been around a lot of Nationalists, I had been around the Panthers, and I'd been around the Nation, and I saw that the downfall of all these efforts was always a character issue, a moral issue. You know it wasn't external opposition, it was internal decay.

When W. D. Mohammed came in his message was get yourself together first and then you can make a difference in the world. So that just switched the whole focus from being outwardly directed to inwardly directed. And that was really attractive to me because as I said I could see all these problems with character, with people not following through, with having their own agendas for their own personal gain rather than looking at the whole community. So I thought, well maybe this is what we need. If we have strong character, if we have a moral base, and we have a spiritual base, that's really the ultimate solution to all these problems. [50]

Maimouna describes the Nation of Islam as a social movement intent on transcending race and class oppression through collective action. The dynamics of the organization were such that members were required to subsume individualism under collectivism in an effort to promote the social goals defined by the leadership. In that context, macro issues such as community viability were being addressed while personal failings and inequities were being ignored. W. D. Mohammed's WCIW placed race and class transcendence in the hands of individuals who embodied the spiritual ideals of Islam, and who then deployed these ideals through words and deeds.

Before addressing whether different forms of resistance praxis quantitatively improve empowerment and agency, one must address the possibility of transcending structural oppression. At a theoretical level, Michel Foucault argues that people are not freely constituted subjects, that transcendence is impossible. Power, according to Foucault, defines the limits of our knowledge and the methods for determining that knowledge.[51] Similarly, one can argue that even if African Americans can address, even articulate the source of their oppression, they might not understand choices like straightening nappy hair, moving into white neighborhoods, joining a violent and nihilistic gang, or beating one's children. Alternatively, James C. Scott positions subjects as capable of slowly unraveling systems of domination. He argues that liberation consciousness exists in utopian and millennial beliefs and "can be understood as a more or less systematic negation of an existing pattern of exploitation and status degradation as it is experienced by subordinate groups."[52]

Within the Nation of Islam, systems of negation were (and still are) explicit both in discourse and in practice, whereas the African American Sunni Muslim community renounced the race-based eschatological and utopian ideology of the Nation of Islam. The Sunni Muslim community attempts instead to adhere strictly to ideals of race-neutrality, political and social assimilation, and economic independence. Some imams, for example, encourage the community to oppose affirmative action despite the fact that, as a system of reparations, it has been effective in increasing the wealth of the African American community.[53] They live according to the belief that the ends do not justify the means, a choice that sometimes limits intermediate actions designed to address specific injustices.

In many ways the Nation from the 1940s through the 1970s was unsuccessful in liberating their community for reasons having to do with notorious abuses of power.[54] Nevertheless, "consciousness raising" about the nature of racist symbolism and prescribed methods for ideological and economic counterattack provided a dialectic to white supremacy and institutional racism. In contrast, the ideology of the Sunni Muslim community has no articulated counterattack, no reasoned approach to achieve utopian goals beyond personal salvation through religious practice. Therefore, one might ask if conversion to Sunni Islam is an act of pure asceticism or if resistance and liberation praxis is present in a form that is often overlooked.

FIVE

Soul Food

Changing Markers of Identity through the Transition

In the early 1940s, living in Boston with his half-sister Ella, Malcolm Little reluctantly accepted a job as a drugstore soda fountain clerk. The soda fountain was in a section of Roxbury where, according to Malcolm, blacks had assimilated much of the values of the white middle-class community. Since slavery, the black community has constructed its own system for assigning social status: a house slave was considered superior to a field slave, a light-skinned black was superior to a dark-skinned black, and, in the case of Roxbury in the 1940s, established New England Negroes considered themselves superior to recent black migrants. The concentration of blacks in segregated urban cities increased the opportunities for black entrepreneurship, and commensurate with an increase in the size and wealth of the black community was an increase in opportunities for social status within black civil society.

In his autobiography, Malcolm X describes the inhabitants of Waumbeck and Humboldt Avenues in the Hill section of Roxbury as woefully unaware that, regardless of their education and social performances, from the perspective of the whites they were undifferentiated Negroes. Throughout his day at Townsend Drugstore, Malcolm Little confronted characters like "the sleep-in maid for Beacon Hill white folks, who used to come in with her 'ooh, my deah' manners," and "the hospital cafeteria-line serving woman sitting there on her day off with a cat fur around her neck, telling the proprietor she was a 'dietitian.' "[1] After work, Malcolm says, "I couldn't wait for eight o'clock to get home to eat out of those soul-food pots of Ella's, then get dressed in my zoot and head for some of my friend's places in town, to lindy-hop and get high, or something, from relief from those Hill clowns."[2] While historians are uncertain as to when the term "soul food" came into common usage, they agree that this excerpt from Malcolm X's autobiography contains one of the first written references to the term.

The origin of the term "soul" can be traced to the 1930s. To describe something as having soul meant that it contained some indescribable essence of "authentic" black culture. Malcolm X contrasts the realness of soul food with the status conscious artifice of the people he meets at his job. The narrative juxtaposition implies that something that has "soul" is beyond politics, like a mother's love expressed everyday in the mundane space of a family kitchen. For Malcolm, escape from status conscious norms came in the form of bodily expressions of social rebellion (the lindy-hop), and the ingesting of mind-altering illegal substances. The constraints of capitalism and status hierarchies are contrasted with the freedom and liminality of soulful expressiveness. Indeed the word "soul" is often used to denote an African American authenticity that exists outside the realm of identity politics. To the contrary, ideas of authenticity, in this case food, are always situated politically and speak to issues of performance and resistance.

SUNNI MUSLIMS IN THE 1990S

Paul Robeson Park was often the designated location for *Eid al-Fitr,* the obligatory group prayer and celebration following Ramadan. Families, predominantly African American, would begin arriving around seven in the morning dressed in their best *Eid* clothing. Well before the crowd began to trickle in, plastic tarps would be positioned in straight rows so that the *salat* could be performed facing the Ka'aba in Mecca.[3] Following the prayer and *khutbah*, the community would hold a celebration that included music, kiosks, and food. While the prayer and lecture usually lasted an hour, the gatherings on the blankets, which included talking and eating, would last up to five hours. At one *Eid* I was situated among three cowives who were enjoying each other's company on several large blankets. Also within the group was Hawaa (one of the few women who veils), Safa, and Fatima, a single mother and engineering student at a local state college. The picnic area was clearly a gendered space, although occasionally a husband would wander by and eat a piece of chicken or a plate of salad. The exchange between husband and wife, or wives, would usually last no longer than five minutes, at which point the husband would find his way back to his group of male cohorts. The majority of the Muslims at this *Eid* were converts to Sunni Islam. The fact that some of the women have chosen to be cowives, coupled with the fact that they perform traditional gender roles hints at the possibility that conversion is a reinstantiation of patriarchy.

Doris Witt argues that within the Nation of Islam soul food signified the role of women in the pollution of the black physical, intellectual, and spiritual body:

> My main line of argument will be that Muhammad used food as part
> of his effort to formulate a model of black male selfhood in which
> "filth" was displaced onto not white but black femininity and thus
> articulated within African American culture via discourses of gender
> and sexuality rather than class. He adopted the traditional Islamic
> ban on pork to pursue this rearticulation, while supplementing it
> with numerous other dietary recommendations which, through
> their stigmatization of the foods associated with "soul," seem to have
> been intended to purify the black male self of black female contami-
> nation.[4]

Witt is not the only one to characterize the Nation of Islam and, by extension, the African American Sunni Muslim community as the producer of new oppressive gendered tropes.[5] Witt's thesis fits neatly into a traditional feminist paradigm that male and female are represented in the following binaries: public/private, culture/nature, and, in the case of Witt, sacred/profane.[6] In these models, male/female relations are points of contestation and competition rather than uniquely situated at the intersections of race, class, nation, and gender.[7] Given that Witt's structuralist gaze lacks an appreciation of how African American Muslim women make sense of their own gender, it is necessary to interrogate the role of patriarchy in the community's discourses and counterdiscourses.

Through food and food taboos, female converts articulate their relationship to a number of oppressive ideological domains including race, class, Christianity, Western biomedicine, capitalism, nihilism, and family. The women enjoying one another's company at the *Eid* were involved in elaborate forms of food and gift exchange that made them more dependent on one another than on their husbands. "Husband" in the case of these women does not denote a particular set of emotional and material dependencies that indicate patriarchy or repression. With respect to this community, the practice of food production, distribution, and consumption clarified each member's relationship to the group and to the intellectual and spiritual project of self-purification. Who brought what food? How much? Was the meat *halal*, or in accordance with Islamic law? Who was eating from whose picnic spread? Who made the best soul food? The answers to these questions defined the ideological and material position of the women, and in this respect the cooking was always socially significant.

Clearly one of the best and most generous cooks was Safa, who for *Eid* brought enough fried chicken to feed five large families. Safa, who often entertained this community of women at her house with large quantities of southern fare, had "come into al-Islam" at the same time she was conquering alcoholism. When Safa entertained it was an expression of joy and commitment to her community and family. As a form of exchange, southern cooking strengthened Safa's bonds with African American converts, whose personal and social histories mirrored her own. Macaroni and cheese, collard greens, fried chicken, potatoes, okra, curried lamb, cornbread, black-eyed peas, hot links, beef kabobs, barbecued beef (not pork) ribs. In every sense of the term, the preceding list represents African American Sunni Muslim "soul food." Most of the list references the community's social history, but the eager adoption of a Middle Eastern cuisine references yet another set of cultural linkages and histories. For the African American Muslim community, eating was always an expression of social, personal, and religious communion. As such, food was not prepared simply to fill one's stomach; to cook was an expression of religious duty, love of community, and love of Allah.

INGESTING IDEOLOGY

Elijah Muhammad wrote a regular column in *Muhammad Speaks* entitled "How to Eat to Live." The journal was such an important educational tool and entrepreneurial venture for the Nation that converts were required to sell papers.[8] The most striking feature of "How to Eat to Live" is the recategorization of foods as healthy, dangerous, sacred, tainted, or polluted according to the physiological and spiritual needs of "Asiatic," or black, people. The Nation's origin myth stated that whites were created by the evil god-scientist Yacub through the removal of genetic materials from black and brown "germs." Claude Clegg III describes the supposed physiological outcomes of this genetic alternation:

> Their bones were fragile and their blood thin, resulting in an overall physical strength one-third that of blacks. Weak bodies made Yacub's man susceptible to disease, and most future aliments, "from social diseases to cancer," would be attributable to his presence on earth. . . . Actually, the grafting process had made the white race both incapable of righteousness and biologically subordinate to the black people.[9]

A corollary of these physiological differences marked by disease and moral pollution was the urgent need for members of the Nation to construct behavioral barriers to potential physical decay or weakened immunity to white "tricknology," or treachery. Limiting ingestion of particular foods, of course, represented one of the most important methods against disease of the physical and social body. In a published collection of food edicts, Elijah Muhammad warns:

> Peas, collard greens, turnip greens, sweet potatoes and white pota-
> toes are very cheaply raised foods. The Southern slave masters used
> them to feed the slaves, and still advise the consumption of them.
> Most white people of the middle and upper class do not eat this lot
> of cheap food, which is unfit for human consumption.[10]

Clearly the Messenger's taboos rejected more than food and encompassed issues of identity, class, and social history. Conversion for Nation followers meant cleansing the body through food restrictions, namely the avoidance of traditional "slave" foods that, Elijah Muhammad argued, poisoned the minds of black folk, making them participants in their own degradation. Food taboos have changed over time and mark an important consciousness shift within the African American Muslim community. In essence, the developing food taboos within the Muslim community relate in complex ways to social history and more specifically to personal feelings of agency over oppressive political and economic structures. Looking historically at the transition of food categories within the Nation, one recognizes that food taboos exist simultaneously as a method for blending the physical and the moral,[11] as a form of social control or a way of delineating order,[12] as a way of reducing ambiguities,[13] as a way of embodying resistance to disintegration (personal and social), and as a method for ascribing sacredness.[14] In the movement's transition in the 1970s from Nation of Islam to Sunni Islam, the dynamic and changing character of food taboos demonstrated that food edicts were mired in a dialectical relationship: historical memory and identity versus social and ideological change. Most food occupied more than one category, allowing fluidity for constantly shifting subject positions.

In one clear example, Elijah Muhammad, who earlier in the text warns that the hog is simply a polluted animal, takes the old adage "you are what you eat" to a new level:

Allah taught me that this grafted animal [hog] was made for medical purposes—not for a food for the people—and that this animal destroys the beautiful appearance of its eaters. It takes away the shyness of those who eat this brazen flesh. Nature did not give the hog anything like shyness.

Take a look at their immoral dress and actions; their worship of filthy songs and dances that an uncivilized animal or savage human being of the jungle cannot even imitate. Yet, average black people who want to be loved by their enemies, regardless of what God thinks of them, have gone to the extreme in trying to imitate the children of their slave masters in all of their wickedness, filthiness and evil.[15]

In this excerpt the hog shifts from a polluted object to a medicine from Allah to an active agent causing loss of control and evil behavior. It is a symbol of the evil influences of the white race, who he claims historically forced blacks to eat hog, as well as a symbol of an appropriated consciousness that stubbornly refuses the Nation's call to join. Finally, Elijah Muhammad warns that eating hog hastens death. What does this taboo represent? The hog stands in for itself, for history, for oppression, for behavior, for a liberated consciousness, and for poor health. Put another way, the taboo organizes multiple political, social, and personal locations, and these food categories shift in priority based upon changing spatial and ideological contexts.

In order to understand the connection between taboos and shifting identities, it is helpful to focus on two individuals: one who transitioned from the Nation to Sunni Islam and another who converted straight to Sunni Islam. The examples show how a radical redefinition of sacred and profane is possible given the right social, political, ideological, and religious circumstances. For the Muslims in particular, the recasting of the African American in history from one of object to one of creative subject meant that southern "slave" food was once again purified and reappropriated as a powerful symbol of political and social resistance.

CONVERSION THROUGH THE TRANSITION: AFAF

I met Afaf at Masjid al-Mustaqim. She was introduced to me by Aida, who described Afaf as someone who "knows her religion." Afaf agreed to allow me to come to her house and tape our conversation after Aida explained that her own interview was fairly painless. Afaf lives in South Central in a house she owns. The middle-class neighborhood is made up of well maintained single-family homes and belies an almost pervasive assumption by outsiders that black families living in South Central are either poor, chronic victims of crime, dysfunctional, or all three.

Afaf's yard and house were meticulous, and furnished simply; the interior was as elegant as she. Afaf is a tall woman who, instead of dressing in Africa-inspired clothing, dresses in flowing, solid print fabrics. Her outfits are always stunning and she accents them with earth-toned headscarves wrapped to reveal her neck but not her hair. She wears bold ethnic necklaces and bracelets that contrast nicely with the simplicity of her clothes. During this interview, we sat for three hours on her burgandy, overstuffed couch and were interrupted by only one short phone call. Afaf, in her mid-forties, had no children or husband and, although she has a large family and is well connected in the Muslim community, her social life could not be described as hectic.

In 1974, while living in Southern California, Afaf joined the Nation of Islam with one of her brothers. Like many converts, Afaf grew up in the South. She was born in Memphis, Tennessee, and raised there until she was five, when she and her brother were "borrowed" for one year by their mother's sister, who was unable to have children. That one year turned into eight, and so until the age of thirteen Afaf lived during the school year in Kansas City with her aunt and uncle, a minister. During the summers she would return to Memphis to be with her parents and their growing family. Afaf is the second child of eight. Her early experience living with extended kin is not unusual among African American families, so in many respects she had not a typical, but a familiar childhood.[16] Again in 1967, at sixteen years of age, Afaf left her parents' home and went to live with her uncle in Southern California.

After high school, Afaf enrolled in Harbor Junior College and upon graduating tried very hard to enter a health profession. She applied to California State University, Long Beach, to become a physical therapist, but was rejected from the physical therapy department. Instead, she earned a B. S. in Health Sciences from Cal State, and upon graduating she applied to Drew University to become a physician's assistant. Rejected from the program at Drew, she went to work instead as a medical transcriber. The pay was poor, so she moved to Cedars-Sinai Hospital, where she educated patients about breast cancer detection. Unfortunately, during a mass layoff she lost her job, so at the urging of some friends Afaf took the post office examination because "they pay pretty good money." At the time of the interview, she had worked for sixteen years as a night letter-sorter machine operator while simultaneously studying alternative medicine and selling alternative health care products.

At the same time Afaf was pursuing a failed career in the health professions, she was also rejecting a lifestyle of drug experimentation into which so many friends and relatives were falling. She said her brother encouraged her to try marijuana and "red devils," which she hated because they diminished her sense of control. After her brother emerged from a six-month stay in a youth facility, he swore off drugs forever, and they both began a spiritual quest within the Nation of Islam.

At first opposed to the teachings, Afaf was finally convinced by her brother to go to the temple, and Afaf claims "something" kept her interested. Initially the visits were sporadic, but eventually she became a regular visitor. Afaf said she had become disillusioned in Kansas with the church, but nevertheless maintained a strong belief in God. Of the church she said, "Just looking at a lot of the people, like my uncle who's a minister, and the hypocrisy of the people, the message wasn't strong to me. . . . And you ask questions, and they handle answers for you they say, 'Oh don't question God's word.' "[17] So Afaf was a woman who sought a professional career in medicine, was thwarted by all her attempts, living in a segregated community, rejecting the 1970s counterculture of drugs in favor of control and order, and harboring a strong belief in God despite her negative experiences with Christianity. In the midst of all these conflicts and rejections, she was introduced to the idea that while black people do not have the same opportunities as whites, they are intelligent, and with hard work, discipline, and community, black people can achieve anything. The message of self-sufficiency and discipline led her to join. Afaf half-jokingly confessed she could not imagine joining the Sunni Muslim community now without having first become a member of the Nation of Islam. When she joined the Nation of Islam in 1975, the political and spiritual message was clear, the community was self-sufficient, and on top of all of that there was spectacle.

> When I came, there was a whole lot of glitter to attract people. So when I see people come in now I say, "Wow I wonder what attracts them." I say, "There must be something to this religion that makes people want to come to it although that glitter that was out there, those flashy cars, and those nice fezs, and those white outfits, and those suits, and that military discipline, and that type of thing, and the stores, and the restaurants that was there when I came [are gone]."

> But I think what made me stay was I just liked it. Even after all the other stuff started breaking down I just like the fact of Allah being the true God, the sense that it made. If you have a question, you want to ask there's no one saying don't question Allah because you know you can ask the question and get an answer if someone knows the answer. I like the discipline still. I like the fact that this religion is about living it. It's not just on-a-Sunday-type religion where you go in and "hallelujah" and come out of there and do everything in the week and don't feel guilty about it. In this religion, if you're not living it right, if you got a conscience, you're going to feel like, "I'm not on my job." And then everyone else is conscious of the fact that we're supposed to be living right.

Even though the Nation of Islam and Sunni Islam differ in ideology, they share a holistic and ritualized approach to life that appeals to converts like Afaf. The similarity between the Nation and the Sunni Muslim movement in America is the desire to alter one's worldview in response to particular social relationships and to translate that consciousness into everyday practice. But social relationships change, and in the 1970s, a decade after the Civil Rights Act and desegregation, there was a political evolution away from separatist black nationalism. After the death of Elijah Muhammad in 1975, during what is referred to as "the transition," the greatest challenge for adherents was not in altering their worldview; their worldview had already been radically altered when they joined the Nation.[18] During the transition the most difficult part was the restructuring of symbolic metaphors giving meaning to self in relationship to society. During Elijah Muhammad's tenure, black nationalism was the ideological foundation upon which a spiritual movement was built, but for Sunni Muslims, Islam has became a spiritual quest within which a radical political, economic, and social agenda for the inner city has found legitimacy. The ideological changes have been accompanied by changes in symbols, rituals, rules, and politics, which have been the result of developments that occurred outside the movement.

Food taboos as symbolic forms represent the type of ideological developments occurring both inside and outside the African American Muslim community. Clifford Geertz notes:

> Whatever the ultimate sources of the faith of a man or group of men may or may not be, it is indisputable that it is sustained in this world by symbolic forms and social arrangements. What a given religion is—its specific content—is embodied in the images and metaphors its adherents use to characterize reality.[19]

In describing the conversion of African Americans to Islam it is essential to acknowledge the symbolic forms that sustained the Nation through its development. From the beginning of his movement, Elijah Muhammad linked eating to purity and control, arguing that blacks, as a result of "brainwashing," existed in a state of impurity. By targeting through political discourse the agencies responsible for polluting black consciousness, the Nation hoped to halt black participation in the reproduction of their own inequality. Elijah Muhammad argued that African American dress, behavior, and diet represented an individual's level of "brainwashing;" and therefore personal and social "recovery" involved understanding the relationship between consciousness and behavior. For the Nation, "lewdness" and shabbiness of dress indicated poor self-esteem. Addiction, sex without marriage, and criminal activity represented a disconnection with one's history and the internalization of racist stereotypes. Finally, consuming certain "slave foods" facilitated the digestion of white-supremacist ideology by weakening the body physically and spiritually.[20] Elijah Muhammad lists dangerous foods:

> The law of nature is the divine law the Creator set for us in the beginning of the creation of the universe. This race (white) of people has ignored and disobeyed this law and has met with disaster. They seek and have tried throughout their civilization to change the very natural religion of the Black Man.
>
> Do not eat any cornbread, it is for your horses and cattle; and the hog loves it. The hog is made for medical purposes for the white man and not for food relishing.
>
> Let the white man eat all the hog he wants. It was made for him, not for us. It was made for a cure—all for many of their diseases and is used for salves.[21]

Elijah Muhammad is arguing that in order to restore social order (economic well-being, self-sufficiency, stable nuclear families, status, and privilege), blacks must begin to follow rules regarding food consumption. He also clearly indicates that different races have different food requirements. By linking consumption to social order, Elijah Muhammad is making the corollary that if blacks and whites naturally need different foods, they must also naturally need different social orders, or put another way, a separate nation. Within a separate nation, blacks could live free from the polluting foods (and ideas) of whites and therefore in a state of purity as ordained by God.

Elijah Muhammad's warnings were not solely directed toward food choice. Controlling eating was also decreed as relevant to achieving social order. Possibly inspired by the Islamic month of fasting, Elijah Muhammad at times recommended that people eat one meal per day. Although he advocated fasting because he believed it was better for the body, it also promoted a feeling of spiritual purity through the tempering of bodily desires. The ability to delay gratification was promoted by Elijah Muhammad as an important skill for blacks not only in terms of curbing addictions, but also in building their separate nation through austerity and hard work. The Nation articulated three important actions necessary to achieve self-sufficiency and engaging in any of these practices represented a purification of consciousness: First, for the community to become economically viable, the first important conscious act must be patronizing black-owned stores. Every African American in the Nation had to understand the importance of circulating dollars within the community. Spending money outside the community along with any behaviors that diminished the economic potential of a separate black nation were understood as acts of selling out the race and yourself. Second was the presentation of self. In *Muhammad Speaks*, non-Muslim blacks are depicted in cartoons looking foolish. In one cartoon a black man wearing platform shoes, a long, plaid coat, and hair in braids sticking straight up is telling a white used-car salesman, "Two thousand dollars for that piece of junk?! I must look like a fool to you?"[22] The cartoon implies that if blacks want respect they will be required to present themselves in ways that demand it. The third and final behavior representative of purity is the worshipping of God in the ways outlined by Elijah Muhammad. Black people who did not accept Elijah Muhammad's decrees were deemed polluted. After Malcolm X broke from the Nation and spoke out against the teachings, for example, he was described as an "Uncle Tom," a term denoting brainwashing and pollution.[23]

Elijah Muhammad's extensive labeling of clean, allowable and forbidden, was intended to stop blacks from reproducing their own oppression. He cautioned that by identifying with European American culture, blacks gave credibility to white-supremacist ideology and furthered black economic and social decline. Therefore, the logic goes, if corn-bread is a dangerous food for blacks, then ritual abstention from that food is required for the "Asiatic black man" or "so-called Negro" (terms used by Elijah Muhammad) to establish a God-ordained, independent nation in North America. That logic accompanies all proclamations of sacred behavior: If such and such consciousness or behavior hinders the development of a God-ordained nation, then it is polluting and must be stopped.

It is remarkable that Elijah Muhammad was able to encourage an entire community to change their eating habits, given the fact that adults have entrenched eating habits and that the permitted foods were costlier and harder to obtain in segregated urban America. It is even more remarkable that after Elijah Muhammad's death in 1975, his son, in an effort to move the community toward orthodox Sunni Islam, slowly replaced Nation of Islam food taboos with Islamic decrees. Afaf describes changes during the transition:

AFAF: I went ahead and joined in July of seventy-four, and it was kind of confusing because at that time they were kind of coming out of that old thing with Elijah Muhammad and really coming into the new religion, so it was kind of like they were like running around like chickens with their head cut off. They didn't know what to do or what to say or what they were supposed to be. And they were still calling them ministers, and they were saying one was saying one thing and another was saying something so I was kind of like. . . .

CAROLYN: Like a mosque versus a temple, and an imam versus a minister?

AFAF: Exactly. At that time when I came in, before I came in, like the book *How to Eat to Live*, you didn't eat certain foods, like you didn't eat greens and sweet potatoes a lot of . . .

CAROLYN: He made them taboo because they were all associated with slavery.

AFAF: Right. So you couldn't eat certain kind of foods, so like this is what I'd heard so now I'm telling you, "I can't eat that, I can't eat that." And then some people say, "You can eat that." I'm like, "No the book said . . ." "Well they said you can." So you really didn't know what to do. I was totally confused, you know. So I was getting kind of confused, but I was hanging in there, you know, and then they started talking in Arabic [laughs]. You know you had to learn your prayers in Arabic. I remember my brother would pray, but they would just pray in a supplication position just standing with their hands like this [places hands face up in front of her, pinkies together, palms facing up]. But like I said, it was like a point of confusion, so I asked a friend of mine, "Well gee why this, why this?" She said, "Well, right now it's kind of confusing because the ministers they don't know what to say because this is different for them." So people just up there talking off the wall, and a lot of people were just totally confused, and I guess the ones who were too confused went on about their business and never came back, you know.

Clifford Geertz asks, "How do men of religious sensibility react when the machinery of faith begins to wear out? What do they do when traditions falter?"[24] For African American Muslims, the machinery of faith had gradually worn out. As African Americans began to make their way into formerly segregated spaces, black nationalism and separatism for Muslims and non-Muslims seemed less appealing. In the 1970s, as blacks began to win institutional reforms, they moved away from seeing themselves as unique victims of racism and instead situated themselves universally as victims of a racist, capitalist industrial complex.[25]

A change in political and social sensibilities paralleled a change in Muslim religious sensibilities. The writings and political actions of the 1970s indicate that a decade after the Civil Rights Act, African Americans tried to reformulate their identities relative to changes in their social status. Oppression, which was once as blatant as a "Whites Only" sign on a bathroom door, went underground. Also, many key political players at the forefront of radical black movements were suspected of unethical business practices or illegality, and ultimately organizations began to decay due to one scandal or another. Many African Americans felt they needed to re-think the origins of their oppression, and many asked, Was it only the "white man," or were blacks responsible in some way for maintaining the system of oppression? African Americans stepped back to reassess the cultural, social, and psychological barriers that kept them from attaining economic well-being and status. The writings by and about African American Muslims during this period indicate that Islam became a tool for framing answers to those questions and redefining self in relation to economic injustice and racism. The belief in Islamic ideals of food consumption and purity still challenged Western norms and engendered self-control, but instead of being used metaphorically as a description of race essentialism, these taboos literally went by the book—the Qur'an. Afaf explains:

> I said I was going to hang on in there and see what's going to happen because, like I said, I liked the atmosphere. Then I started learning things. Matter of fact I came in maybe a couple months before Ramadan started, and that was my first time going on a thirty-day fast. But I was fasting right, and I would get up early for my *suhur* and make my *salat*.

> And it was so funny he [my brother] said, "Remember that time we used to be in the closet trying to pray?" Because they say if your house is dirty or something's not clean that you have to get in a clean spot. And then I think they were sleeping in the living room and the bed wasn't made up and so we're like, "We can't pray. The bed's not made up." So we have this big closet [laughing], and we'd all be around it bowing. I said, "Yeah, wasn't that the dumbest thing, you know." It's so funny now that I think about it you know.

> I think I started learning a little bit of Arabic, so I was kind of like trying to teach them and it was just a mess [laughs]. So we'd all be

jammed up in that closet. I'd lead the prayer because they didn't know what to say [laughs].

So finally I remember Imam Washington, his name is Kamal now, he was well versed in Arabic, so he was down at the mosque one day trying to show us how to pray, and we were just going up and down like, "What is he doing?" I had never seen anybody do that. He'd just stand up there and people trying to follow him. It just looked like we were doing exercise or something [laughs loud and hard]. I'll tell you. So then Imam Hussain said something about if people don't know what they're doing, they shouldn't be trying to show other people [laughs]. I said, "That's a lot of nerve" [laughs long and hard]. I tell you the truth. You should have been there. I'm like, that's a lot of nerve at least the man does know a little something. He's trying to show them. What can you show us, right [laughs and stamps feet]?

I don't know how I finally learned how to [pray]. I'm trying to re-member, I guess because I like to read. I had this little book called *The Muslim Prayer Book*. Matter of fact here, it is now. Sitting here. This is my second copy because I gave the other one away to some-body. So I took this little book, and I used the book. And that's how I learned a lot of my Arabic, out of here.

The transition for African American Muslims involved a change in the sacred and profane. Afaf describes the change from English to Arabic in naming and prayers, ritual ablutions, designation of sacred spaces, the elimination of certain food taboos, Ramadan, and the use of the Qur'an as the sacred text. It was an incredible time that tested the ideas of the Nation of Islam. What survived was not the dictates of Elijah Muham-mad, but the intent and social impulse behind them.

POSTTRANSITION EATING TABOOS: HUDAH

Hudah ran a marriage class for single and married Muslims. She taught individuals and couples how to work out problems and divide responsi-bilities according to the teachings in the Qur'an and hadith. Although she was a divorced single-mother and was living (at the time I interviewed her) with her twice-divorced daughter and two grandchildren, she was very conservative with regards to women's roles. Gender roles, faith, food, and discipline were the tools, she thought, for struggling against social and personal decay and chaos. Hudah was in her early fifties but looked to be in her seventies. She was a cancer survivor living well beyond her predicted demise. I thought perhaps her combined use of prayer and herbal and alternative medicines had worked, as well as her following the Prophet's advice for eating as outlined in hadith and Qur'an. Her dietary requirements were stringent, and during each of our interviews we would have to break every two hours for a meal. Ultimately, our discussions were always peppered with Hudah advising me to eat lamb, honey, meat in moderation, fresh vegetables, shiitake mushrooms, and an assortment of food regimens.

Hudah's apartment was a stuffy but clean one-bedroom located on the borders of two different ethnic communities. Living with her extended family meant space was limited. The children lived in the bedroom while she and her daughter slept on their dark-blue fold-out couch. Much of the space was used for storage, so free space consisted of several different paths allowing a person to move from one room to the next.

Hudah, who was extremely thin, dressed in a head covering that hid her hair and draped over her chest. She wore a traditional full-length long-sleeved garment over her clothes. She had grown up in a Christian household that attended church almost every day of the week. Her mother (at the time I met her) was still one of the most active leaders in her church in Mississippi and had even received an honorary doctorate from a local Christian university. I imagined Hudah's commitment to Islam rivaled her mother's passionate commitment to the church. According to some converts, Hudah was a bit too self-assured (self-righteous) about Islam. Nevertheless, people in the community respected the work she put into activities for the children and her outward demonstrations of faith.

Hudah, who was raised in the South, represents the newer convert.

She has appropriated her southern identity not as a source of shame, but of pride.

> We were too poor to have a lot of meat. We were raised mostly on beans and I would eat the vegetables coming up. As a result of that, having gotten the potassium I need, when I developed colon cancer that brought me through.[26]

Hudah credits her southern diet with contributing to a lasting physical strength rather than pollution and decay. Unlike with Elijah Muhammad's entanglement of food and race purity, converts to Sunni Islam observe traditional Islamic eating practices.

> The Prophet Muhammad (PBUH) told us to practice preventive medicine. In other words, we should eat the proper foods so that we don't get sick. He tells us in the forty-fifth chapter and the thirteenth verse, Bismillah . . . , "He has subjected to you from himself all that is in the heavens and all that is on the earth." And then in the twentieth chapter and the eighty-first verse he says, "Eat of the good things we have provided for your sustenance, but commit no excess there in." Then in the second chapter and 158th verse he says, "Ye people eat of what is on earth lawful and good." So there are laws that we have to follow in eating. In *The Prophet's Medicine*, it says that lamb, for example, generates blood that we need. Barley, the Prophet recommended, we give to the sick because it's good for digestion and honey and has all the trace elements. It helps elimination. It helps to prevent diarrhea. It cleans the arteries so you don't have to have surgeries if you eat honey and the other proper foods that go along with it.

> When I was in the hospital and I had heart palpitations, I had my daughter sneak some honey in the hospital and it stopped the heart palpitations. The doctors couldn't believe it.

For Hudah, prescriptions for eating go literally by the book, and she characterizes the Prophet's prescriptions as more scientifically advanced than modern Western medicine. While she never claims that American food is designed to weaken a specific population of Americans, she does say:

I had a friend that went to the Sudan, drank the milk, and did not get gas. They put some pork products in the milk [in America], that's why it makes people sick. God said he made milk pure and agreeable. God does not lie, so it's not milk, it's ilk in many cases, as we say. *Halal* milk you can get from the *halal* market and it doesn't have all those chemicals in it, and it won't make you sick.

Hudah's statement is tied to her critique of the American capitalist system, which, she believes, allows food to be tainted in order for businesses to increase profit margins. In other words, food is conceptually situated within economic, social, political, personal, and religious domains. At the end of my interview, Hudah said to me:

When you first came to me and said, "I want to talk about holistic medicine," I thought I was just going to be limited to just foods and herbs, but holistic medicine is spiritual medicine, physical medicine, mental medicine, it encompasses all of it. It encompasses our prayers, how we treat each other, the role of mother and father. Holistic medicine includes our education, our mental development, the foods that we eat. All of that is holistic medicine because it's going to affect our entire body. How we feel physically is going to affect how we think. Children can't concentrate in school because they're getting too much candy, too much sugar.

Cancers and tumors are a result of blood stagnation and not having proper circulation. God said he subjected the whole creation to us. If we know the foods that we should eat, the laws we should practice in dealing with our children and our marriage, we will have peace because Islam means peace. . . . This is holistic medicine, submission to the will of God, to the laws that he left us.

Elijah Muhammad's food taboos, intended to challenge established norms and engender self-control, were replaced by the Islamic concepts of *haram* (forbidden) and *halal*. Elijah Muhammad taught his followers that everything they knew about themselves and the world was designed to make them participants in their own oppression. Even the food was understood to aid in the brainwashing. When W. D. Mohammed took over the leadership, he told his followers that instead of abiding by the purity guidelines established by his father, they must now use the Qur'an. As a result, *Eid* festivals, Islamic religious festivals, and feasts in the African American community now include fried chicken, ribs, sweet potato pie, black-eyed peas, and collard greens, foods forbidden by Elijah Muhammad. What happened to the original consciousness equating traditional black cooking with slave foods and slave mentality? The elimination of certain food taboos has a strong correlation to changes in the understanding of self and society.

Food taboos represent the development of African American Muslim economic, social, and personal consciousness. In the early years of the Nation of Islam, food was linked to brainwashing and oppression. For a member of the Nation of Islam, changing one's diet was tantamount to accepting self. Like Nation members, Sunni Muslims appreciate the link between avoidance of certain substances and spiritual and physical strength, but purity now is not orchestrated around themes of race segregation, race essentialism, and rejection of a past identity. The Sunni Muslims embrace their slave roots. Accordingly, southern black cooking has been reappropriated as a point of cultural pride. This change accompanies the adoption of American patriotism. African American Muslims identify as Americans and demonstrate the reappropriation of their national identity by placing the American flag at the top of their weekly journal, the *Muslim Journal*. When Muslims give *dawah*, Islam is represented as complimentary to mainstream America. Eating *halal* is described as easy, not very different from the American diet. It is as though they are telling people to join them because they present little modification of values and behaviors. Accordingly, the Sunni Muslim position on America is a non-confrontational one. The Islamic movement now asks that African Americans try to change the American cultural landscape from within. Under W. D. Mohammed's leadership, the edicts of separatism had lost validity in the face of increasing integration and black economic and educational success. That means their identity as Americans is a point of pride and not shame, and their reappropriation of southern cooking represents that shift in identity.

The Nation of Islam's taboos against traditional southern (black) cuisine were representative of the Nation's historical reading of African Americans as objects and not subjects in American history. As such, blacks were understood to be entirely oppressed objects, which relieved them of all responsibility for their actions prior to conversion, but also meant a clear rejection of an African American identity. Instead, they were essentially a lost-found tribe of Africans requiring a separate nation and by corollary, separate cuisine. This conversion, therefore, came at a price; it meant relinquishing certain identities and suppressing dispositions toward things converts had grown up with, like southern cooking. With the transition from the Nation to Sunni Islam, an understanding of African Americans as creative subjects was adopted, and with it southern cooking gained status as an example of a creative, empowered, and independent African American spirit during slavery and Jim Crow.

SIX

Conversion

La ilaha ill-Allah
(There is no deity but Allah)
Muhammadan Rasool Allah
(Muhammad is the messenger of Allah.)
                                        The Shahada

With the utterance of a belief in monotheism and a commitment to the teachings and revelations of the Prophet Muhammad, a person becomes a Muslim. At Masjid al-Mustaqim, in a given month anywhere from one to twenty-five people stand in front of the congregation and take the *sha-hada*, or the witness of faith. In the early 1990s, al-Mustaqim was one of about twelve predominately African American Sunni Muslim masjids in Los Angeles county and the surrounding regions.[1] If the same statistic holds true in other masjids, up to three hundred African Americans convert to Islam every month. My estimate was that at times as many as sixty African Americans converted monthly in Los Angeles county, which means the adult Muslim population increased by about 720 yearly.[2] At other times, I witnessed very few take the *shahada* in a given month and, losing confidence, I estimated that the number must be closer to twenty. Do the high or low estimates represent a significant increase in population? Without any contextual information, the statistic sheds very little light on Muslim conversion in the region. Is it a phenomenon? Not on the scale of the Nation of Islam in the 1950s and 1960s, but it is a quiet movement poised, perhaps, to change the way low-income African Americans look at themselves, their race, their gender, economics, and politics. I estimate the number of active adult African American Sunni Muslims in the county to be somewhere between fifteen and twenty thousand. Twenty thousand is enough to establish an economic enclave and a voting block, and perhaps enough to affect structural change. But is that what they want?

One could characterize the community's priorities as (1) promoting Islam, (2) fostering family and community, (3) supporting general and Islamic education, (4) expanding and creating services for the poor, and (5) developing an economically viable community. I could name several individuals who might want to include promoting health, supporting women, or redistributing wealth, but the five priorities represent agendas that virtually the entire community owns. The ideas are not unique; most mainstream American religions promote a similar agenda. What is unique is the Islamicly informed ways of addressing each of these priorities.

By virtue of community membership converts accept the implicit goals of the group. While at times there is disagreement, there is rarely outright dissension from committed converts. At some level, community membership requires a priori agreement with these values, engagement within the community to try to change the values using particular protocols, or the suppression of heterodoxy and self-censorship. It is the suppression of individualism that most frightens non-Muslims who want to know if female converts accept orthodoxy at the expense of their own liberation. While community membership does not require the sacrifice of female agency in order to promote an imagined social, political, and spiritual consensus, it does require surrender to a number of authorized discourses that issue from the *shahada*, as well as the emerging political discourses that circulate within the membership. Zipporah described her conversion in an interview at her home:

ZIPPORAH: I came to Islam the same way that everyone else did, except I wasn't a member of the Nation of Islam. But my family was. My oldest sister and her husband were very involved in the Nation of Islam. Of course they tried to recruit me several times but, for a lack of a better term, the person that I was, it just didn't suit me. But there were things about it that I always liked.

I had really begun this search for my spiritual self in 1984. I call it my ascension to Allah. Part of the change for me was to go and live with my father in Minnesota. Even though he and my mother had been divorced, I had been involved with him in my life: summers, vacations, the kind of things that divorced parents do. But I had never really lived with him, and I wanted my children to know him.

I began to learn a lot more about who I was because I was learning a lot more about who my father was. The thing that was interesting is my mother and father had appeared to me to be quite a bit alike. I saw that really as a conflict. After divorcing, my mother married a passive man and that made her have a successful marriage, and my father was married to a very passive woman and that made for him a successful marriage. I learned that the role my mother had, . . . which was this kind of aggressive, assertive woman . . . the reason her role was not accepted in society was because of her being a woman. But my father, when I went to Minnesota I saw it from the patriarchal point of view, he was very well respected for his outspokenness. I also realized the advantages in the relationship between my mother and her new spouse, and the disadvantages of my dad being the patriarchal domineering man that he was. My mother died in 1992, and my stepmother died in 1991.

Now my mother and father both had been educated

people and had worked. My mother when she came up, as an African American woman, you either taught or you were a nurse and she didn't want to be either one of those. So she ended up being a medical records secretary, which is something that she really liked. And my father, who had a degree in psychology, he was a counselor. But their spouses, my stepfather was in the military and my step- mother never worked.

When my stepfather lost my mother and my dad lost his wife financially it was quite interesting to see their cir- cumstances. My father was the dominant person in his household, but his wife being the passive person never made any decisions, recommendations about money, or anything. He would give it to her and she would just pay the bills. My mother on the other hand, being this kind of aggressive woman, assertive I should say, who really didn't know a lot about financing, but had some savvy, always stuck money in places. And when my mother died, now her and my father I would say their incomes were parallel, but my stepfather is in much better shape financially than my dad.

My dad is suffering. He's on a fixed income, social secu- rity, strictly this one little lump sum of money, that's all he has. On the other hand my mom, we found I don't know how many savings plans and things. No more than ten thousand dollars, eight thousand dollars here and there, in places. Also, even though they did not have a high income, their credit worthiness was just tremendous because she had A-1 credit. It was very interesting to see that dynamic take place because my father, he's suffering, we have to as- sist him. My stepfather travels, he has all of these things, he's financially sound. It was probably then that I really began to see the strength that she had.

It's like you can't get one without the other. You know what I'm saying. A lot of times you can't be what society considers this passive, submissive, docile woman and make some moves internally in your household. Even though my mother was always criticized for that. There were times in their marriage he would say things to us and we, all of us, even the children [would say], "She just bosses you around, she runs everything she blah, blah, blah." We didn't always see it as a good thing, but he says now, she balanced so many things that he never knew until she died.

Those are the kinds of things that led me to al-Islam because I had a need to be appreciated for who I was, like my mom should have been; accepted because I had a lot of the qualities that she had. I had all that fire from both her and my dad, and I had to channel it in positive ways that seemed to be acceptable. So I think that was part of my ascension because I believe firmly Allah puts us in places. We think sometimes it's a very bad spot, but we have to figure out the lesson that is to be learned in this spot.

When I came back from Minnesota my brother-in-law, who was very engrained in the Sunni community here, was in my ear everyday. I mean he and I used to have talks until the morning because I wasn't working when I came here. So I was home, and they always used to say I was his second wife because I did all the house stuff while my sister worked. Being there with my children I didn't have any money so I had to do housework, and cook, and those kinds of things. My brother-in-law had his own business, and he was in and out of the house during the day. So we used to talk endlessly about al-Islam and he took me to the masjid. He took me to al-Mustaqim when al-Mustaqim was little. He would take me there to *Jumah* and I still wasn't quite getting it. At the time, still being kind of stub-

born about it because I didn't know what I had to give up.
I mean, "What do I need to give up?" At the time I wasn't
ready to give up any thing [laughs]. I guess that's what it
really was.

I had moved out and I was working when my brother-
in-law was killed [pause]. In 1992 my brother-in-law was
murdered. Something really kind of stirred up inside of
me. I had read in the Qur'an someplace that it's not just
that Allah puts you in the place, and there are reasons behind you being there, but there are signs for those who
will reflect. And when my brother-in-law was killed I saw
it as a real direct sign.

CAROLYN: And he was building the masjid [when he was shot].

ZIPPORAH: I looked up to him. Everyone in our family looked up to
him. Because my other sister and I had been single parents, he was kind of the man of our boys. He was someone
who I thought was basically sinless compared to me, who I
thought was pretty much a sinner. It was a sign to me that
I really needed to make that move right now. I mean I had
been teeter-tottering for years.

Actually the day of his *janazah* [Islamic cleansing ritual
for the dead] I was there with a couple of sisters and I was
laying across my bed and they were talking to me. One sister says to me, "What is it that you're afraid of leaving?"
And I remember thinking. . . now that I think about it, I
think it's kind of silly . . . that really seemed to be kind of
serious to me, covering, *hijab*.

CAROLYN: *Hijab?* Interesting, because you speak on it now.

ZIPPORAH: It's interesting that that's one of the first things that I
learned about [in Islam]. But that was the thing that I was
afraid of because I worked in the public, I had to speak in
different places. I had never seen any women in *hijab* other

than being some place where there were some Muslims. I had never recalled seeing a Muslim in some work place. Never, never, never! [laughs] And so I thought that was what was holding me back from it. So when she asked me the question, and I really didn't have a legitimate answer, I said, "I think I'm going to take the *shahada*."[3]

CONVERSION AS NARRATIVE THERAPY

The power of conversion is the control one has over the recreation of a personal history. This history, as we see in the case of Zipporah, explains contradictions between internal and external realities; in this case a sense of oneself as feminine set against the social sanctions against female assertiveness. Repositioning oneself within both a personal and social narrative is usually very therapeutic, which is why some therapists use narrative therapy in place of psychoanalysis. Narrative therapy extends the cure for psychological distress beyond the borders of the body. Whereas Freudian therapy locates pathology within individuals and the ways in which they frame and process their experiences, narrative therapy frames pathology as the result of the interaction between individuals and their community. What is missing might be an understanding of patriarchy, class structure, and other social dynamics that might lead to, for example, anorexia nervosa or depression. In other words, narrative therapy externalizes and sometimes politicizes personal distress. The Muslim community believes strongly that slavery and racism have left deep psychological scars. They believe these scars, in part, thwart the community's ability to prosper. In *Sisters of the Yam*, bell hooks similarly situates personal experiences such as substance abuse, anxiety, feelings of inferiority, and powerlessness within social context. Speaking about addiction, hooks says:

I have found it meaningful to connect the struggle of people to "recover" from the suffering and woundedness caused by political oppression/exploitation and the effort to break with addictive behavior. In contemporary black life, dis-enabling addictions have become a

dangerous threat to our survival as a people. . . . It is no mere accident of fate that the institutionalized structures of white-supremacist
capitalist patriarchy have created a modern society where the vast
majority of black people live in poverty and extreme deprivation—
most often with no hope of ever changing their economic status.
Living without the ability to exercise meaningful agency over one's
material life is a situation that invites addiction. [4]

In a number of ways, bell hooks uses narrative therapy like the Nation of
Islam: to find within African American social history a different story
from the one Americans are generally taught. Another important part of
narrative therapy involves members of a person's community who affirm
the legitimacy of this new identity. Community after all is where stories
are distributed and, in the recreation of self, consensus building by others seems to be effective in eliminating negative self-constructs.

ZIPPORAH: I'm telling you, Islam has empowered me. I didn't know
             that I have the right to be who I wanted to be, and that
             some of the things that I thought were negative qualities
             about myself were really not.

CAROLYN: Can you give me some examples?

RASHEEDAH: Well, this desire to be out front, to speak publicly. I was
             always chastised about my loud voice, about my aggres-
             siveness. To me, aggressive is a term, and I think that I
             use it because this is society's way of describing a woman
             that is not meek and mild. In feminist terms, it's as-
             sertiveness and it's good. And it was something that I had
             been growing up with. I played sports and worked in
             jobs that were not feminine. And so I thought all the
             time in society when you did those kind of things either
             you were a lesbian, potential or lesbian want-to-be
             [laughs], or you know or something that wasn't positive.
             But Islam taught me that that wasn't negative. Even
             though scholars, and a lot of folks who teach about

Islam, they teach what the world knows about Islam is that they think women are second-class citizens and all this. Well, it worked quite the opposite way for me. I did not fall into that at all. It brought me right out.

CAROLYN: And what do you think in terms of the rest of the community? I mean do you think a lot of the women just come right out?

ZIPPORAH: Uh-huh. I think that women have been empowered to do things. Sometimes it is set where you can only do things with women, and I have mixed feeling about that. I think women could teach men a lot more than they are allowed. But I think the women in the Islamic community that I've met all feel that "paradise is at the foot of the mother." And that we're the women. And the position and power that Allah gave us to teach and nurture and raise society as a whole makes [Islam] an empowering kind of thing for me.

What it said to me is, "You got it going on." Okay. Allah says we got it going on. He says that we're supposed to teach the world. Maybe I'm able to teach certain things from the roster here at the masjid. Sometimes yes, sometimes no. But I am able to go out in the world and teach men and women.

CONVERSION AS NARRATIVE PRAXIS

Important elements of conversion stories include new concepts of body, purity, and health; redefinitions of gender and family; positive acceptance of race; and belief in the doctrines of Islam. These narratives of transformation contain a number of consistent elements, including:

1.   Pre-Muslim Activities: Conversion narratives almost always include a description of preconversion activities and ideologies. Either

Islam affirms her values and ideals (strong family, no drugs, the work ethic) or radically alters what she now sees as destructive, "brainwashed" behavior (drugs and various dependencies):

I was seeing families decaying, and I was seeing disrespect for human beings, disrespect for black people. Going to school in Hollywood, taking a bus, I was constantly propositioned by men when I'm just sitting on the bus with my schoolbooks. . . . And for me that was degrading, and it was humiliating, and I found it very offensive. And this religion was emphasizing that black women needed to be respected, they needed to be treated like women.[5]

A traumatic event can also frame a preconversion story. One informant, for example, describes how she was arrested for drug possession and sent to jail for a short time. The event of almost losing her children made her want something else for her life. For others, the trauma is a long-term prison sentence, divorce, or severe depression.

2. Values Reinforcement: Sometimes the situation is as tragic as losing custody of your children because of drugs, but more often than not the situation is simply political, social, or personal dissatisfaction: "I had first gone through a period of saying I was an atheist, and then I went through a period of saying well maybe I was an agnostic. So I was searching for something. I didn't know what."[6] Or:

So when I went to the mosque and Ayman Majeed called the *adhan* [call to prayer] . . . I always say that's my testimony that when he called the *adhan* it was like a far-off song that I'd heard before, but I hadn't heard for a long time.[7]

For many women, the choice to convert to Islam holds some mystery, but their descriptions almost always connect with the current political discourses. Usually, the convert finds continuity between Islam and lessons taught to them by important figures in their lives. Aida describes the Nation of Islam's community development and family empowerment, "They emphasized the moral values that my family had already taught me as a child."[8] Nadia describes her affinity to Angela Davis and other radicals of the time, "When I'm listening to the oldies radio station, now I know more what they're saying consciously than I did before. I say, 'Wow they were political!' [laughs]"[9] I think that for many, the ultimate reason they converted has so many dimensions, it's hard to define, but looking back they recognize that the ideas that influenced their decision to convert were part of a developing consciousness within the African American community.

3. Rereading Western Feminism: The conversion story addresses mainstream American concerns regarding Islam and gender. Within that story are comparisons to Christianity and its (negative) influence on Western constructions of gender and race. Most converts describe the double binds that Western society places on black women, including the necessity for women to be employed *and* take primary responsibility for domestic work. The burden is such, these converts contend, that the ability to parent and partner effectively in this society is diminished.

4. Radical Social Ideals: The story often addresses the issue of where African Americans are socially, politically, economically, and personally, and how Islam challenges many of the social structures that, they believe, perpetuate these social weaknesses. "I saw a lot of problems in our community. I thought, 'It's really up to us to take care of ourselves. We could build businesses, we could do it. We could have schools. We could have what we needed to establish ourselves if we worked together and we had an organization.' "[10] Many converts, in fact, were socialists prior to converting.

5. Proof: Finally a conversion story addresses what the convert sees as an empirical example of the religion's power in their lives: "When I found Islam I stopped using drugs," or "My cancer went into remission by the healing powers of the Qur'an," or "I felt at peace with myself and the world." The pattern of responses maintained this basic outline and, as I said, the cohesiveness of the sto-

ries, the power of the rituals, and by all outward appearances the un-questioning faith of the adherents made the religion particularly attractive to me as both a research project and a personal challenge. A personal challenge because I allowed my perceptions about liberation to be held up to scrutiny by my informants.

Knowing the reasons people choose to convert or the fact that converts express a sense of empowerment as the result of converting does not negate for some scholars that "objectively" these women are accepting patriarchy and diminished social roles. In order to address the issue of the legitimacy of these claims of empowerment we first need to explore how accepting religiously prescribed limits on our individuality differs, if at all, from accepting other cultural and social limits. Societies place limits on the ways in which people can express themselves, from language to dress to laws regarding behavior. Societies, in essence, define the rights and responsibilities of its members to one another. Are these cultural limits different from the limits imposed by religion? While the cultural relativist approach, which mandates that we not evaluate one culture's moral standards against another's, helps anthropologists avoid some of the Eurocentrism and even racism of the past, there are clearly examples where women are oppressed. Under the Taliban in Afghanistan the women were denied numerous rights under the guise of religion. The methodological dilemma posed by the need to locate power and oppression with the need to recognize the validity of different moral universes has made it difficult to develop a definitive statement about conversion to Islam in late twentieth and early twenty-first century America.

A RELATIVIST PERSPECTIVE ON RELIGIOUS CONSCIOUSNESS

When it comes to understanding the conversion experience, it is crucial to recognize that the religious impulse and the symbolic structuring of a worldview exist in other cultural realms. Geertz, for example, goes beyond simply defining religion as sacred acts and objects imbued with meaning, uncontested doctrine, and collective rituals.[11] For Geertz, religion is any strongly held belief and orientation to the world. Religion is:

> (1) A system of symbols which acts to (2) establish powerful, pervasive, and long-lasting moods and motivations in men by (3) formulating conceptions of a general order of existence and (4) clothing these conceptions with such an aura of factuality that (5) the moods and motivations seem uniquely realistic.[12]

According to Geertz's definition, at one level all individuals are religious because a strong belief in what is real and meaningful provides one with a sense of authority to act. Included in this definition could be atheism, secular humanism, Marxism, and of course Judaism, Christianity, and Islam. But even for people who follow traditional religions, the meaning of any theology in terms of an individual's orthodoxy and orthopraxy varies. Therefore if, as Geertz implies, cultural orientation is religion then how can we understand Marx's assertion that religious consciousness is false consciousness?

Perhaps the best approach is to analyze specific examples. There are, for example, women reproducing oppression by "circumcising" their daughters or binding their daughters' feet. Edgerton candidly addresses this issue, arguing that extreme cultural relativism limits one's ability to judge important dysfunctional social norms.[13] So if reproducing one's gender, economic, social, and political oppression is obvious at such extreme levels (circumcision and feet binding), then more subtle ways in which women reproduce their own oppression must exist.

Richard Shweder paints a very compelling picture of suttee in India, challenging the idea of false consciousness. Suttee is the practice of widows burning themselves on their husband's funeral pyre. It is an act of purification believed to free the woman from guilt in the next incarnation. Shweder questions whether the anthropologist's explanation can come close to the emic understanding of suttee, which aside from being "imaginative," positions the widow metaphysically in a world that makes sense to her. Shweder discusses the lexicon of suttee, arguing that it is necessary to understand how individuals paint their world using a complex symbolic grammar.[14] Their response to the world they create has internal consistency and therefore rationality:

> If we insist platonically that the very idea of reality suggests something independent of any one of its particular material realizations as a "thing" in time and space, independent of our involvement with it, independent of our verification procedures, of our presuppositions and theories, of our purposes and interests, then to represent suttee as a rational practice we would have to invoke the notions of conditionalized universals and of time-dependent or space-dependent truths.[15]

So if truths are not universal, then all ideas and practices must be understood in context. This cultural relativist model contradicts the premise of false consciousness, or the idea of universal ethics, morality, and economic and political justice. Shweder goes on to say:

> That romantic conception of an interpenetration or interdependency of objectivity and subjectivity, of pure being and existence, has been variously expressed: as the idea that nothing in particular exists independently of our theoretical interpretation of it; as the idea that our measuring instruments are a part of the reality they measure; as the idea that the world is made up of "intentional" objects, such as "touchdowns" or "weeds" or "commitments" or "in-laws." Intentional objects have real causal force, but only by virtue of our mental representations of them and involvement with them.[16]

In other words, culture must mediate our knowledge of the world. Therefore, it is impossible to try to derive an objective universal truth about the ways in which people can or must be empowered.

Cultural relativists argue that we should not judge one culture's values against another's. Applying the same theoretical standard, we should not attempt to compare cultural definitions of empowerment. For some women, a high-paying job is empowering, for others, the ability to raise their children full-time is empowering. While the cultural relativist approach to the study of culture can sometimes blind the researcher to issues of power and reluctant acquiescence, the relativist approach may work better with respect to understanding a women's decision to convert. It works well because the women in the preceding examples are not physically in danger as a result of their choices, and more optimistically, many of the women have improved their material lives as they have developed an alternative vision of social justice and personal responsibility. Improvement in their material life goes beyond making more money or living in a better house. It also means that they have contributed to their children's success or improved the lives of their neighbors by, for example, founding a clinic. The standards by which we judge individual empowerment cannot be rigid, but must emerge from the ideological and social context of the individuals or community. For most converts into the Nation and into Sunni Islam, redefining everyday symbols is the beginning of the process of reinventing self. Ideas of sacred and profane, *halal* and *haram*, and legitimate and illegitimate are the starting point toward consciously remaking self and society. For African American converts to Islam, this process continues with new social realities contributing to a different sense of intent with respect to religious practice and belief.

WHY ISLAMIC FEMINISM?

Although Muslim women understand themselves to be empowered, many black feminists criticize the ideological foundation of the Muslim movement, be it Sunni Islam or the Nation of Islam, for revisiting patriarchy. Often American Afrocentric movements idealize Africa's cultural history and therefore encourage the adoption of African clothing, rituals, and customs. The leaders of these movements often look toward Africa as a kind of mythical location where a natural and essential order exists, and therefore if traditional African society is patriarchal, then patriarchy must be the natural order. Even in organizations dedicated to liberation, the Black Panther Party, the Student Nonviolent Coordinating Committee (SNCC), and Congress on Racial Equality (CORE), female leaders such as Kathleen Cleaver and Angela Davis were criticized for assuming what Ron Karenga and other male leaders deemed to be the man's role.[17] The Muslim women in this community are often forced to contend with this idealization of patriarchy. The sisters believe, however, that most brothers, as they learn more about their faith, begin to understand that their ideas of masculinity are Western ideas of masculinity. The sisters also believe that although men may flaunt a machismo in public, they argue that privately these men have such damaged egos that they are almost incapable of sustaining relationships. The beauty of Islam, many converts claim, is that it recognizes the importance of defined leadership roles for men in the community and in the family. For African American men these roles were lost, many feel, because of racism. Many hope that an added benefit of conversion is an increase in men's self-confidence so that they can become good husbands, fathers, and/or leaders.

Why, given the overwhelming acceptance of Western feminist ideals, are African American women choosing to perform gender roles as defined in the Qur'an? Western feminism is, after all, the simple assertion that women are as intellectually and morally capable as men of participating in the social, economic, and political life of a society.[18] Black women's distrust of "feminism" can be said to be forged over centuries. Fannie Lou Hammer described her relationship to white women as such:

> You've been caught up in this thing because, you know, you worked my grandmother, and after that you worked my mother, and then finally you got hold of me. You thought that you was *more* because you was a woman, and especially a white woman, you had this kind of angel feeling that you were untouchable.[19]

Many white women in the suffrage movement were openly racist, and this history informs the distrust many black women have of white feminists.[20] Another reason some African American women have a difficult time identifying themselves as feminists is that feminist paradigms in the 1960s were constructed by an articulate and socially elite group of white middle-class women who were rebelling against a particular "Western" set of gender roles and ideas of femininity.[21] Second wave feminism finally took shape as an activist movement at the tail end of the civil rights struggle and developed simultaneously with the black-power movements of the mid- to late 1960s and early 1970s. This historical synchronicity meant that African American women were participating less in the development of women-centered discourses than in theorizing about the intersections of class and race oppression worldwide.[22] People prioritize identities for particular reasons at particular times, and during the 1960s black women, more often than not, chose to align themselves ideologically with black men in an effort to liberate their families and communities.[23]

Clearly the race and class politics that accompanied the rise of second-wave feminism are responsible in part for inspiring an ideological counterframing by many middle-class "persons of color" who supported the basic premise of universal gender equality but rejected the prioritization of gender over race or class. Poorer women of color, who were largely on the sidelines of these discussions, did have a role in the development of new gender ideals, but they did so at a pragmatic level as they tried to negotiate structural barriers created by racism and classism. As such, their feminist theory emanated from the practical needs for security. Many Muslims today, for example, believe that security comes from parental involvement in their children's lives, protecting them from certain forms of materialism or "street culture." This means, of course, that women sometimes prefer to work at home and devote time to educating their children.

By the 1970s and 1980s, black radical and working-class women were challenging hegemonic feminist discourses emerging most notably from the National Organization for Women (NOW), which had grown increasing bold in defining a national agenda for women.[24] The targets of a lot of criticism were middle-class feminist activists who insisted that their liberation ideology was universally applicable, an assertion that required ignoring ones own class, race, and therefore privileged gaze. Objections by Third World scholars of women's issues were to the agendas set by privileged members of an already privileged society who, in a sense, took ownership of "feminism," defining the perimeters of female power and liberation. In an effort to demonstrate the universality of women's oppression and patriarchy, Western feminists appropriated the stories of Third World women or women of color without understanding the diversity of women's experiences.[25]

I hesitantly use the term "Western" especially when applied to the word "feminism." Ultimately, I use it as Chandra Mohanty does:

> My reference to "Western feminism" is by no means intended to imply that it is a monolith. Rather, I am attempting to draw attention to the similar effects of various textual strategies used by writers which codify Others as non-Western and hence themselves as (implicitly) Western. . . . Similar arguments can be made in terms of middle-class urban African or Asian scholars producing scholarship on or about their rural or working-class sisters which assumes their own middle-class cultures as the norm, and codifies working-class histories and cultures as Other.[26]

I use the term "Western" in general to distinguish hegemonic discourses in which the authors colonize or appropriate the cultural production of the " Third World" and essentially diminish heterogeneity in favor of sweeping generalizations about the powerlessness and oppression of the Other. These generalizations often ignore the local challenges to hegemonic discourses as well as the opportunities for resistance and agency at the level of the everyday. Missing from most hegemonic feminist discourses, according to many black women, are important discussions around the concept of multiple identities and roles. Gender oppression is only part of their struggle.[27] Patricia Hill Collins describes the black feminist paradigm shift:

> Black feminist thought fosters a fundamental paradigmatic shift that rejects additive approaches to oppression. Instead of starting with

gender and then adding in other variables such as age, sexual orientation, race, social class, and religion, Black feminist thought sees these distinctive systems of oppression as being part of one overarching structure of domination.[28]

The tension between white and black progressives plays itself out on many different levels—academically, politically, and socially. Ultimately, the choice of a particular gender ideology situates itself within the realm of identity politics, and as such many black women are uncomfortable identifying themselves as feminists. Black women lawyers, doctors, engineers, and teachers protest the label "feminist" despite the fact that their educational attainment, career aspirations, income, independence, and ideas about gender equality are evidence that they are in fact feminists.[29] Such a distinction denotes an allegiance to a narrowly understood idea of feminism, thought to reject a "femininity" associated with nurturing children, loving men, family first, a female aesthetic, and cooperation over competition. Also, women of color who were maids and janitors when middle-class white women were protesting their domestic roles object to the assumption that earning low wages is better than raising one's own children full-time. Another issue for poor women is the assumption that to be a feminist one must possess the drive to succeed in the market place, but Muslim women often reject this idea of feminism and liberation for the same reason they reject capitalism for defining people's worth by their earning potential.[30] Instead, full-time motherhood and marriage are viewed by many as a privilege.

Hudah, whose food prescriptions are discussed in chapter 5, argues that Western feminism is the wrong approach to liberation because social problems have only become worse since the 1970s. After I asked her why domestic roles should be determined solely on the basis of gender, she countered:

> In terms of the feminists, the feminists are not our guide for living. The Holy Qur'an is the guide for living for all mankind. Many women are working, many women are political leaders, many women are secretaries, doctors, lawyers, and look at our society, look

at our children. The proof is in the pudding, as they say. If you want to know if our opinions are working, and the feminist ideas are working, then look at the society.

Apparently the feminists don't have the answers because the society that they're living in has the worst of problems with [respect to] our children. We have AIDS, we have the gangs, we have the drugs, we have the teenage pregnancy, we have the high divorce rate. We have all these problems that you don't have in countries that don't use feminist guidelines.

We didn't create ourselves. God, who is such an intelligent entity, would not put us here without giving us guidance, and he gave us the Qur'an as guidance. We're not smart enough to follow our own guidance. This society is proof of that. So the Qur'an is our criteria. There's a chapter in the Qur'an; the title of it is *Al-Furqan*. [31] It is our criteria, not our whims, not our emotions, not our opinions. Everything that we need to know is in that Qur'an to protect us and prevent us from having to experience the high divorce rate, the gang behavior, the drugs, the teenage pregnancy, the economic exploitation. All your money goes toward rent and food. The Qur'an has the answer to all of that.

Allah tells us in the thirty-third chapter and the thirty-sixth verse, "It is not fitting for a believer, man or woman, when a matter has been decided by Allah and his messenger, to have any option about their decision. If anyone disobeys Allah and his messenger he is indeed on a clearly wrong path." We can see that. We have disobeyed. We have not fulfilled our role. We've gotten away from our roles. We've disobeyed the guidelines, that's why we have a high divorce rate. That's why we have the crime. That's why we're scared of drive-by shootings, that's why we're scared for our sons. That's why we have such corrupt politicians because we're not following.

We have a *shariah*, the law of Islam that tells you how to run the government. A portion of our wealth doesn't even belong to us, it belongs to the downtrodden, to the homeless down there on the streets of downtown L.A. To our children. We need to follow those guidelines if we want to avoid the problems that we're having in this society. So we don't have any options. So that's my answer to the feminist stance because the feminists have not solved the problems of this society.[32]

The interesting and typical part of Hudah's perspective is her attempt to place herself and her beliefs in a wider social context. That context has primacy over self, a strong theme in African American "feminist" consciousness.[33] Hudah is arguing that there is a larger class issue that has yet to be addressed by feminists and that Islam for her balances the needs of women and men with the needs of children and the poor. In this sense, Hudah's perspective, although she rejects the label "feminist," is similar to black feminist theory in that it demands the recognition of injustice against all subgroups. The black community is not understood, as in the market model, as a place for competition and mistrust. According to Patricia Hill Collins, the black feminist model identifies community as a place where people work together, share in successes and struggles, and care for one another's families. This model of community solidarity resonates with most female converts, which is why for Muslims the goal of a stable family is not simply for personal satisfaction. Muslims argue that a stable family requires that the husband has access to consistent employment, which helps to create a more stable family and helps to recirculate dollars in the community. In addition they feel that society needs to make sure that with two incomes, families can afford to live in a decent location with good schools. With this social support it is assumed that children have more opportunity to do well in school because they have both parents to raise and educate them. The hope is that the successful products of these families and neighborhoods will eventually prosper in the communities in which they were raised. The vision is one of cyclical wealth versus cyclical poverty, with parents and society sacrificing in order for all individuals to be able to live in safe and self-sustaining neighborhoods. Parents sacrifice by positioning their children ahead of their need for status or career fulfillment (some parents can "have it all," but many must make choices), and society sacrifices by encouraging the circulation of wealth rather than the concentration of wealth.

Many African Americans view feminism as an ideology that assumes a natural antagonism between men and women. In response, a number of black women scholars, including Alice Walker, advocate the use of the term "womanist." Womanists and Muslim women share a desire to empower both genders. According to Walker, a womanist resists all forms of oppression, respects all people, and adopts all of humanity as "people of color." The presumption that a womanist can simultaneously attend to ethical principles of universal justice and pluralism differentiates Muslim feminists from womanists. Muslim women are unabashedly clear about the methods they use to arrive at truth, while Walker articulates no clear method for determining a womanist agenda. Indeed, it is questionable whether a womanist stance can methodologically mediate the contradictions between universalism and particularism. Womanism is a highly idealized approach to liberation that even Walker struggles to uphold. In her outspoken condemnation of female circumcision, Walker emphatically prioritizes the implementation of universal human rights over respect for regional difference.[34]

Muslim women in the community agree with Walker in principle that female circumcision is wrong, but the methods they use to reach that conclusion are based on *tafsir*. Situating feminism within the authorized discourses emerging from Islamic exegesis does not eliminate the conceptual contradictions between universalism and particularism. Muslim women similarly attempt to differentiate what they consider the normative from the contextual edicts in Islam. What Islam does that feminism and womanism does not is situate calls for reform within a faith that men in the community accept. Shared beliefs can strengthen the community's consensus and resolve around enacting social change. What feminists and womanists can do that Muslim feminists cannot is innovate beyond the perimeters established by the Muslim community (local and/or international). Each approach to women's rights has a unique discursive potential, but notably none is objective or conceptually free of the issues of gaze and power for which second wave feminism was so condemned.

The differences between black feminist intellectuals and "everyday" black women are troublesome to black feminists because they fear that by privileging the intellectual's worldview they are making the same mistakes as second-wave white feminists. Black feminists want the production of feminist consciousness to originate in the lives of ordinary women. Therefore, for Patricia Hill Collins all black women are feminists:

> Black feminist thought consists of theories or specialized thought produced by African-American women intellectuals designed to express a Black women's standpoint. The dimensions of this standpoint include the presence of characteristic core themes, the diversity of Black women's experiences in encountering these core themes, the varying expressions of Black women's Afrocentric feminist consciousness regarding the core women's experiences, consciousness, and actions. This specialized thought should aim to infuse Black women's experiences and everyday thought with new meaning by rearticulating the interdependence of Black women's experiences and consciousness. Black feminist thought is of African-American women in that it taps the multiple relationships among Black women needed to produce a self-defined Black women's standpoint. Black feminist thought is for Black women in that it empowers Black women for political activism.[35]

Collins makes a delicate attempt to articulate the interconnection between black feminist intellectuals and "everyday" black women. While I disagree with Collins's black feminist essentialism, her approach to framing an understanding of the evolution of feminist consciousness is similar to Michel Foucault's "genealogies" in *Power/Knowledge*.[36] Foucault proposes that any analysis of power must join local knowledge and history with erudite macrotheory. "Genealogies" acknowledge that in daily life people are able to negotiate power by knowing their political, social, and personal landscapes. If the project of black feminists should be, as Collins argues, to remove issues of gaze and power from feminist discourses, and to recognize the truth value of subjugated knowledges, then I assume the role of black intellectuals is not to formulate truths, but to imagine possibilities. Margo Badran recognizes that a woman who cannot imagine a life without oppression limits her ability to empower herself. Badran argues that the development of feminism in Egypt was in part the result of conceptualizing heterodoxy:

> Upper- and middle-class women observed how men in their families were freer to innovate while they were more restricted. As women expanded their female circles, they discovered different ways that they *as women*—across lines of class, religion, and ethnicity—were controlled. As they imagined new lives, women began to withhold complicity in their own subordination.[37]

If women who believe in and seek out their own empowerment should be considered feminists then African American converts are feminists. They fulfill the feminist ideals of producing local knowledge and articulating an erudite Islamic scholarship that imagines numerous possibilities, including, at times, acquiescence to patriarchy. Therefore, black feminists could and should include Muslim converts in their ranks because in consciousness and action they have many of the same characteristics, and fulfill many of the same roles, as feminists. Muslim women recognize Islam to be the first "feminist" monotheistic religion, and therefore when they choose to identify as Muslims, as opposed to a feminists, it is more for political reasons rather than any clear objections to women's equality as defined by the West. Most African American Muslims work, end troubled marriages, and work toward greater gender equality within their families and community. The difference is that African Americans acknowledge that there are alternative ways to view the importance of women, and that maybe the model of men and women performing the same roles is not the best way to organize a family or a society.

Perhaps the most significant way in which female converts fulfill the feminist ideal is in their personal sense of empowerment. According to bell hooks, "Oppressed people resist by identifying themselves as subjects, by defining their reality, shaping their new identity, naming their history, telling their story."[38] African American converts certainly do all those things in their struggle to recreate their personal narratives. Their struggle is to find a balance between personal empowerment and community empowerment, and about prioritizing the family and spirituality. A convert's transformation is often in response to personal crises and has little to do with trying to reestablish the patriarchy of yesteryear. In these ways, African American Muslims parallel in consciousness modern Muslim feminists who, according to Saddeka Arebi, contest any feminism predicated on ideas of universality.[39] Muslim feminists and womanists share a common critique of certain Western feminist assumptions including, (1) family ties do not hinder women's liberation, (2) the problem is not Islam but specific interpretations of Islam, and (3) for Third World women, wages for work performed within capitalist markets are only occasionally the means for liberation as predicted by second wave feminists.

There are a number of men in the community who use Islam as an excuse to seclude and beat their wives, and women who allow this. These converts, most women in the community contend, do not understand Islam, but that does not provide sufficient reason to call all female converts disempowered by their faith and praxis. Muslim women's interest in transforming notions of gender again is much more complex than simply making the man the head of the house. Islam, according to my informants, actually has a very different perspective on women's roles, power, and position in the family and community than most non-Muslims would assume.

SEVEN

Performing Gender

Marriage, Family, and Community

Marriage in Islam is prescribed to channel sexuality: "Whoever of you has the means to support a wife, he should get married, for this is the best means of keeping the looks cast down and guarding the chastity; and he who has not the means, let him keep fast, for this will act as castration."[1] Marriage for Muslims is the nexus of physical desire, culture, and divine law, and according to some traditions, "The man who marries perfects half his religion."[2] Some African American Muslims say the ideal Islamic marriage requires that the husband and wife cooperate to manage a household with the rights and responsibilities afforded each gender organized around maintaining that ideal. They contend that as opposed to the patriarchal European organization of gender in which women traditionally occupy the private and men the public spheres, Muslim women are allowed to occupy both.[3]

When most Americans imagine Muslim gender roles, they envision the 1950s white, middle-class wife at home fulfilling all the domestic duties to the satisfaction of her employed husband. In fact, the public/private division along gender lines is not the Islamic ideal. One informant, Aisha, told me, "A woman's role is not to cook and clean," and most authorities on Islam agree.[4] Aisha also says that within marriage a man has exactly two rights: the right to know where his wife is going every time she leaves the house (but not the ability to restrain her) and the right to sex when he so desires. She has other rights, including the right to distribute her husband's income how she sees fit, the right to work, to keep all her earnings for herself, to own property, to inherit, to educate and raise the children the way she wants. Aisha argues that a woman does not lose her rights because she enters marriage, but she is required to take on other responsibilities. The African American convert's perspective on gender organization can best be described as two branches of the American government: His tenure as president does not preclude her own authority and power as Speaker of the House.

For African American converts, the Prophet Muhammad's marriage to his first wife, Khadija, represents the ideal union. The forty-year-old Khadija was a successful businesswoman when she proposed to the twenty-five-year-old Muhammad.[5] Khadija had employed Muhammad on one of her caravans and was so impressed by his trustworthiness that she proposed to him. For Khadija this was her third marriage, for Muhammad, his first. The fact that Khadija (1) did not ask permission from any male member of her family before proposing; (2) was an independently wealthy and successful business woman who freed Muhammad to pursue his own interests; (3) was older than him; and (4) was his only wife while she was alive, represents for Muslim converts the respect, independence, and status women are afforded in Islam.[6] Others argue that Khadija proposed to Muhammed ibn Abdullah in pre-Islamic Arabia in "the time of ignorance," or *jahiliya*. They disagree that Islam ushered in great feminist reforms and that Khadija's independence and agency were the result of the pre-Islamic social order.[7] The accuracy of Islamic exegesis is not as significant as how that Islamic exegesis is authorized, or legitimated, by those who convert. In order to understand Muslim feminist praxis, it is simply enough to know that African American female converts identify Khadija as an exemplary role model with respect to the rights and responsibilities afforded women in Islam.

Since culture meets nature and divine order in marriage, success in a relationship requires the careful balancing and nurturing of all three, an important challenge for African American converts. However, statistics in the African American Sunni community on divorce and out-of-wedlock births are high, and the social expectations and pressures keeping these statistics high are at odds with the Islamic ideal.[8] In response, leaders in the African American Muslim community focus a considerable percentage of their talks on Islamic marriage, including redefining gender, delineating male and female roles, and in a sense changing marital expectations in an effort to help Muslims get married and stay married. Many people would dismiss the intentions of the men in the community as an obvious attempt to reinvigorate the male patriarchy of yesteryear. In terms of the women, many might think they are being duped into believing that by giving up certain rights they are strengthening the community. These assumptions do not acknowledge that the Islamic prescriptions regarding marriage are subtle and malleable, while also being informed by ideals of gender equality.

Four professional women in the community demonstrate that performing faith, marriage, and career is possible. These four leaders represent for many of the women in the community the ideal: They are committed to a faithful reading of Islam at the same time that they have tremendous agency within their marriages and within the secular community.

BALANCING RELIGIOUS PRAXIS AND CAREER: AIDA

If there is a faith gene, an innate capacity for spirituality, Aida has it. As a young and extremely gifted student, Aida went to private religious schools, and at each one she accepted the faith.[9] Her parents even took her out of an Adventist school because in the fourth grade she tried to convert her family and demanded them to turn off the radio and television on the Sabbath. In her junior year of high school, at the age of fourteen, Aida met members of the Nation of Islam. Her sister was dating a member of the Nation who wanted her to convert before they got married. He would bring literature to Aida's family, and while her sister re-

mained unimpressed, Aida, the avid reader, became interested. Origi-
nally intent on knowing enough about the Nation to argue against the
faith, Aida found the Nation's emphasis on family life attractive. The Nation was advocating the adoption of clean living as a form of resistance
to racism, and the reawakening of an "essential" African identity. After
careful consideration, Aida converted more than a year before Elijah
Muhammad's death in 1975. Aida who has white friends and never saw
the Nation's theology as racist, believed one of the Nation's greatest contributions was to the advancement of black economic self-sufficiency.
When she joined the Nation there were bakeries, a large market, restau-
rants, and other businesses in one African American neighborhood. I
asked her if she had trouble maintaining her commitment during the
transition. She replied that her faith was not shaken when Elijah
Muhammad died; she was more disturbed when he was alive and people
treated him like a deity. Aida's family vehemently objected to her joining
the Nation, which meant in order to visit the temple she had to surrep-
titiously take a bus and change into her white uniform at a stop along the
way. Aida credits economic class as the number-one reason her family
objected so strongly to the Nation, and argues that the Nation's mission
to rehabilitate society's "rejects and undesirables" turned off many
middle-class Christians.

At Fisk University at the age of sixteen, Aida was happy to have her
faith as an excuse to reject alcohol, drugs, and sex. She would say, "In the
Nation of Islam, we don't drink and put poisons into our bodies and
smoke cancer sticks from the white man."[10] At Fisk, an historically black
university, it was "cool" to be in the Nation, so people allowed her to
hold her values without labeling her a "square." In her second year, Aida
met Sunni Muslims who had transitioned from the Nation, and through
a close relationship with another female student she was introduced to
traditional Sunni Islam. After college and before medical school in
Southern California, Aida worked in a lab and met her husband, who was
studying chemistry. Aida wanted to marry a Muslim, but her husband, although very supportive of Aida's faith and religious practice, has never

wanted to convert. Aida says that although he has never taken the *sha-hada*, she believes he acts more Muslim in his responsibilities to his family than most men she knows in the Sunni community.

Aida's medical practice serves a diverse clientele, but mainly poorer African American women and Latinas. Many of Aida's clients are Muslim women from the community, and, like Imam Khalil, Aida is intimately familiar with their personal tragedies. During a phone call Aida and I discussed marriage.[11] In referring to an extremely devout Muslima, Safa, who put up with abuse from her husband for years, Aida said, "It's funny, I look at Safa and hope one day I'll have that much faith. Why can't I just obey my husband and submit to him. Instead I'm mouthing off and having an attitude about everything? I say, 'Al-hamdulilah, I will be such a good wife and mother.' I keep thinking that some day Allah will give me the patience and humility." How could Aida idealize a woman who for years wanted to divorce her husband, but was powerless to do so? Aida objects to the idea that Muslim men have the right to abuse their wives.[12] So what does Aida admire about Safa? Simply that given a nonabusive and supportive husband, Safa's patience and compassion are, Aida believes, the ideal.

At some level, Aida is overexaggerating her desire to be like Safa. Aida is happy to have a relationship with a man who respects her and gives her the freedom to make her own choices, but at another level she is quite serious. Although she recognizes that she will probably never change, she believes that in Islam women are supposed to submit to their husbands. "The Qur'an is clear on that; man has a degree above women. If he fulfills his obligation to provide and protect, then we owe him that. Otherwise we don't give him that. But what does that mean? It says *a* degree and all I know about degrees is there are 360 of them, so one out of 360 is not a whole lot above me and that's if he provides and protects." Aida argues that the significance of that dominance is quite small and, she qualifies, that degree is only on the condition that he is asking her to do only that which is allowed within Islam.

Aida loves her career and despite having disabling high blood pressure following the birth of her third and last child, she refuses to contemplate giving up her career. Her illness is such that it forced her to reduce her hours by half and threatened the financial viability of her practice. Nevertheless, Aida maintains that quitting her profession is out of the question. In order to test the limits of Aida's desire to submit to her husband, I asked what she would do if her husband demanded she stay home and educate their three daughters. She said, "Theoretically Islam gave women the right to work and the responsibilities of the house and family. Technicalities like that mean you must follow the spirit of Islam. That's a touchy subject. For me, I'm not automatically obedient. I probably shouldn't make excuses for why I do what I want to do. To this day I can say I've never disobeyed my husband." Her husband overhears and gives her a look. "When I said that he just looked at me, but I haven't. I don't ask, I just do it. And if he says he didn't like what I did, I tell him, 'You didn't tell me not to do it. It's done.'" Her husband, who commutes three hours a day for his work, loves his family and pampers the women in his life, but he does not have the time to invest in the management of the daily schedule. Aida is clearly in control of the organization of the family, both financially and socially, and hires nannies full-time—usually Muslim women from the African Diaspora, including a Ghanaian-Parisienne, a Jamaican, and numerous African Americans—which means that she fulfills her gender obligations through a surrogate. These nannies provide a level of care for her children that frees her to be on call, which for an OB/GYN is vital. Regardless of her very hectic schedule, Aida has been responsible for educating her children in significant ways. Her oldest daughter reads and speaks Arabic and can recite numerous *sura* by heart. And interestingly, all of her daughters speak fluent French to their mother. Aida does not come from a French-speaking family, but she decided that she would teach her children French in case they ever move to a French-speaking African country.

The personalities of Aida and her husband are such that they are well suited for each other. "When I think about our biggest arguments, I re-

alize I need to listen to this man or be divorced. I may not come to him
for permission, but I'm patient with him. If I wasn't, we wouldn't be married anymore. He doesn't give a lot of orders. He makes it easy to get
along with him. He doesn't harass me. If he were the type of husband that
did, it would be a problem." My hypothetical question regarding Aida
staying home is truly hypothetical. Her husband has no desire to see Aida
home schooling her children. "We've talked about home schooling and
he says, 'No way!' It's a recipe for death. My blood pressure is going to
go through the roof. He says we would spend all our time fighting and
arguing. It would be a challenge. We have this mother/daughter thing."
In fact, Aida does virtually none of the cooking in the house, and by all
measures Aida is one of the most liberated married women I know. Despite that, she is committed to the idea of a wife's submissiveness, and she
wears *hijab*: "For me *hijab* is a personal thing. It's based on fear of Allah,
not because of my father or my husband. It's because you know that that's
what Allah wants of you. It's the same reason you make *salat* and fast. If
you don't think that's what was meant, don't do it."

Several years after this phone conversation, I sat down with Aida to
show her what I had written about her in the preceding passage. In that
interview she summarized what an Islamic marriage means to her:

> Marriage is referred to in Islam as a fortress. That's the literal trans-
> lation of the word. You join together in unity to form a protection
> for yourself and your family unit against everything that is out there.
> Not just the material challenges, but the spiritual challenges as well.
> Following the rules of what you say you are submitting to, in other
> words, the Qur'an and hadith, that strengthens your fortress,
> strengthens your relationship, increases your protection against
> problems from the material world, problems from the financial
> world, sociological problems, and spiritual problems. If a spouse is
> just going to tell you what to do based on what they feel as opposed
> to what they have learned in the Qur'an and hadith, then you're both
> going astray. And that weakens your relationship because in the ef-
> fort you think you're pleasing Allah, but you're really pleasing man.
> And everything is supposed to please Allah.[13]

EMPOWERING WOMEN: ZIPPORAH

Zipporah has successfully assimilated her Islamic exegesis into her private life, but has been thwarted at times trying to translate that private success into public agency.[14] Prior to moving to Minnesota and getting her bachelor's degree at the University of Minnesota, Zipporah was a single mother in a nontraditional job in Portland, Maine. She worked as a laborer for General Electric and eventually was trained to become a machinist in an affirmative action program. As a result of a layoff she decided to attend community college where, she says, "I found out I could learn." As a result of her performance at community college, she received six scholarships to attend a four-year college. She chose the University of Minnesota in order to reacquaint herself with her father.

Through a combination of human resource experience, a business degree, and experience in nontraditional employment, Zipporah has been tremendously successful working and consulting for women's job training programs. About six years ago, Zipporah and a group of women formed CARE, an organization devoted to training women for nontraditional employment. CARE is a nonprofit whose mission is to "encourage and support women's training, placement, and retention in high-wage, high-skill jobs." Zipporah described it:

> We do outreach to women, we recruit them, we assess them for barriers that they have to employment and training, we work with them to put them in training, focusing on these high-wage, high-skill jobs to try to help women become economically self-sufficient. We see women who are transitioning from welfare. We see women who just want to transition in terms of jobs. We help them by providing them with skills to go on into nontraditional employment. We help them by providing them with a high school diploma program or GED program that we have. We help them by providing them with support services to help deal with child care.[15]

CARE was Zipporah's dream, and she became the executive director after receiving more than a million dollars in grant funding.

Zipporah converted and eventually married a Muslim after a long courtship during which they strictly adhered to the Islamic regulations regarding contact between unmarried men and women. "I met my husband at al-Mustaqim. . . . I had kind of watched him for maybe about a year and saw that there were qualities in him that I was interested in. So being the assertive woman that I am, I sent him a note saying I would like to meet him and get to know him better." Her approach was reminiscent of the Prophet's first wife, Khadija, who also took the initiative of identifying a man who had the qualities she desired. Wanting to abide by the tenets of her new faith, Zipporah chose to use a *wali* (friend, matchmaker) as an intermediary. She found out that a woman could be a *wali*, so she chose her sister.

> We would have dinners. [My *wali*] arranged for a time for him to be invited so that we could kind of be in the same place without dating per se, so that we could get to know each other a little bit. He proposed after a year of this. He had been invited to my sister's retirement party, so he came and he said to me 'What kind of wedding do you want?' I thought, okay I'll just play along, and I described it. He goes, 'So when do you think you would like to get married?' I said, 'I don't know.' He said, 'How about in the summer?' So we set a date for June 23. Well, once you have made your intentions, Allah says that we should hasten to the wedding. Well, we didn't think we should hasten, we thought we should just wait.

Ultimately, Zipporah learned that there was something at stake for the future bride and groom, and for the community in making sure that proper Islamic etiquette is followed.

ZIPPORAH: Once we had made the intention, it escalated our feelings toward each other. It was the first time in my life experiencing something like that. I had my first child at sixteen, and so this was really completely different. This is a man I didn't even know if his hand was rough, or if his hand was soft. I think the pressure started to get to us. To me it was like a fairy tale, knight-in-shining-armorish kind of thing. [In a mock young girls voice], "We're going to get married and we're going to have a honeymoon and ahhhh." It was kind of a big issue for a forty-something year old woman who had three children and a grandchild. But one day all of a sudden right after *fajr* I get a phone call and it's him, and Imam Khalil and my sister. And he has said to them that we need to move the marriage date up. And I guess they had had some kind of conference before they called me, and they tell me I'm getting married in a few days [we laugh].

I said in three days! This was in March, this was right after Ramadan. And I said, "In three days! What are you talking about?" And so Khalil counseled, and they all kind of said what was happening and that we should move toward the marriage right away. And I said, "Well alrighty then. I'm a new Muslim. You guys know best." So we proceeded to get married March 30 instead of June 23. We had done a lot of talking about a lot of things. I asked questions that probably women just don't. I think people just don't do this. We discussed everything. I wanted to know how he felt about more than one wife, I wanted to know how he felt about the degree above. What did he feel even about *hijab* and his wife covering? What did he feel about makeup? I mean all these things. What was your financial circumstance? What is your credit worthiness? How many children do you have from somewhere else? Where are they? What do you do? Do you support them financially? Do you support them emotionally? These are the things I encourage other women to do. I asked about him in the community. I inquired of his ex-wife. I did because I wanted to know. I had just seen, in my year or so in the community, so many devastating kinds of things happen in that area.

CAROLYN: Like Zainab? [She was beaten by her second husband.]

ZIPPORAH: I had just seen so much of those kinds of things that I didn't want to be that. So I really thought I did fairly well in the preselection process. It was important that I had someone who would be patient and understanding. I mean fourteen days after I married my husband, I was gone to Kansas for a five-day business trip. What is considered normal in society is that the woman usually stays home and the man usually travels. He told me that men actually said to him things like, "Brother, you ain't going to be able to control that sister." He had a lot of that, but he was able to handle that because he didn't see those qualities as negative, he saw those as positive qualities. He's been very supportive of the work that I've done with CARE. He's been very supportive of the work that I've done with women period, and all of that. He's not demanding. All these things that are really important to me he understands that they are important to me, and he's very supportive. He's not a demanding husband. I don't cook dinner every day or every other day or every five days [we laugh].

You know. It's not important to him how the house looks. It's more important to me than it ever is to him. He does fret sometimes because sometimes I get a bit busy. Like he said yesterday, "My, are we actually leaving here together in the same car going to the same *Jumah?* Are we actually going to spend a day together as mates?" You know [laughs]. I go, "Okay, okay what are you trying to say?" But he has a life of his own. He has his own aspirations and his own dreams.

CAROLYN: What does he do?

ZIPPORAH: He works in retail. He's a manager. But he does a lot of work with the brothers. He works with the security at al-Mustaqim. He teaches at the county jail. He does *Jumah* at the county jail. He's a very giving kind of guy. He really is. The thing that I think that I always saw in him was how he seemed to treat everybody the same. I have a very diverse staff. Some people have issues with that diversity. I mean I have Latinas that work for me. I have lesbians that work for me. I have all kinds of folk. For some people, especially those who came from the Nation of Islam, there are issues with those kinds of things, and he doesn't have any problem. . . . I work with a lot of men. Everyday there are a couple of them that I have to work with. One gentleman he calls me here in the morning at 7 o'clock, 6:30 in the morning if he needs to reach me, and my husband is okay with that. And a lot of men would not be. A lot of men period, let alone Muslim men.

But he's secure in who he is. He's secure with our relationship so he doesn't have a lot of problems with that. That's been very important because in fact I may have to travel from one place to another with a guy. Because we're going to the same place it doesn't make sense for us to not go together. I don't do it as a habit, but it's something that happens. Usually when that happens I always explain it to him first so that some person doesn't happen to see me going down the street with somebody and say, "I saw your wife!" [laughs] The fundraiser. He's there. He helped me when we had to move. He's there. When we need things he tries to help us find them. That's important because that's my passion.

Zipporah and Aida have marriages in which the ideological and personal dispositions of their husbands allow them to experience Islam the way they idealize it. These women have a number of qualities, like intelligence and endearing dispositions, which have allowed them to create satisfying careers for themselves. They have chosen husbands who encourage them to pursue their passions sometimes in lieu of fulfilling domestic responsibilities, or maintaining rigid walls between the Muslim and non-Muslim worlds. They successfully cross borders while maintaining a sense of who they are: Muslim women. Zipporah maintains a diverse staff; Aida is unfettered. They do not believe that the pollution, so to speak, of the secular world in any way dilutes their faith. In fact, Zipporah and Aida present themselves in the hospital, or in Washington, D.C., as Muslim women by wearing *hijab* and finding time to make *salat*.

Aida and Zipporah do not simply submit to things because they are "Muslim." Aida's first two children, for example, attend Los Angeles charter schools rather than Muslim schools because of their educational needs. Her second child, for example, is extremely gifted, and the Muslim school wanted to advance her two grade levels. Aida felt that her daughter would benefit more by being with children her own age and therefore made the decision to move her. Similarly, Aida broke ties with a masjid that she had supported for more than a decade because of one imam's lack of proactive engagement with women's issues like divorce, abuse, and poverty. Now her daughters study Islam and Arabic in an environment that Aida feels reinforces, rather than contradicts, Aida's Islamic exegesis.

Aida is teaching her children to maintain a strong sense of who they are in order to cross spatial and ideological borders without losing their faith. In contrast to some Muslim women who construct the world outside the Muslim community as tempting and impure, Aida shows her children that there is good and bad within any community and that faith must rise above the failings of individuals.

INSIDE THE MASJID

Ther are two important arenas in which Muslim women from this community subvert hegemony: in secular Southern California and in the masjid. In the secular arena, the struggle to unseat hegemonic discourse on race and gender occurs through Islamic exegeses. There are two equally important arenas both within the family, as described above, as well as in the masjid, where Islamic "feminist" discourses are created to subvert patriarchal discourses. Using Islamic *tafsir,* female converts first reject mainstream hegemonic discourse regarding race, gender, and class; using the same tools for critique, they create a feminist agenda within the Muslim community. This phenomenon can be described as dialectics within dialectics because the women use Islam to negate sexism within the Muslim community while the community itself is a negation of essentializing ideas of race and class. The methodologies and concepts used to create agency in women's lives have an indigenous character that to outsiders seem like the replacement of one form of oppression with another. At the local or personal level, however, many of their ideas capture the imagination of a community with a shared history and identity. Ultimately, these ideas might have the capacity to change relations of production, but in the meantime if they are not altering life materially, at least they are providing these women with sufficient ideological weaponry to engage in a battle over symbols and legitimacy.

Surrendering to Islam in the context of a community also means women must contend with Qur'anic exegesis that threatens women's empowerment. Zipporah illustrates the difficulties of being part of a community where one's interpretation of the religion is not necessarily the consensus. She struggles to make community praxis mirror what she believes to be the correct treatment of women as prescribed in Qur'an and hadith. Zipporah describes why she took "a break" from the community:

ZIPPORAH: I was running into some walls, and I thought that for my husband and for me, I need to back up a little bit. I would have to put my husband in a position to have to defend me, and he would happily, but it wasn't necessary to do that. So Allah gave me the freedom to choose what I wanted to do at the time.

CAROLYN: How do you feel about your faith having to be part of a consensus when you're in the community? You know a kind of consensus faith? Or is there such a thing? Or is everyone an individual?

ZIPPORAH: No, I think there is a consensus faith. I think you're right about that aspect. I think that there are times that I'm not with the consensus. That is the place that I was in. That I wasn't in with the consensus and so I had to move away a bit and kind of regroup myself and refocus myself on what I need to be focused on in terms of the religion. And kind of begin to understand that I didn't really carry the banner for all Muslim women, so to speak. And that it wasn't just my responsibility to make people accountable for things that they were doing because I was running into a lot of problems. I had a lot of issues around accountability in the mosque, about things happening to sisters and people not doing anything about it. I was running amok [laughs]. I think I had expectations that were way too high for the capabilities of what I was dealing with. I think that that's a good way to put that. That my expectations were not necessarily above or below or whatever they were, my expectations were beyond the capabilities of the people I was looking at.

CAROLYN: Do you think that is the experience of many of the women that have been there for a number of years?

ZIPPORAH: Yes, I think we get disillusioned. It kind of seems like there's this circle that you go through; you know when they tell you go full circle. Hopefully, I'm on my way back to the place where I was before when I was much more active in the community. I think you do have that transition that you go through. I think it was a shock to me to learn, number one that people had this religion and the knowledge of this religion and were treating women in the way

that they were doing. I think that was a shock. I think that
I was disillusioned by the fact that al-Islam said one thing
and people were teaching something from the rostrum and
then they didn't do it. It was not a part of everyday. Because I was an activist, women would come to me with issues and I would think that they needed to be addressed,
and they were not. And I was burning with that. It was like
they wouldn't address them with certain people. They
wanted to try to fall back on things that Islamic law says.
And when a situation would come up and a woman would
say she had been raped or abused, or domestic violence or
incest or any of those kinds of things and they would say
things like, "Well, that's hearsay, that's conjecture." "Look
all I'm asking you to do is investigate." I had a personal in-
cident with the mosque, and it really disillusioned me,
where a brother actually physically hit me. And everyone
assumed it was my fault because of the person that I am—
assertive. They just assumed it was my fault.

The refusal of the leadership to reprimand the man who hit Zipporah has
many disturbing features, including the men's desire for control, the
"blame the victim" approach to women's issues, and the utter disregard for
a member of the community based on her personality and gender. One
can only wonder why she returned. The answer lies in African American
social history and the desire of both men and women to heal the devasta-
tion racism and poverty have inflicted on the urban community. In the
case of women who convert, community solidarity supercedes the desire
for individualism, or the belief that individualism is freedom. The community instead looks to Islam as a religion that, if followed correctly, balances the needs of the individual and the needs of the family with the
needs of society. For Zipporah, Muslims are not perfect, but Islam is and
therefore she prioritizes her needs in order to continue to enact her dominant personal narrative of Muslima and community leader.

Identities are ensconced in the service of preserving other agendas and priorities; the performance of identity does not always correlate with an embodied sense of self. Zipporah eventually returned to the masjid and continues to support women, but now she is less assertive and silences her criticism. She still believes that Muslim women are supposed to be assertive, but now she believes the men are simply not ready for what she sees as Islam's radical empowerment of women. Zipporah explains it to herself in this way, "I had expectations that were way too high for the capabilities of what I was dealing with. I think that that's a good way to put that. That my expectations were not necessarily above or below or whatever they were; my expectations were beyond the capabilities of the people I was looking at." Zipporah believes that many converts are on a trajectory, and she understands her failure as her attempt to move people along too quickly. She has a "you have to crawl before you can walk" argument that puts her in the position of adapting her performance to suit a community with whom she desires to belong.

For most Americans, Zipporah's choice to limit the full expression of her identity challenges the belief that agency is the attainment of unencumbered individualism. The dual ideals of democracy and meritocracy situated in a capitalist (free?) market system continually feed an illusion that through the liberal state and consumption we can be anything we want to be. Baudrillard discusses how consumption is tied to the understanding of social mobility through individualism:

> There is a double mystification. On the one hand, there is the illusion of a "dynamic" of consumption, of an ascending spiral of satisfactions and distinctions toward a paradoxical summit where all would enjoy the same prestigious standing. This false dynamic is in fact entirely permeated by the inertia of a social system that is immutable in its discrimination of real powers.[16]

Americans generally have faith that if you can think it (within legal limits), you should be able to do it. Zipporah, for example, believes that assertiveness in women is a quality sanctioned by Allah, and most Americans would assume that if the Muslim men are forbidding what she knows to be right, she should move on, or commit radical acts of rebellion. Most Americans, however, are firmly tied to communities where the material and social realities are not easily transcended, and there is a question whether they can be transcended at all. Therefore, Zipporah's choice to engage with the community by ensconcing parts of her identity reflects that she connects community redemption with individual salvation.

This story indicates that the way some women embrace Islam as a tool for liberation, and the way some men embrace Islam as a tool for regaining respect, pride, leadership—manhood—are sometimes at odds. Qur'anic exegesis, or *tafsir*, becomes, as a result, a mechanism whereby women legitimate their concerns. The reason Zipporah continues to struggle within the community is because a Muslim community where men and women work together toward common goals is something she desires. Zipporah even characterizes Masjid al-Mustaqim as one of the only mosques where the congregation is empowered. In other words, for Zipporah al-Mustaqim has the greatest potential for fostering personal and community transformation. She sees other masjids as racist, being run by a family, or as noninclusive in their leadership. Masjid al-Mustaqim has had several boards and seeks the input of the community for development projects. She describes other masjids, "All you do is just go there and you pray and you leave." Most important, the male leadership is not entirely unresponsive to women or women's issues, and leaders educate the community about gender in Islam knowing that even though female converts to Islam might reject "Western" feminism, they act and think like feminists. The way in which these tensions are resolved, through *tafsir*, speaks to the use of an authorized discourse as a tool for grounding transformation. Change results from the dialectic of "accommodating protest,"[17] "contestation and reinscription,"[18] "complicitous critique"[19] and "engaged surrender."[20]

HISTORICAL EXEGESIS: MAIMOUNA

Maimouna is a divorced mother of three and owner of a very successful law firm (see chapter 4). Her understanding of the history of women in Islam is that the women were political and social leaders. Far from the ideal of a wife secluded at home, Islam reaffirms for Maimouna that being a mother, wife, and professional are indeed compatible. Islam for her is about women's empowerment and mirrors the sentiments of modernist Muslim feminists who feel it is necessary to insert a new voice into scholarship on Islam.

> I was blessed to be able to make *hajj* in 1992. When you go to Saudi Arabia, in the shops you can see some with signs that say, "Women not Allowed." I looked at that and it kind of hit me in the face and I said, "Wait a minute? Doesn't this sound familiar? Isn't there something from home that I remember, you know, "No Colored"? I said wait a minute, I just went through that[laughs]! Why am I in this place where there's this whole new battle and I've got to almost start all over again?
>
> And I thought, well there is a reason. There's a reason that I'm here. There's a reason that this is happening to me, and maybe this is our battle. This is the time. Somebody's got to do it. There's got to be a change, and maybe that's what I'm part of. There's a change that's going on and I really believe that once women understand the power of Islam, and cut through all the nonsense and all the cultural garbage, it's so empowering.
>
> You know we need sisters to go into the Qur'an and translate those *ayat* that are not translated correctly. You know, the ones about the husband can beat you. That's the most blatant one. But there's got to be a translation to that that's different than what we're getting. I believe that sincerely 'cause Allah would not oppress us.
>
> That's why we need women to be Qur'anic scholars because I think the translations are messed up. Even the Arabic translations. Because despite what they say, "The language hasn't changed," in fourteen hundred years language changes. So the usage of a word that might

have been prevalent fourteen hundred years ago may not be the same meaning now, so somehow or another we need scholars to go back and look at those things.

A lot of it is just cultural baggage from Islamic cultures. It's just gobbledygook! It's gook! In fact, I shared this with someone. I was at a Muslim wedding and I was sitting next to my daughter. And my older daughter was about eleven or twelve at that time and the imam was giving the *khutbah*. He was talking about the roles of the husband and the wife. "The husband has to be the maintainer of the family and the spiritual guide and blah, blah, blah." And the woman, he says, "Well, the woman has to serve, you know take care of her husband, and wear a pleasing dress." I wasn't paying too much attention to him, and my daughter she says, "Mommy, do you think Allah would keep you out of the *Jannah* [Paradise] just because you wore an ugly dress?" That was the whole point of the *khutbah*, you get to Paradise if you're a good husband or a good wife. At her young age she could see through that. I mean this is not what our lives are about, serving our husbands and wearing pretty dresses.

We're trying to get to the *Jannah*. You look at the four perfect women in Islam. There's ʿAsiya who was the wife of the pharaoh. She became exalted because she went against her husband, not because she served her husband. Her husband was the pharaoh! She was granted Paradise and an exalted position over all women not because she was this doting wife, but because she was a believer, and she put that above anything else.

The second one was Mary, the mother of Jesus. She didn't even have a husband in the beginning. What does that tell? She's exalted because she's a mother and she dedicated her life to raising a righteous child who became a prophet. What does that tell you?

The third is Khadija, who's a wife. Yes, she's the wife of the Prophet, but more importantly she's the first convert. She believes the revelation her husband receives. That's why she's exalted.

And the fourth is Fatima, who is the daughter of the Prophet and the only one who survived him. We know least about her, but none of those is exalted because they were good wives, except perhaps Khadija. But it wasn't because she was a wife, but because she was a convert to this new religion.

Men aren't going to get their salvation by being good husbands. They get some blessings. We'll get some blessings for being good wives. That's important. I'm not trying to male bash or anything, but let's keep it in perspective. Our ultimate salvation is not serving our husbands. It's serving Allah.[21]

PRAGMATIC INDEPENDENCE: AFAF

The last example is Afaf, who is in her late forties and very devout (see chapter 5). Her reluctance to get married is based on the fear that she might marry a Muslim man who interprets Islam as a reaffirmation of patriarchy. She embodies the ambivalence of many women in the community.

CAROLYN: So do you want to be married? Because I imagine you've gotten proposals.

AFAF: Yes, I have. I want to be married, but I have this fear [laughs]. Matter of fact it has probably become a phobia by now [laughs long and claps hands]. Yes, I do want to be married.

CAROLYN: The fear of men.

AFAF: Not the fear of men, the fear of being married to one [laughs]. You know. The fear of getting some nut who's going to try to splatter me against the wall. I hear so many horror stories; it's just like I said, "Gee, I don't want that." And among Muslims no less. My brother told me from the beginning, "Now don't come in here thinking it's going to be a utopia because the word is perfect; the people are not perfect." Now I understand what he's saying, but I thought it would be a lot better then it was out there. But I come in here and find out that we got some psychopaths in this community.[22]

The descriptions of these four women demonstrate—from the personal empowerment expressed by Aida, to the material and community goals of Zipporah, to the historical exegesis of Maimouna, to the pragmatic ambivalence expressed by Afaf—that African American converts use Islam to shape and/or confirm their understanding of the best role for women in society. On a personal level they use Islam as a standard that their husbands and former husbands must reach. The roadblocks to liberation are seen not as Islam, but poor readings of Islam. For the majority of the women I interviewed, Islam has given them peace. The fact that their families and communities are in turmoil confirms for them that people are not understanding the religion, not "getting it." It confirms for them that some Muslim converts are in fact disempowered.

EIGHT

Searching for Islamic Purity
In and Out of Secular
Los Angeles County

A year and a half into my research, my husband, daughter, and I traveled to Abiquiu, New Mexico, to the "Second Annual North American Muslim Powwow." Dar al Islam, the mosque in Abiquiu, was a gift from a wealthy Middle Eastern industrialist who along with an American-born Muslim dreamed of establishing a religious community in North America. Several conferences are held yearly at the mosque, including the June powwow, an open forum on Islam.[1] About 50 percent of the Muslims who attended that year were European American, 45 percent ethnic American (African American, Native American, Pakistani American, Mexican American, and Puerto Rican); and 5 percent foreign (British, German). I was told that when the mosque at Abiquiu was first built, about forty American families moved to this remote city outside Santa Fe to live simply and Islamicly. Unemployment around Abiquiu is very high, so most families, out of economic necessity, were forced out.

Dar al Islam sits near the top of a hill and the location provides an almost 360-degree view of a beautiful and sparsely inhabited section of New Mexico. When we first arrived it was sunset, and families were looking for spots to pitch their tents. There was a driving wind, not dampened down by hills or chaparral, which made setting up the tents difficult. Ultimately, we decided to establish camp away from the mosque and next to our friends from Los Angeles.

Dar al Islam is truly magnificent, from the domed ceilings to the tile to the woodwork and ornamentation. The designer, Hassan Fathi, chose a North African style of architecture so that the mosque retains heat in the winter but remains cool in the summer. During the hottest months, the wind is directed through the mosque by opening certain doors and windows, providing natural air conditioning, a welcome relief when the temperatures rises above one hundred.

On the evening we arrived, after settling in, people began entering the mosque in order to perform *wudu* and *Salatul Maghrib* prayer.[2] The women performed *wudu* in a large basin surrounded by a bench intricately crafted in beautiful blue and white tile. After completing *wudu*, the women entered their prayer space, behind the men's and separated by a short wall and carved wooden slats. The women prayed individually and then headed back to their families to continue unpacking. I stayed in the mosque and watched the children who regularly attended the Dar al Islam *madressah* (school). The children, who ranged in age from eight to thirteen, were running around playing a game that one girl described as jihad—a name that evokes many things to most Americans, but which simply means to strive or struggle. The most important jihad for any Muslim is the struggle for spiritual purity and self-improvement. Regardless of how well schooled the children were in Islam, the boys and girls, in their dirty pants and long-sleeved shirts, were given tremendous room for self-expression and social independence. The mission of Dar al Islam is to educate Americans about the complimentarity between Islamic and American values, including respect for individuals. In that sense, through their play the children demonstrated that the mission of Dar al Islam was, at least in one respect, being met.

Immediately what struck me about the visiting families, as well as the families from Abiquiu, was their diversity. The fact that Islam resonates with people from such disparate backgrounds and communities in America speaks in no small measure to the power of the faith. The event was overwhelming for me personally: from the intellectual idealism of the Muslims to the beauty of the mosque to the *dthik* (spiritual chanting) under the stars. I felt that if Islam was this—communion with a group of people devoted to social justice, nonmaterialism, and spirituality—then maybe I want to be a Muslim. This trip marked an important turning point in my research not only because I was forced to confront the methodological conundrum of the ethnographer's gaze, but I was required to imagine what it means on a day-to-day level to be a Muslim. Particularly, I had to acknowledge the daily identity politics of Islamic religious practice in a non-Muslim country. Up until the powwow I was able to move in and out of the Muslim community, not as a Muslim, but as an African American committed to understanding Islam. After teaching Muslim children and interviewing adult converts, I would drive down Adam Clayton Powell Boulevard and become a graduate student learning to make film. At one level, it never occurred to me that Muslims do not make the same drastic shifts.

The ritual and symbolic requirements of the faith determine decision making at minute levels of time organization. Prayers are practiced five times a day, according to the sun's movements, and the first conscious act for Muslims is the preparation and performance of *Salatul Fajr*. While the first prayer before sunrise is both humbling and inspiring, it is also difficult. One of my informants, a European American who converted, lived with a Shia Muslim who would chastise her every morning if she failed to perform *Salatul Fajr*. While most Muslims would feel that this roommate's comments were inappropriate ("Allah judges"), it still put this convert in a difficult position of having to defend her faith.

My Muslim friends like to remind me that Islam is not "a Sunday-type religion where you praise God one day and then go about your business the rest of the week." One must choose employment that allows for daily prayers and extended Friday lunches in order to attend *Jumah*. If one wears *hijab*, one must contend with "glass ceilings" and possible job loss because of discrimination. One is frequently called upon to defend his or her faith, or worse, one is scorned as being anti-Jewish because African

American Muslims are all thought to be either in the Nation of Islam or anti-Israel.[3] In addition, non-Muslim women wonder why female converts chose sexism over feminism, and the potential assumptions, misreadings, and hostile reactions continue.[4] The choice to throw oneself into the contentious arena of religious identity politics seems overwhelmingly problematic, but then again one must remember that African Americans are already deeply engaged in racial identity politics. In this respect, the qualitative differences between being conspicuously black and being conspicuously black and Muslim are negligible. The difference is religious identity, which unlike racial identity, is a choice. Therefore, choosing to self-identify as Muslim could be considered a form of liberation: freedom to pick your political battles.

Performative issues aside, in order to decide whether to convert I needed to confront how I felt about Islamic exegesis. I understood the sociopolitical elements of a convert's faith, but what would it mean to actually have to live by the five pillars and follow the edicts? And which edicts would I decide to follow? Throughout my research, I had wished that I had the capacity to have faith, to give myself fully to an orientation on the world reliant on the unseen. Ultimately, my own nagging ambivalence made that impossible. The Muslim concept of a creative force beyond the reach of the human imagination was easy to accept, and the rules surrounding how to successfully organize a society impressed me. Nevertheless, profound questions plagued me: Does *Shaitan* really exist? Could I ever describe my periods as a pollution? The Abiquiu powwow forced me to distinguish politics from faith, the act of social engagement from the act of spiritual engagement. In the end, I recognized that what I had grown to respect about Islam was partly the theology, but mainly the people who accepted the theology. The majority of Muslim converts in America are intellectuals with a passion for community solidarity and personal excellence. Acknowledging that there is a difference between a convert's political idealism and their faith enabled me to grasp the distinctiveness of the African American Muslim experience.

AMBIVALENCE

Based on my experience in Abiquiu, I decided to look more closely at a subgroup within the community who has adopted such an extreme interpretation of Islam one would expect the absence of ambivalence. My data reveals quite the opposite. Through this research, I finally realized that ambivalence is part of faith, and it is within this ambivalent space that followers transform and adapt their religion to meet personal challenges. African American Muslim women authorize, or legitimate, their feminist exegesis by reading the Qur'an, hadith, and secondary sources; some even learn Arabic. While the women's exegesis is at times quite radical, tethering beliefs in social justice to a faith with very specific rules of interpretation limits the ways in which converts are able to challenge social relations and material structures. I argue that ambivalence occurs when there is a disconnect between a convert's common-sense view of the world and the community's exegesis. Most converts will search to find the connections between their sense of reason and Islam using all the methods mentioned above, including finding new translations of the Qur'an. While this method helps converts develop stronger connections with their faith, it does not always help them develop stronger connections with the community. Converts must deal with other Muslims who may or may not share their view of the faith, and because Islam is a religion that turns certain forms of social engagement into a practice of faith (marriage, *Eid, Jumah* for men, *salat*), Muslims cannot avoid the community. Muslim women will sometimes employ silence and acquiescence as a method for dealing with their ambivalence. We see that in the case of Zipporah, who chose to limit her outspokenness in order to function in the community. Some women have made choices to practice different forms of asceticism. It is about self-imposed limits placed on individualism, or self-censorship, for the sake of family or community. But is silence and acquiescence a ceding of power or, put more directly, disempowerment?

Unlike career-oriented converts, there are those who favor asceticism over assimilation. These particular expressions of asceticism, predicated on ideas of orthodoxy and purity, have their roots in the transition from Nation of Islam to Sunni Islam. Elijah Muhammad set up elaborate categories of sacred and profane, and during the transition, orthodox Islam replaced the rituals of race and food purity that had developed within the Nation (see chapter 5). This shift created an ideological space for assimilating and reconciling Islam with the American social and political landscape.

Within the subset of converts, who have what I call an "eastern gaze," are many men and women who decide to live an extreme version of sunnah. These families usually live without material comforts; the wife tries not to work outside the home, and typically wears conservative *hijab*. They are poor and sometimes socially isolated from non-Muslims, including, at times, their families. Many Muslims object to this choice of lifestyle, arguing that the Prophet and his wives did not isolate themselves socially and in fact were politically engaged. Nevertheless, I have seen this isolationist interpretation of sunnah repeated by different families in Southern California. The practices of these women arguably represent the greatest challenge to the assertion that Muslim converts are not falsely conscious.

Carving out a marginal existence in a highly materialistic society invites a whole host of problems related to boundary issues. Imani's (see Chapter 1) experience with her oldest son, for example, demonstrates that families without sufficient means butt up against a pervasive political, economic, and social system, which is sometimes invited, but more often than not unwelcome. Imani's asceticism could not compete with her son's desires for power and wealth, clearly a product of his social environment. While one of my informants lives in a country that allows polygyny and does not discourage poor women from having many children, the families in America that choose to live by an alternative set of social codes must contend with a system that discourages those choices. Polygynous marriages, for example, go unrecognized. Cowives in part benefit from this law because it means they can continue to collect AFDC, now TANF (Aid to Families with Dependent Children; Temporary Assistance for Needy Families), but their families are under the scrutiny of the system. If the families were independently wealthy, this would not be a problem, but for poor families the boundary issues wreak havoc, sometimes for good reason, on their ability to sustain an alternative lifestyle. But does this mean that the choices these women have made are bad ones?

BORDER CONFLICTS: SAFA, AMINAH, LATIFAH

Safa, Aminah, and Latifah were in a polygynous relationship with an abusive man, and the compromises they made in order to remain faithful to their religious ideals are troubling. In contrast to women who live in a Muslim society, these three women only imagined and tried to create the experience of living in a society where there is continuity between the personal and the political. It is these women who most Americans would see as disempowered because they maintained a rigid religious identity regardless of the negative social consequences.

I had known Safa for several years in various contexts, but this rather somber meeting took place at Aida's medical office. Safa was there for her prenatal appointment, and I sat with her in the waiting room before she was called. I felt awkward, as did she, because I was there to give her money to help her out during a particularly difficult time in her life. In all of our encounters, I had never directly asked her about her conversion. Feeling at a loss for words, and realizing that talking about the past at this point would be far better than talking about the present, I finally asked her why she became a Muslim.

Safa told me that she met her husband, Ali, after she had already had her first child, Amber, now fourteen years old. She lived across the street from a masjid, heard the *adhan*, and wondered why this happened at the same time everyday. She was able to address her questions to Latifah, whose children were being babysat by Safa's mother. It was through Latifah, Ali's first wife, that Safa met her husband, the same Ali. Safa's mother was not happy with her decision to enter a polygynous marriage, however Safa enjoyed it. She liked it because polygyny gave her time away from her husband, a break from cleaning and cooking, and a chance to snuggle with the kids in bed. I am thinking, "Of course she wanted time away from him, he is miserable and controlling," but Safa separates the man from the institution of polygyny.

Enter Aminah. Aminah attended a prestigious college and was working in a lab when she met her future husband, Mustafa. Although Mustafa was a Sunni Muslim who performed the five pillars of his faith, his political and religious sympathies rest with the Nation of Islam. The next part of Aminah's story is part interpretation, part fact, perhaps revealing more about the Muslim women who tell it than about Aminah. Aminah became the object of Ali's desire. Ali already had two wives, but he wanted Aminah and pursued her behind the back of Mustafa. He did so by convincing Aminah that her Islam was not pure and that her husband was not willing or able to dedicate himself to the purest of Islamic lifestyles. Ali convinced Aminah that together with her two children, and his ten or so children, they could build a better Muslim family. So Aminah left her husband and became Ali's third wife.

The three wives appeared to have a terrific relationship. At one *Eid al-Fitre*, the celebration following Ramadan, the wives spread out many blankets, pulled out baskets of food, and sat together joking and laughing. But a year after this *Eid* celebration, I noticed that the first wife, Latifah, was missing. It turns out Ali almost beat Latifah to death after discovering she was taking money from Ali's sister for babysitting her nephews and nieces. Ali wanted Latifah to provide her services for free, but because Ali was marginally employed, Latifah arranged to be paid without Ali's knowledge. For years Latifah put up with extreme poverty, which her husband framed as righteous and purifying. Finally, she recognized that she must support the family financially and accepted money her husband wanted her to reject. Ali was trying to create a social network for himself modeled on gift exchange and barter, which runs counter to capitalist Los Angeles, and Latifah, who was responsible for making sure her children had enough to eat, knew this. When Latifah rejected this model of exchange, which forced her to be dependent on her marginally employed husband, she experienced the most serious conflict. When he found out that Latifah had gone behind his back, he discovered that Latifah had lost faith in his moral universe. The only way Ali could control his wives and children was to make them believe and abide by his righteous paradigm. To Ali's dismay, Latifah was able to separate her reality from that of her husband's and to move beyond his use of Islam as a tool for creating dependence. He was angry that Latifah lied and used his interpretation of Islam to justify a severe beating. He beat her so badly that the police pressed charges despite Latifah's refusal to press charges herself.

Latifah moved out of California, Ali went to jail, and Safa and Aminah along with their twelve children waited for his release. The second wife, Safa, wanted to end the relationship as soon as she could, but Aminah wanted to stay married. Aminah had already demonstrated a need to submerge herself deeper and deeper into the rituals of Islam and went from wearing *hijab* to veiling, and from attending *Jumah* in the more mainstream al-Mustaqim to attending a masjid where separation between men and women was more highly enforced.

Finally, Safa got her wish to end the relationship, but not without tragedy. Latifah called to warn her that her oldest daughter accused Ali of sexually molesting her. Social Services was required to interview Safa's daughters, two of whom told similar stories. As far as Safa knows, Aminah's children had not been sexually molested. Safa told Ali that she was going to press charges. She spoke to Aminah on Friday and on Sunday went to Aminah's apartment to find her furniture still there, but clothes and suitcases gone. Ali, a wanted felon, had fled, taking Aminah and their children with him. Safa thinks Aminah might come back. Safa thinks Ali must be telling Aminah that "everybody's lying on him." In other words, he continues to craft narratives in order to rationalize his actions to others. A month after I saw Safa in the doctor's office, she gave birth to their eighth child, a girl.[5]

Mary Douglas defines "pollution ideas" as either instrumental or expressive. At the instrumental level, "We find people trying to influence one another's behavior. . . . At this level the laws or nature are dragged in to sanction the moral code."[6] Alternatively, at the expressive level "pollutions are used as analogies for expressing a general view of the social order."[7] Pollution symbolizes the relationship between different social entities. For many female converts, purity rituals are expressive, while for their husbands, like Ali, they are often instrumental. Ali used and manipulated Islam to give credibility to actions that are not credible, and his wives accepted his oppressive behavior for a number of years. In this sense, they were disempowered, but that is not the end of the story. None of the women has lost her faith; in fact, Safa and Latifah use the Qur'an to criticize Ali's actions. Therefore, was their religious ideology making them participants in their own disempowerment, or did a myriad of material circumstances and beliefs make it difficult to extract themselves from an oppressive marriage? Ali offered his wives very little room in which to maneuver socially, and his ideological goals kept crashing up against the reality of secular, capitalist Los Angeles. Even if he had been able to support all three families without government assistance, his pathology made it impossible to create boundaries against the encroachment of secular life. This meant that his reality was disconfirmed outside the ideological walls he erected around his domestic life. In this instance, the border conflicts between Ali's asceticism and mainstream American understandings of justice were welcomed by the two women, who used Ali's imprisonment as justification to leave. With other families where pathology does not exist, however, border conflicts hinder rather than empower those who choose asceticism. With all the families who tried to forge a culture of purity separate and distinct from mainstream America, the success rate was low because there was pathology, ambivalence, or poverty that put the family at the mercy of the government.

This family scenario is not typical in the Muslim community. The frequency of this type of dysfunctional marriage/family is probably equivalent to that in the general population. Aminah's story, however, has become a morality play within the community, an example of what is wrong with some men and women's interpretation of gender roles and rights within Islam. Aminah is the model of what most of the women fight against. Her divorce, her position as a third wife, her total submissiveness to her husband, her family's poverty, and husband's marginal employment, dependence on government support, physical abuse, and social isolation from the community represent the opposite of who the majority of Muslims want their families to be. Aminah, the two other wives, and the husband are part of a minority of Muslim women and men who seem to ignore the context of Los Angeles in order to perform what they imagine is the most perfect practice of Islam. What is Aminah's moral reasoning? Is it liberating? Does it challenge the assertion that the Muslim community uses Islam to liberate poor inner-city folk? What does it say about the limits of our consciousness to alter our material world? Richard Shweder and Nancy Much write:

> Cognitivists tend to search for the objective foundations of moral judgments in an abstract-formal-logical realm far removed from everyday thoughtful talk. Our neorationalist approach shares with cognitive approaches the assumption that natural or objective moral entities exist and that moral understandings are a form of knowledge about some objective moral world. Our neorationalist approach is defined by three distinctive assumptions: that genuine objectivity can be, in some measure, subject dependent; that the existence of moral facts and moral knowledge is compatible with the existence of multiple objective moral worlds and alternative forms of postconventional moral reasoning; and that each of those several objective moral worlds is found in, and maintained through, the ordinary conversations of everyday life.[8]

When Franz Boas encouraged anthropologists to adopt the cultural relativist approach at the beginning of the twentieth century, most anthropologists accepted the view that cultures followed an evolutionary trajectory from barbaric to civilized.[9] In this respect, cultural relativism acted as a theoretical intervention for some questionable methodologies and presuppositions. About eighty years later, Shweder and Much argue that when approaching the "foundations of moral judgments," anthropologists should use a cultural relativist approach that validates the moral reasoning of subjects "in some measure." In other words, they make the case for a modified cultural relativist approach that does not paralyze discussions of human universals. Without modification, a cultural relativist approach allows that as long as there is a cultural explanation for behavior, it exists in the realm of the morally acceptable. Using the example of Bali before the Dutch outlawed the practice of *suttee*, it is quite possible that devout Hindu women leapt onto their husband's funeral pyre despite objecting to the practice. Pure cultural relativists do not have a critical language in which to engage discussions of the simultaneous practices of complicity and critique.

The only way to truly understand the moral worlds of the wives of Ali is to take the neorationalist approach, which engages the native's point of view while also problematizing that emic wonderland. Ultimately, the only way to understand the choices of these women is to examine their reasoning in light of their social and material environments. There is one caution, however, which is not to confuse "reasonable" with "rational." A woman may decide that entering into a polygynous marriage is better because she believes her husband is less likely to have an affair outside of his quasilegal marriages. This is her reasoning, but it is not necessarily rational. I certainly cannot claim that staying with an abusive man is rational, but it may be reasonable in light of other factors. James Scott criticizes modernist political economy theorists, including Karl Marx, for failing to recognize that participation in a system, in this case a marriage, does not equal capitulation.[10] Paul Willis similarly critiques Antonio Gramsci's representation of hegemony as a billiard ball with no cracks, smooth and impenetrable.[11] Safa and Latifah's acceptance of Islam, but rejection of their husband's interpretation, demonstrates the cracks in the billiard ball. Notably, Islam provided both the thesis and the antithesis to life with Ali, and became the space in which they resisted their husband's oppression and validated their claims against him. For this community, Islamic exegesis, or the science of interpretation, is a method through which people advocate for themselves and promote new ideas.

Regardless of its limits, Islamic exegesis acts as a mediating discourse empowering women, like Safa, who feel powerless.

What is both wonderful and problematic about Marxism, and any political economy theory predicated on a belief of what ought to be, is the presupposition that transcendence is possible. During a talk where I discussed Safa, an audience member thought it ridiculous that any women should have to rely on religious exegesis to validate divorce from an abusive man. Why not simply transcend the religion rather than try to reform it? In order to come to this conclusion this audience member must believe that social facts are objective facts: That we know objectively that women and men are equal and are deserving of equal rights. I argue that when it comes to the construction of a moral universe, there are very few objective truths. Put more directly, there is no natural law. Moral truths, like Western feminism, must be nested by other ideological domains, and in the United States, feminism finds validation through the domains of individualism, democracy, and meritocracy. Some ideological domains exist in the realm of what Bourdieu calls *doxa*, or the realm of the undisputed, while others exist in the realm of heterodoxy, orthodoxy, or opinion. In order to move a concept from heterodoxy into the realm of *doxa*, one must nest it in undisputed concepts.[12] For the Muslim community, belief that Muhammad is the last Messenger and slave servant of Allah is *doxa*, therefore to move feminism into the realm of *doxa*, one must validate it through Islamic exegesis.

When Safa's husband was released from prison, she asked an imam to grant her a quasilegal divorce from her quasilegal husband. The imam refused, so Safa was thwarted not by her faith, but by an imam's exegesis. This refusal disappointed Safa so greatly that she stopped attending Masjid al-Mustaqim. Ultimately, another imam granted her a symbolic divorce.

INDEPENDENCE: HAFSA

Hafsa was the mother and matriarch of a matrilineal-extended family who moved from Philadelphia to the Mojave Desert in order to live sunnah. It was yet another family searching for religious purity in secular Southern California. The women practiced *purdah* through social isolation; when in town, they covered their entire bodies. Hafsa arranged the marriage of her two teenage daughters, who also lived in the same home in the desert. Their dedication to living "pure" was so intense that the mother gave up gardening because it took too much time away from studying Islam and worshipping Allah.

Whereas the other families kept butting up against the secular space of urban Southern California, this family created an isolated domestic enclave. While they were spatially independent, Hafsa's husband and the husbands of the daughters were economically tied to secular life. Hafsa's husband, for example, traveled more than an hour to do construction at a rapidly growing desert community. In many ways, this freed them to organize their family life according to their beliefs. The women were able to stay at home with the children and dedicate themselves to Islamic scholarship without the need for public assistance, gift exchange, or barter. Ultimately the family moved to a small urban community because their living conditions had been harsh, and employment in construction had been seasonal.

The teenage daughters, particularly the oldest, were extraordinarily dynamic and outspoken. They felt empowered by their arranged marriages and early childbearing and felt superior to the "Kaffirs" (disbelievers) with whom they interacted in town. Their isolation seemed to have diminished much of their ambivalence to their way of life, perhaps because they spent less time comparing themselves with others their age. Their environs confirmed rather than disconfirmed their religious idealism. Clearly there were limits to the girls "freedom." Hafsa, for example, did not encourage her daughters to go to college and therefore limited their ability to be independent of the family. Nevertheless their relative success, independent of secular urban America, highlights the fact that some of the ambivalence experienced by the first and second generation of converts is related to physical proximity to a secular and capitalist community.

The example of Hafsa highlights that one's sense of liberation is related to a discursive context. In particular, outside of a secular context, Hafsa can easily make sense of Islam to her children. She eliminates opportunities for her children to challenge their faith by removing enticements. Therefore, it is difficult to evaluate the oldest daughter's sense of empowerment given that, according to some people's standards, it is based on a lack of knowledge. However, many Muslim women with advanced educational degrees have converted to Islam. It is easy to see them as empowered because their approach to conversion, through education into various faiths, is something most Americans can understand. The fact that these women are part of the secular world means that their faith is constantly tested, motivating an empowering engagement with Islamic exegesis. Would a college education, for example, increase the daughter's personal agency by encouraging a similar questioning of faith? If Islam is empowering to Zipporah, Aida, Maimouna, and Afaf, why does Hafsa's need to be "worldly" in order to be considered empowered? These questions about empowerment are difficult to answer. The fact that Hafsa began looking for husbands for her daughters when they were fifteen is not in itself proof that this matriarch disempowered her children, nor is the fact that she sheltered them from alternative educational and social trajectories. The best approach to gauging the choices made by this woman and her daughters would be to study them longitudinally. Unfortunately, I lost track of this family when they moved and therefore have no data on what early marriage and limited secondary schooling has meant in terms of their transitions to adulthood.

AMBIVALENCE: JAMILAH

Perhaps the best example of the relationship among context, ambivalence, and empowerment is the example of Jamilah. Before converting to Sunni Islam, Jamilah's mother, Hind, was addicted to drugs. Hind would have parties where she would openly use drugs and sleep with various partners, all witnessed by her four preteen children. Finally, one party ended with Hind's arrest for drug possession. As a single mother, Hind had very few options, she either had to change her lifestyle or lose her children. Hind chose to change.

After converting, Hind married Abdul Muhammad, also African American, and accepted a very rigid interpretation of women's roles in Sunni Islam. To prove to herself her commitment to her new faith and family, Hind chose to cover herself in full *hijab* and *niqab* (face veil); in addition she draped black lace over her entire head to hide her forehead and eyes. The covering made sense to Hind. She had married a devout Muslim who wanted Hind to perform her domestic duties as prescribed in Islam. The covering demonstrated Hind's entitlement to, and Abdul's ability to provide, what many African American converts to Sunni Islam say is one of the most important marital benefits in Islam: a woman's freedom from wage labor. Abdul Muhammad was proud of being able to financially support his family, and in many ways, Hind's covering was symbolically important to both of them.

In an effort to educate the children to become Islamic scholars, the family moved to the Sudan, where the teenage boys attended a school where children memorize the Qur'an. Without being explicit, it became clear that the boys had had a miserable experience. The brothers ultimately memorized a significant percentage of the Qur'an, but their sister, Jamilah, indicated that they learned very little about Islam. After one year, Hind grew tired of the difficult living conditions in the Sudan, and so Hind, Abdul Muhammad, and their youngest son returned to the United States. Jamilah, who was thirteen years old, and her teenage brothers decided to stay in Khartoum.

During Ramadan in 1992, Hind told me about Jamilah, then twenty-four. I was at a fast-breaking, *iftar*, at a sister's house in South Central. The party was lively with excellent fried chicken, macaroni and cheese, and greens. Being pregnant, I sat around the buffet table with an excuse to overeat, and sitting next to me, equally indulgent, was Hind. She told me that her daughter was also pregnant and lived in the Sudan. Hind "married her daughter off," at thirteen and left her in the Sudan. Intrigued, I felt compelled to pursue this story, but unfortunately lost track of Hind, who lived an hour and a half from my house. Fortuitously, in the fall of 1993 I crossed paths with Hind, this time at a conference on Islamic education and home schooling. I asked about her daughter Jamilah who, it turned out, had come back to the states for ovarian surgery and would continue living with her until December. Without prompting, Hind invited me to visit.

In the fall of 1993, I traveled every Friday to spend time with Jamilah and a small, close-knit community of African American Muslims from around Hind's neighborhood. The economic status of Hind's neighborhood, poor to lower middle class, is more clearly represented by the desertified lawns than by the cinder-block housing. Hind grew up in her current house, and on the sidewalk by the front chain-linked gate, written in cement, is Hind's preconversion name alongside the names of her five brothers and sisters.

The first time I arrived, Jamilah was alone with her children. Jamilah's appearance surprised me. Hind is dark skinned but Jamilah, whose biological father is Irish American, is light skinned with black curly hair. What surprised me even more was when Jamilah and I would talk alone, she would appear to be a typical, young American with soft facial features expressing hope and eagerness. When she was parenting or talking with her family, however, her expressions and manner reflected a different identity. During my visits with Jamilah, there were moments suggestive of her life in the Sudan. At these moments, I was reminded that she sweeps her dirt floors after *fajr* (prayer); that she prepares food and home-roasted coffee for visitors who drop by unexpectedly; that one of her most joyous times is sleeping under the stars with her children; and that she gages her acculturation to Sudanese culture by her ability to understand Sudanese Arabic gossip—an important, as Michel Foucault might say, technology of power. In different contexts she displayed different personas, laying claim to the fact that she was truly between worlds.

Hind's small cinder-block house was decorated quite sparsely. The living room had a cement floor painted black, and off of the living room was a small kitchen. When I entered the kitchen, Jamilah's three youngest children, the only ones with her during this trip, were sitting on the floor and in a very Sudanese way using their hands to eat spaghetti out of bowls. Samira was four years old, Karima three years, and Elijah was one year old, the same age as my daughter, who accompanied me. Jamilah spoke to them in a combination of Arabic and English, and the two older girls were so quiet they said nothing to their mother when I was present. Jamilah told me that Sudanese children are taught not to speak around older people. Even when Hind's friends visit, Jamilah said she barely says a word. Jamilah said her mother's friends think it is strange, but she says she cannot help it, it is her custom.

By Sudanese standards, Jamilah's daughters are considered beautiful. In the Sudan, Arab descent holds status, so their café-au-lait complexions and curly, not kinky, hair are the revered norm. While the ideal for women and girls is long hair, Jamilah insists that her daughter's hair be cut in short afros in order, she claims, to make it grow back thicker. As a result, her daughter's are teased, but Jamilah remains undeterred, believing that her daughter's sacrifice now will be rewarded with more beautiful and desirable hair in the future. Little did I know upon first meeting Jamilah that her daughters' haircuts were symbolic of Jamilah's approach to social empowerment through the rejection of specific cultural and ideological norms in the hopes of something better. Jamilah simultaneously desires and rejects aspects of both the United States and the Sudan. Being aware of each system's benefits and drawbacks, she has tremendous ambivalence, as expressed by her moves back and forth between the Sudan and the United States. At a more personal level, Jamilah works to create a world for herself that is consistent with her social ideals, but not to the exclusion of future social and material rewards.

During our first meeting and interview, Jamilah ironed her family's clothes for Friday prayers at the mosque while her children took a bath.

JAMILAH: My brothers were in India. They were learning the Qur'an and the hadith, and in India they are really strict. So they brought them back to America, but after two years here they kept losing it. Because they kept losing it they decided to go to another country in Africa . . . so they picked the Sudan.

My stepfather took my two brothers over there. He built a house in a village and brought me, my mother, and my youngest brother. My mother, she couldn't deal with it [life in the Sudan], the fact that you can't just jump up and go out. Like here [in the United States] you can jump up and go shopping for food. And even if you have a car over there, you might not have gas because you can't just go to a gas station over there. To buy gas you have to wait in line. And she just couldn't deal with that stuff. It was too much. So she only stayed a year, and I decided to stay.

CAROLYN: And when you first went over you were eleven, right?

JAMILAH: Yeah, I liked it, but at first they wanted to put me in an Arabic school and stay with some friends. But when they talked to the sheik and stuff, there was no way that an unmarried person without parents could stay that way. It was their custom, so I ended up getting married. I was thirteen.

CAROLYN: How did you meet your husband?

JAMILAH: Oh, it was done through my father, my stepfather. I didn't meet him until afterward.

CAROLYN: Did you know you wanted to be married, before you got married?

JAMILAH: Yeah, I can say that. At the time, now when I think back on it, it was just the excitement of staying here [the Sudan]. I didn't know what I was really getting myself into. I just wanted to stay there at all costs. Marriage was like a big idea. Me, thirteen years old, getting married, nobody around me. If I went back, I don't think I would have done it. I would have waited. I would have tried to figure out other ways to stay.

CAROLYN: Because it was too much responsibility at such a young age?

JAMILAH: Yes. At the time it didn't seem like it. At the time I could swear it was the best thing I was doing. But now I realize that it was different. Seeing my age, [they] got an older man. He was eighteen years older and he was a lot more understanding.

CAROLYN: Had he been married before?

JAMILAH: No. So and then I just kind of stayed there. My mother and my stepfather came back, and my youngest brother. My two oldest brothers stayed there. At this point the *khatwa* in the Sudan it was just hard, it was horrible. So we moved to the city with my husband, and we got them into a standard Arabic school.

CAROLYN: What is a *khatwa?*

JAMILAH: A *khatwa* is an Islamic place where you learn the Qur'an. But it's kind of remote. They do it in very remote parts and villages. It has to be in seclusion, like the monks. So there won't be any distractions for the children. And mostly orphans go there. My brothers told a lot of tales, they can tell you more than I know. But I wouldn't send my sons there. It's okay to learn the Qur'an, but it's kind of hard because they *only* learned the Qur'an. They didn't teach them how to make *salat.* They didn't teach them to clean. That was it. As long as you learned the Qur'an, it was okay. I don't think I would have been into it. But at the time they thought it was the best because they knew the Qur'an, they were just forgetting it. As the boys got older they wanted to go to school.

They didn't speak standard Arabic when they were learning the Qur'an. They spoke Indian. But they learned quick because they stayed at the *khatwa*. When I got married they came to the city to live with me, and when they were living with me, my brother, he was all over Khartoum, he knew everyone. So they were speaking Arabic.

CAROLYN: How old are they?

JAMILAH: Right now they speak Arabic, they're both older than me. They're twenty-seven and twenty-six. So they were sixteen and fifteen.

CAROLYN: But they left, so you were all alone?

JAMILAH: Yeah they left after I gave birth to my first son. Yeah, after a year and a half they left. They came back here, and one's in college and one's working. So yeah, they made their lives here.

CAROLYN: So you're all alone?

JAMILAH: I'm now by myself, and it's kind of difficult because you deal with the customs and the people, and no matter how much you make friends. . . . To me they're the type of people, they're very nosy. It's like this community, if you move to this community, this town right here, they know everything about you. I mean they will pander you with questions until you tell them. And they know everything about you.

In a way it's nice, in a way it's not nice. Because in a way this is my best friend and living next door. When she gives birth I go over there, I see her whole family. So one day I can be in another town and I can get in some trouble, but the lady living down the street can be my neighbor's sister-in-law, so she will automatically help me. So in a way when you know each other it's like a big family. All through the Sudan, it's like the biggest country in Africa, but you always have somebody you know or somebody who knows someone who knows you. So they will automatically open the doors and feed your children.

My mother she always says, "The year I lived there I never cooked," and I know it's true. Each day just for being a foreigner, American, who wanted to learn their religion, we had breakfast, lunch, and dinner provided to us. I mean they're very giving. But as you come to live and marry one you wouldn't know that they live on their customs.

If your daughter got married, and you invited me to the wedding, just like in America, I would go over to the wedding. They have a lot of rules. I would give the mother something, the daughter something, the father something, the groom something. Plus if I gave you two hundred dollars, I would expect three hundred dollars when my daughter gets married.

CAROLYN: So you have to give more each time?

JAMILAH: I have to give more each time. So each time I give birth, like when I first gave birth, they were giving me ten pounds. And now with my youngest son when I gave birth they gave me ten thousand pounds. Some give me two thousand pounds, it depends on how much I gave her. That's how they do it. In some ways you can see it as they do it to get back. You know some people you don't pay back, but they will come and give you it anyway.

CAROLYN: So do you rely on that sort of giving?

JAMILAH: I rely on something like this: An unexpected guest shows up. There are no invitations in the Sudan. You can wake up and there's half his family with suitcases. You take them in. I can rely on my neighbors to help me that whole first day until I get myself [what I need]. I can rely on them.

If there's a death in the family, I can rely on all my neighbors in the community to feed each and every one of my family [members], and wash all the dishes. When there's death over there, you can just sit in a room like this. The household people, they just grieve. The neighbors take over your house for forty days.

And when you're giving birth you just stay in a room because you're circumcised, you just lay down all the time. Your best friend and your mother and your neighbors take care of you, your husband, and your children.

CAROLYN: Because you're circumcised?

JAMILAH: Yeah, most girls there are circumcised. So they can't move. They have to learn how to walk all over again. It's that painful. They're cut and then they're sewed again, so it's just like a C-section but it's underneath, so it's very painful. I think it would take a strong girl—who has the will to move around—two weeks. The first two births, they make sure to be with her parents, or her parents come to her in her house. It depends on how much income the man has. The third and fourth times around sometimes they don't have that much money so she gives birth in her house and she relies on her neighbors. And the girl, if she has the will to get up, and she has kids and doesn't want to rely on her neighbors too much, it will take her two weeks. She really has to want to. But most girls their first time, they're so scared and in pain it will take them two months.

CAROLYN: So when are you circumcised?

JAMILAH: When you're six. It's just so painful when you give birth, it tears again. Well some girls have a problem when they start their period and on their wedding because . . . they show you a video of how they do it. They would leave a hole just like this [she holds up a finger to demonstrate the size of the opening]. So it would take at least four months for them to ever have sex with their husbands. So all the time she's in pain. It would take four months. If he's kind.

CAROLYN: Why do they do that, make it the size of a pea?

JAMILAH: They say because it protects . . . they would know if the girl is pure or not. It protects the girl from doing unlawful things. By the time you first have sex all the pain is gone because they've spent so much time trying to get in. So by the time they have sex there's not so much pain. It's like a regular person I suppose. They talk about it a lot. Right now they're trying to clear it out.

It's restricted. They would take the license away from the lady who did that. It's restricted. They hide it too. It's mostly the grandmother. It's the custom no matter how much education the family has. If this is how we did it in the old ways, they're going to do it. Especially the old people. And they force their children. Because one thing about Sudanese, they call themselves half-Arabs, one thing about them is the children absolutely have to respect and listen to their parents. So if the mother comes in here and says, "I don't like your wife," he's seriously going to think about that. And she would seriously have to think about finding out what went wrong between her and her mother-in-law just because her mother-in-law doesn't like her. They respect their parents very much. So they respect their families, they have a whole sense of family. You have to be careful with their families. Most Sudanese are married to each other's cousins, so you respect them anyway because she's your aunt or your uncle or something like that.

CAROLYN: So you're on good terms with your mother-in-law and your father-in-law?

JAMILAH: Yeah. I'm not. . . . His mother, I'm okay with and his sisters; two sisters and his mother. His brother, I don't like. I don't think he doesn't like me or anything, but whenever he comes in the house it's like we argue all day. We can never agree on nothing. He's very modern, very Sudanese. Sudanese, one thing, if they give birth to sons, they teach the boys to do nothing but go to school, come home. The girls are the maids to the boys. And it's very hard for me because right now my sons are over there with their grandmother, and they teach them that. See when I have to go home now, I'm going to have to wean them off of that. Before I left them, one boy—because I had all boys before my two daughters—one washed dishes, and one would sweep. One would help, and one would go to the market. But now that they're at grandma's house they won't be doing anything. And believe me, I know my husband is a very spoiled man. They're used to it. He can be lying around, he says, "Go get me water," and it can be right next to him, and you have to give it to him. They put it in their heads they don't have to do nothing but go to sleep, get up, eat, go to work, go out, get an education. That's what they teach their men. And it works, it works, it's not bad, but it's hard on the girls.

CAROLYN: How did you learn that when you were thirteen?

JAMILAH: Oh, I didn't. I got in a lot of scrambles, a lot of arguments. I would say, "I'm not doing this. " And when his family would come over, one would go out, and another would come in, and another would go out. And I'm pregnant nine months, and I'm washing some old man's clothes just because he's some uncle or something like that, and it's hard. So one day I just went in there and I screamed. This was in some hotel and this and that. And now to this day I very rarely . . . it can be only his sister or his mother with his family [when they visit]. They took it as an insult. They will come and visit, but they won't spend the night.

My husband was kind of mad at that, but to make coffee you have to get the beans, you have to burn the beans, you have to ground the beans, and remember there's no electricity, you have to ground it with your hands, just like Indians. You have to do all that stuff, and for all the extra work you have to do, believe me, living here in America is like paradise. This simple life right here that my mother has, believe me, it's paradise compared to over there because I have to get up early after *fajr*. You clean the whole house. Right at ten o'clock in the morning, a sandstorm comes and you have to clean it all over again and more. So the life over there, it's kind of hard, but you get used to it. I like it most because I feel more safe over there, more secure, and . . .

CAROLYN: Your kids can go out and play in the street?

JAMILAH: When, I came here four years ago I didn't want to leave. I would have done anything at all costs to stay here. I was tired. I wanted to stay here. But now as I look at it, when I came this time I think maybe because I'm older I think I've started to like myself a lot better. I look at girls my age [in America], the way they talk to their parents, the way they are. Just little things that they do, which any other person [in the Sudan] wouldn't do. Like my brother. A lot of people accuse him of trying to be white because he has a lot of white friends and he says, "I'm not trying to be white, I'm just trying to be civilized." He says, "I grew up in Africa, and in Africa people are civilized. They're not white they're Africans." Most of these black people over here, they don't understand that they come from Africa. And just because you're civilized, they think you want to be white. So I look at these girls [in America] and if I said, "Do this," they would look at me like, "This is cool. What I'm doing is okay." But it isn't. You know when I'm around my mother I don't speak much because I listen to her and consider her with her friends as grown-ups.

CAROLYN: So you grew up in this area?

JAMILAH: Until I was eleven, yeah. I don't remember much about it, but I remember some, and I came back four years ago, and I spent two years here. I had my twins here. First I had my son, named Ahmed, then Muhammad, then I had twins here.

CAROLYN: Twin boys?

JAMILAH: Yeah, their names are Hassan and Hussain. All four of them now are at their grandma's house. We have a ten-, eight-, and six-year old.

CAROLYN: And then these three. Seven kids at twenty-four?

JAMILAH: Yeah. At first when I come back it would be kind of embarrassing, but then I started looking at it in an Islamic way. Allah said the woman is to produce. And then right when you look at it Islamicly, you want to have more. You say, "Wow, I'm bringing Muslims into the world." It's hard here. Over there we always have hired help because it's very cheap. And then you always have your neighbors, you know you depend on them no matter what. So over here it's just you and your immediate family. And if your family is not Muslim, or are upset because of something, you don't even have them. So basically it's just you and the other Muslims. They don't have that quality of families. So it's kind of different when you're used to one way. I think if an American would go there she would have a lot to complain about. I don't consider myself so much American because I think I grew up over there and most of my customs are like them. As I try to correct the wrong ones, I still see myself more [like] them than American.

But, it's difficult. The Sudan's a nice country. What I

most miss [when I'm in America] is you can sleep outside right underneath the skies. I mean, if you don't mind the mosquitoes you can sleep outside. It can be so hot in here [at my mom's house], so stuffy, and you just can't go outside. You can't let a little girl go outside at ten o'clock. I'm too scared to go out and put the trash out 'cause you don't know what would happen.

I think most people at eleven and thirteen are mature. They say here it's a problem, but I don't think so. I think they're very mature; they know what they want. They can make their own decisions, and if they have good role models, I think they should. They just see what everybody else is doing, you know. [In America] they teach kids . . . they say, "Mommy, do you think there could be a child so evil," you know that movie *The Good Son*. I mean why would they put those kind of thoughts into kids' heads. So I think the television creates most of it.

CAROLYN: There's television in the Sudan.

JAMILAH: Yeah, but they restrict even kissing. It's just only two, one station. You have to have your own video equipment. Don't get me wrong, I would say the Sudan, it's like it has a little piece of America in it, but they do it undercover. That's the difference between here and there. If a girl gets pregnant over there, they're going to kill the man who got her pregnant. And either they kill her after she has the baby, [or] some people have mercy and they won't kill her but she's like a prisoner, and she'll go crazy because she got pregnant unmarried. So they have drugs. They have all kinds of stuff, but you would know the environment it is in. It's mostly in the city [Khartoum], you know, where the corners are. So over there, for your kids to get involved with something, you would have to not have taught them in the house.

Jamilah's ambivalence about the Sudan is clear. She tries very hard to separate what is cultural from what is religious in order to feel safe rejecting certain customs. Initially, for example, when Jamilah got married she started veiling with a headscarf draped over her entire face, like Hafsa. To the objections of her husband, Jamilah slowly moved away from the custom, and when I met her she was throwing a transparent scarf loosely over her head. She told me she responds to her husband's pressure by explaining to him that she must veil for Allah and not for him. She resists some of the customs, like circumcision and excessive burdens placed on women, but she enjoys the safety and, more so than not, the community.

Six years ago, after returning to the states for the birth of her twins, she decided she wanted to move back to America. Unfortunately, soon after she and her husband made the decision to stay, Jamilah's younger brother was gunned down in a drive-by shooting, and within two weeks her family was back in the Sudan. For her, the Sudan represents a safe place, a place away from the violence and drugs that are a part of her family's life in America. She is torn between wanting the security of the Sudan and the freedoms of America. For Jamilah, freedom is represented by two models: The American version of freedom, individualism and materialism; and the Sudanese version, safety and control over families. Put another way, Jamilah's ambivalence can be framed as a definitional question of freedom. Is freedom owning a gun and living in a violent society, or is it controlling guns and restricting depictions of violence in the media? The assumption that there is a rational and universal definition of freedom and liberation, and that Western society is "progressing" in that direction, is an ideology deeply embedded in Western consciousness. Converts for the most part have deconstructed American myths of freedom, but for converts such as Jamilah, no matter how committed they are to their religion, they must consciously reaffirm their choices daily. The seductiveness of materialism and individualism in Los Angeles causes ambivalence, which Jamilah suppresses by living in the Sudan.

Jamilah's conflict between her Sudanese half and her American half is a metaphor for what most African American female converts confront. Jamilah is trapped between wanting the extensive social networks and religiously informed community policing of the Sudan, and the individualism and materialism of the United States. By keeping her children in the Sudan, she insures that they will avoid the same conflict in values that she experiences. Jamilah's search for purity is really not for her but for her children, and she connects her children's chance for purity (freedom from drugs and violence) with their ability to feel at home in the Sudan and with Islam in a way that she never will.

Jamilah and Hind's tremendous ambivalence about the Sudan, America, Islam, and family represents itself in complicated decision-making that is sometimes rational, sometimes irrational, and sometimes nonrational. On a daily basis, converts must choose with whom to align themselves, what ideals to uphold and advocate for, when to be silent, when to speak up, and when to think in short time frames or long ones; and a convert's choices and social performances are often contradicted by other choices and performances. Decisions including where to send your children to school, how to dress, and which eating restrictions to enforce are difficult for many woman. The difference is that women in the African American Sunni community are attempting to resist, through their faith, dominant American discourses on race, religion, gender, and class. The difficulty results from trying to adopt non-Western economic and community models while at the same time defining individuality and freedom in a peculiarly Western, capitalist way. For example, "Islamic socialism," a system in which money circulates, or is redistributed, "like blood" through the social body, is often represented in the African American Sunni Muslim community as the ideal. Capitalism, however, has made many Muslims wealthy, complicating conformity to the ideal. Even if Muslims are not rich, decisions about whether or not to play the stock market, or whether or not to pay or charge usury fees, are complicated, given the current economic system. At the same time, ambivalence, rather than a rigid interpretation of one's faith, is sometimes necessary for negotiating complex social systems where one's capacity to deal with social contradictions can prove useful. This is why women step in and out of *hijab*, in and out of marriage, even in and out of different countries.

The proximity of Muslims to the secular world affects their *tafsir*, or religious interpretation. It is much easier to convince your children that *purdah* is a good thing in the Mojave Desert where there are very few distractions. In the desert, Hafsa erected a wall around her moral world, one that was so high that even her sixteen-year-old, Haneefah, could not climb out. Haneefah had already divorced the first man her mother set her up with and told me that she refused to let her second husband touch her. She asked me for advice about how she could learn not to loath this man. What she probably should have been asking me was how to liberate herself from her family. Haneefah, however, saw no other trajectory for her life and even discussed wanting to move to the Sudan in order to get away from the "Kaffirs."

In the city, building such a wall to protect one's religious idealism is impossible. Instead, the urban community recognizes that its moral idealism shares space with other moral worlds that cannot easily be dismissed or ignored. Confronting difference, as Jamilah does in her moves between countries, can pique an ambivalence that then forces a reengagement with Islamic exegesis. This ambivalence is also tied to this postmodern moment, where cultural hegemony is confronted in the court of popular culture; where performative strategies giving authenticity and power to political agendas have been or need to be rearticulated; and where hybrid forms and dialogic strategies are, as Stuart Hall argues, an essential part of the new black Diaspora aesthetic. Belief in pure forms, or essentialist notions of identity, has given way to the creation and enactment of new dispositions and impure forms.

> Always these forms are the product of partial synchronization, of engagement across cultural boundaries, of the confluence of more than one cultural tradition, of the negotiations of dominant and subordinate positions, of the subterranean strategies of recoding and transcoding, of critical signification, of signifying.[13]

In other words, ambivalence is a product of the performative require-ments of postmodern identity politics where the stakes are control over cultural hegemony.

The story of Jamilah is an example of this ambivalence expressed through ellipses, silence, and through her strategy of shifting between two cultures. Her movement is motivated by the differing limits imposed on her social agency within the United States and the Sudan. She shifts when she becomes frustrated with one context and then shifts back again when it suits her. In either context, she represents herself as a product of, and participant in, that social arena, laying claim to the fact that she en-sconces a portion of her identity in each setting. Nevertheless, within each context she carries within her a sense of self that dictates resistance praxis at moments of profound personal significance; for instance, avoid-ing female circumcision in the Sudan or street violence in the United States.

THE PURITY SPECTRUM

In Islam, the family is the location where individual religious idealism can become constrained as partners contend with class issues, housing, schooling, religious education, personalities, and personal goals. Safa, Hafsa, and Jamilah balance religious purity and asceticism with their de-sire to achieve the goals of self-sufficiency and political empowerment in a secular environment. Some converts decide that a further retreat from secular life gives them greater power and control over their lives, while others feel that assimilation is better because material success leads to fi-nancial independence and social legitimacy.

In the African American Muslim community, converts tend to range between two camps. Some want to purify Islam of its cultural baggage, meaning they reject the idea that American Muslims should try to imi-tate Middle Eastern Muslim practices. These Muslims generally desire compatibility between Islam and American society. The others want to purify themselves of American culture. These converts try to recreate the Prophet's material and spiritual life, usually described in this community as "living sunnah." Where an individual falls on what I describe as the "purity spectrum" usually correlates with their material wealth. Those who seek social recognition within the mainstream tend to be rewarded materially. What comes with that assimilation is often an abandonment of efforts to alter America's economic and political system. But is participation capitulation? Some African American Muslims try to resolve the conflict between the desire to live religiously pure, and the desire for the power and privileges that come with assimilation.

There are four broad categories that help describe the ways in which African American women often adapt their religion to secular Los Angeles:

1. Converts in high-skilled professions who do not wear *hijab* outside of the masjid: They either do not believe that *hijab* is prescribed, they simply prefer not to wear it, or they fear the "glass ceiling." Usually, these women converted well after the split with the Nation of Islam, or they are second-generation African American Muslims. Assimilation of Islam into American capitalism is assumed, and their faith usually does not include a radical sociopolitical agenda. Identification with career is usually quite high. Support for the community includes attending *Jumah*, lectures, and giving *zakat*.

2. Women with careers, and if not careers, well-paying jobs: At their job, they perform their faith by wearing *hijab*, usually West African inspired styles, and in so doing they provoke a range of responses. The choice to express their faith overtly requires an ability to engage with people who react either positively or negatively. This usually requires more than a passing familiarity with Qur'anic exegesis as well as American job discrimination law. The choice to identify oneself symbolically as Muslim means that career choices must conform to interpretations of Islam. Women who wear *hijab* believe that by doing so they represent their faith to others. Therefore, presentation of moral character is required and is understood to be a

form of *dawah*. Also, by being career women and wearing gendered clothing, these converts express to the world that Islam does not exclude women from the public sphere, or from wage-labor. Marriage is 50 percent of the practice of the faith, so coupling is desired. Nevertheless, these women do not maintain marriages at the expense of their happiness, freedom, or well being. Divorce is acceptable and occurs as frequently as it does in the non-Muslim world. In addition, many are very active in, and supportive of, the community regardless of what they believe are the community's failings. They continue to support the community despite the negative ways in which some of the men reject female leadership. Occasionally, the tension between the female leaders and certain male members becomes so difficult that women change masjids, or they simply retreat from the community for months or years in order to conduct inward soul searching. Gender conflict requires reconciling one's understanding of Qur'an and women with the practice of gender oppression within their community. While the men frustrate them, they are truly disappointed by the women in the community who interpret Islam as submission to men instead of submission to Allah. The reason these women reenter the community is that they have an overriding belief that Islam is a path to liberation. Their self-defined role is to renew continually that message to other Muslims. These women tend to get involved in development projects such as establishing a clinic, hosting a conference, lecturing, or writing on Islam. Generally, these women are economically middle class.

3. Married women who are economically poor and full-time mothers: They live in poorer neighborhoods for economic reasons as well as to maintain social networks. They often have more than the average number of children, sometimes as many as ten. Most wear Middle Eastern inspired *hijab*, and some wear the face veil, or *niqab*. Their husbands often work more than one job to support their family or families, and, in their quest to create the ideal Islamic environment for their children, they either home school or enroll

their children in a Muslim school. They are dedicated to educating their children, and the wife chooses to fulfill this goal at the expense of other luxuries. They rely on their friends in the Muslim community for support through gift or barter. The symbolic performance of their faith through dress in poor neighborhoods is usually understood to be an act of resistance. For most of these women, conversion to Islam is as much a profound opposition to the sociopolitical structures of the inner city as it is a belief in the tenets of Islam. Remaining committed to this act of resistance often requires putting aside personal aspirations and performing their faith for the sake of their children, husbands, and community. Any ambivalence must be suppressed or dealt with in the context of deep readings of Qur'an and hadith. They also often limit their social engagement to the Muslim community, where their practice of the faith is recognized in positive ways.

4.   Families that live quite marginally because the husband makes very little in wages and the wife is a full-time mother: They often have many children, which is part of the husband's image of himself as pious. They sometimes express a desire to live sunnah, which in this community means trying to live as the Prophet did, according to need not surplus, and through daily devotion to prayer and ritual. The women often depend on city services and the community to feed their families. Even though the wife may not particularly want more children (again sometimes as many as ten), they believe that birth control is forbidden in Islam. These families must rely on gift, barter, or *sadaka* (charity). Often, the community is very willing to provide the assistance.

The community is mixed, with each end of the purity spectrum enacting identities that are acceptable to all. The professional, career women find somewhat enviable the women who forgo wages and economic independence, and who refuse to compromise their religious idealism for the sake of their family and Allah. However, women who choose large families and home schooling in lieu of material accumulation respect the energy the career women put into hosting conferences and teaching Qur'anic exegesis in sister education classes. It is important to emphasize that neither identity is understood to be inferior, and each brings legitimacy to the community's sense of purpose and quest for both purity and assimilation.

The ideal types—career assimilationist and *purdah*-seeking ascetic—are not representative of binary opposites. Instead, Islam for African Americans is a contradictory space occupied by overlapping Muslim narratives of orthodoxy. A convert's choice of religious performance and exegesis in the overlapping public and private spheres represents important dialogic strategies of sense-making and signification. It is through these strategies that converts author a social space for themselves where authenticity—social, political, religious, gender, race—is theirs to determine. Therefore, these roles are not in opposition to one another, but offer alternative ways to dislocate race and gender essentialism in identity politics.

Finally, aside from Aminah, I am loathe to say that any of these women are disempowered. Because Aminah has chosen to put herself and her children in physical danger, she is the exception, but the other women are trying to make sense of urban, social complexity and have a personal desire for empowerment and spiritual fulfillment. When a convert chooses how to practice faith, whether she chooses asceticism or not, particular forms of agency open up while others become closed off. Freedom is, after all, definitional.

NINE

Conclusion

During Ramadan in 1996 I went with a friend, one of my white female informants, to a fast-breaking, *iftar*, on the Night of Power, *lailat al-Qadr*.
The event took place at the house of a fabulously wealthy Pakistani family. The patriarch of this family bought houses for his children in an ex-
clusive neighborhood of million-dollar homes, and it is not unusual to see
women dressed in *hijab* running back and forth between the houses. The
family had converted the room above their garage into a masjid, and every
night during Ramadan they invited any Muslim connected to friends, family, or the Muslim community for *iftar, Isha* (the last prayer of the day), and
prayer. There was food for people to break their fast, and the imam, who
usually recites 1/30 of the Qur'an each night during Ramadan, recited the
entire text by heart. There was a real sense of community at this event. I
watched in awe the spirit of exchange and celebration and was reminded
about the religious importance of giving and community building in Islam.

Upstairs in the masjid, I was conscious of my child squirming from
boredom. I would have left the space sooner except there were several
Pakistani American children who played in the women's section without
being disciplined for being too loud or too playful. Despite the leniency,
the mothers performed their prayers with a speed I had never witnessed,
picked up their children, and left.

During the middle of the recitation of the Qur'an, I decided to relieve my daughter's boredom. We headed down to the house where a group of women, intimately connected with the family, sat discussing which catalogs have suitably modest clothing that can easily be adapted to fit their standards for covering. They also discussed pregnancy and parenting. Despite the things we shared in common as women, we unfortunately had very little to talk about. My outsider status was something I had never experienced at Masjid al-Mustaqim, Masjid Ummah, or any of the predominantly African American masjids I have attended. Islam is supposed to be a religion that bridges cultural borders, that defies regional identities. While these cultural differences are bridged with respect to the ritual practice of the faith, most notably the five pillars of the faith— prayer, fasting, *zakat*, *hajj*, and *shahada*—outside of those rituals, there are bridges that have yet to be crossed. Clearly there are cultural differences with respect to the intent and impulse behind being Muslim.

Certainly both at Masjid al-Mustaqim and within this Pakistani American community there is a renewed sense of purpose toward the end of a month of religious purification, but how would each group define that purpose given their stark historical, political, and material differences? I think about al-Mustaqim's *iftar*, where the poorest families come so their kids can eat a good meal. The religiously prescribed practice of *zakat* means different things in different contexts, particularly in terms of how it is hierarchically valued relative to other religious edicts. While I did not know enough about this Pakistani community to understand how they position themselves as moral actors in their moral universe, I did wondered if *zakat* is viewed less as an ideological justification for profound economic redistribution and more as a method for stabilizing social relations. Victor Turner describes how in all major religions there are "metaphors of anti-structure." Turner argues that without anti-structure, structure could not exist. He says:

> The great religious systems harmonize rather than oppose structure
> and communitas and call the resultant total field the "body" of the
> faithful, the umma ("comity") of Islam, or some similar term which

reconciles love with law, communitas with structure. In fact, neither law nor love can be such when they are implacably opposed; both are then hate; all the more so, when masked as moral excellence.[1]

Islam clearly has this magnificent, hologramlike, polyvocality. It can and has been used as both a stabilizing and a destabilizing force, with different Muslims attaching more or less weight to the metaphors of anti-structure and structure.

A Muslim's historical, cultural, economic, and political subject position always informs his or her Islamic exegesis and approach to social relations. These nuanced differences expressed themselves in the social gulf between myself and the other people gathered at this house. At the *Lailat al-Qadr*, I recognized that what drove my intense interest in the African American Sunni community relates to how they use the faith to address the particularities of the African American experience. While Islam articulates a body of laws and definitions of moral excellence, the ways in which individuals use Islam to frame meaning and purpose are entirely indigenous. Feeling slightly out of place, my friend and I decided to leave early, and no one noticed us leave.

THE RELIGIOUS SELF

> The human mind is tripartite—it has rational, irrational, and nonrational aspects; and, comparing our ideas to the ideas of others, we will always be able to find some ways in which our ideas are like the ideas of others (universalism) and some ways in which our ideas are different. Sometimes those differences will suggest progress (developmentalism) and often they will not (relativism). The task for the ethnographer is to decide what's rational, what's irrational and what's nonrational and to know when it makes sense to emphasize likeness, difference, or progress.[2]

This book is an attempt to conduct the ethnographic task described by Richard Shweder. The importance of the task is that it forces the ethnographer to confront the troubling ethnocentric assumptions he or she makes when engaged in anthropological projects. It is difficult to get away from personal biases, but this step is crucial before making any claims that others are disempowered, irrational, and/or dysfunctional.

The African American Sunni Muslim community was a great challenge to me partly because I was raised to view faith as irrational, and partly because I was schooled in the virtues of "Western" feminism. At first, the female converts seemed to be not only irrational, but participants in the reproduction of their own oppression. After I entered the community, things made sense. Pierre Bourdieu in *Outline of a Theory of Practice* talks about the intricate cultural maps of nuance, gesture, space, and time, which ethnographers must study in order to understand how informants manipulate cultural symbols in the interest of acquiring power or resisting oppression. As soon as I learned the cultural map of the female converts in this community, I understood that these women are attempting to empower themselves by engaging in Islamic exegesis, or put another way, by situating a discourse of liberation within the authorized discourse of Islam. Surrender is to a faith in Allah and the belief that the Prophet Muhammad was Allah's last and final Messenger. But surrender does not happen in the absence of engagement with the sources of faith, the texts, and the community.

Tacit acceptance of "patriarchal" interpretations of Islam by particular men in the community does not always mean that one is disempowered. Often the ellipses, silences, and seeming capitulations to power are not the result of external forces of oppression, but are related to ambivalence about the extant exegesis, or to competing personal interests that make it difficult to set priorities. As I said earlier, the women try to fit under one rubric family, personal empowerment, and economic and social uplift. This is an overwhelming task given that these goals often compete with one another, and it is very difficult to mediate the resulting contradictions. Clearly there are women who choose submissiveness at the expense of themselves and their children, but for the majority, their beliefs are, I believe, appropriately responsive to their personal and social needs.

Thus I explored how the women negotiate at the local or personal level; a place Michel Foucault recognizes as an important location of power. I found that they do so by being part of a community that surrenders itself to Islam; and Islam, as the religion and as a community, in turn has become the location where people feel free to transform themselves and others. Many of the converts felt disempowered before Islam, and it is through Islam that they feel they can be engaged in affecting their material, personal, and political environments. There are some women, like Safa and Latifah, who have limited agency but use Islam to construct a resistance discourse. I believe that they are materially disadvantaged, but by refusing to assimilate ideologically they subvert the social premises that confer status on some, vast wealth on others, and jobs and security on others. The women who adopt the veil, domestic responsibilities, and/or poverty are resisting at one level the materialism and subsistence wage-labor of capitalism. Even the ones who accepted AFDC, or TANF, those seeming to capitulate to the system, are in essence forcing the government to support upward of six Muslim children, which has some features of resistance.

Dismissing religion as an opiate, Karl Marx was unable to appreciate the value and meaning of the superstructure for the oppressed. The superstructure provides an orientation to material and social relations. In essence, it confers meaning and value onto things that otherwise have no inherent meaning or value. In anticipating the eventual end of religious ideology in favor of scientific socialism, Marx failed to recognize the seemingly inevitable ontological and cosmological questions that extend beyond the question of human history. Science provides some of the answers, historical materialism a few, but faith for these converts provides both answers and direction.

What surprised me, and what I think is missed by most people who believe that African American Muslims are revisiting patriarchy, is that for people following religious doctrine there is room for questioning and ambivalence. Among religiously committed women, the extent of ambivalence surprised me. In fact, female converts to Islam confront ambivalence all the time, and it is in this space of trying to resolve the dissonance between common sense and religious ideology that women attempt, through discourse, to alter community consensus on exegesis. In this way, they bring about a communitywide zeitgeist as opposed to merely an individual epiphany. The women attempt to revolutionize from within by rereading historical documents on Islam and challenging the authenticity of some hadith using modern translations of the Qur'an for their *tafsir*. Unfortunately, modern interpretations of Islam are often challenged as personal opinion instead of as religious truth, or *haqq*. This challenge to authenticity, however, does not deter African American Muslim women from creating an indigenous American version of Islam that speaks to a particular set of liberation ideologies.

The border delineating the Sunni Muslim community from secular Southern California can best be described as a discursive filter. The potential Muslim women have to enact change both within and outside the community is tied, in part, to how they negotiate this border. Zipporah hired a non-Muslim lesbian to work on her staff. In response to the criticism she received from the community, she argued that she was forging a bridge of understanding between the Muslim community and the gay/lesbian community. She made it clear that she was not endorsing homosexuality, but she was trying to demonstrate to those outside that Islam encourages understanding and acceptance. Most poignantly, she initiated an open conversation about homosexuality. The position she took within the debate was informed by what is often described as the spirit of Islam, which some women argue can be gleaned from the sunnah of the Prophet.

I think scholars critical of religion, and/or believers in universals of justice, ask why one even needs to frame things religiously. "Isn't it easier," they wonder, "just to say, 'A husband should not be allowed to beat his wife,' or 'A wife's role is not to dress nicely for her husband?' Why waste time having to authenticate these ideas about personal liberty through Islam?" The answer to this question is more complex. I have found that people who are religious want to feel that their beliefs have legitimacy outside of self. Put another way, they want to objectify, and therefore validate, their consciousness. The majority of religious people are driven in part by the desire to do the right thing and think the right thoughts, but they feel that personal subjectivity is fallible whereas religious theology is objective and timeless. I have heard women in the community say over and over again when expounding on a challenging *ayat* or hadith, "We are not to judge what Allah says." Women reason that edicts about gender roles, ritual obligations, and community organization tend to appear right over time. As Fatima says in chapter 3, "Some people say that you can read a *sura* over and over again, but when Allah's ready for you to understand it, you understand it." So they surrender themselves to the teachings because they feel that some of what might not seem reasonable in the present might later prove to be very wise.

Another criticism of religion pertains to the difficulty of distinguishing the religious from the cultural. Some argue that in an attempt to change any religion to suit present needs, one simply innovates beyond the bounds of the religion. Therefore, all these adaptations of Islam to American life would not be included in what Karl Marx defined as "religion." The religious ideology Marx criticized was unresponsive to the personal realities of the adherents, and was stuck in staid ritual and ideology that reproduced the material structures of oppression. We know, however, from British history (knowledge that Marx must have had) that there had been religious foment and persecution of people who worshipped differently well before modern capitalism. Religion can keep people complacent in an oppressive system, but there are always religious adherents who are challenging the system and redefining the faith. In fact, two of the most trusted collectors of hadith, Ismail al-Bukhari (d. 870 C.E.) and Muslim ibn al-Hajjaj (d. 875 C.E.), disputed each other's collected traditions. Islamic *tafsir* has, since the Prophet's death, been contested.

African American women have surrendered to Islam because of the way Islam has been used in the community as a legitimate framework for challenging racism, sexism, and economic exploitation. Islam is their epiphany. It is the nexus of their social history, personal reality, and liberation ideology. I believe the indigenous American adoption and rereading of Islamic ideology simply validates what most African American converts feel about the capitalist orchestration and legitimization of their own disempowerment. Before their conversions, most lacked the language to express their anger and resentment at a racist and sexist social system. Self-hatred and personal distress for most of the converts before their epiphanies were embodied at a preconscious level. Islam gave them a language and methodology for challenging those systems of oppression. Therefore for converts, surrender to Islam is surrender to the truth. Most of my informants believe that allowing themselves to be transformed by any other regime of thought would be potentially disempowering.

African American Muslim ideology situates its authority not within state-sponsored ideologies, but through the cross-referencing of discourses on race, gender, and political economy theory. Muslims interpret the Qur'an as antiracist, feminist, and as a blueprint for a redistributive capitalist system. In other words, this "counter-hegemonic faith" is considered good because it promotes mainstream American values. In *Weapons of the Weak*, Scott observes that the poor often rely on conservative ideologies more so than the wealthy. "Subordinate classes are often seen as backward looking, inasmuch as they are defending their own interpretation of an earlier dominant ideology against new and painful arrangements imposed by elites and/or the state."[3] Were it not for the fact that Islamic exegesis is nested by other more accepted ideological domains, the Muslim resistance rhetoric would have no legitimate anchors. Dependence on stable domains to upset other domains is a strategy used not simply by the powerless, but by the powerful as well. Referencing these authorized discourses, these ideological domains, limits what converts can say and do at the same time it gives them the legitimacy to be taken seriously.[4] This authority means they are better able to affect change.[5]

Among members in the Nation of Islam, the most significant ideological changes took place in the transition to Sunni Islam. Notably, the community shifted from an ends orientation to a means orientation. A member of the Nation of Islam, for example, was supposed to purchase goods at black-owned stores. The action, they thought, would result in monumental economic redistribution. Alternatively, for Sunni Muslims, one is supposed to purchase *halal* foods from a *halal* market in order to avoid eating *haram* foods. The intentions of the members of the Nation of Islam differ from those of the Sunni Muslims, although the effect is the circulation of wealth in the affiliated community. Even with a shift in purpose from economic redistribution to spiritual (bodily) purity, the more ascetically oriented praxis of the latter does not lessen the redistributive power and effect on manufacturing and production. By objectifying borders between the self, defined as a religious and sacred body, and the external world, one cannot help but alter social relations. For converts to Sunni Islam, the daily rituals of *wudu, salat,* and avoidance of *haram* while embracing *halal* asserts self into the material world. By objectifying through action what they deem is Islamically permissible, converts reshape economic and social relations. These women are resisting the deep structure, the internalized racism, sexism, and classism, a process I believe that is fundamental for lasting sociopolitical change.

The Sunni Muslims have clarified that objectification and habitus, perception and practice, play crucial roles in both religious conversion and resistance praxis. Religious rituals, taboos, presentations of self, social organization of space, and intentionality determine both the physical and the sociopolitical world of the convert. The body is, as Thomas Csordas argues, not the object of culture but "the subject of culture."[6] As a cultural subject, the embodiment of religious perceptions and practice, particularly with a large and vocal group, has the effect of negating oppression and redefining the social order at the local level. Religious embodiment and ambivalence dialectically form a liberation praxis that rescues converts from perceptions of powerlessness and aids in the creation of a very personal form of agency.

Epilogue

In 2002, I visited the women and Imam Khalil to show them what I had written and renew their consent. The visit was important because I became aware of how deeply disturbing the events of September 11, 2001, have been to the African American Sunni community. The community in Southern California has responded in a number of interesting and subtle ways. Imam Khalil, for example, who has always encouraged his community to separate Islam from the cultural baggage associated with the faith, now is much more strident in his condemnation of oppression committed in the name of Islam. He, and his new wife of a few years, repeated a number of times, "There's a difference between Islam and Muslims."

In some respects the events of 9/11 freed the African American community from the shadows of the immigrant Muslim community, which, many African Americans felt, tried to claim ownership of Islam. In fact, one brother mentioned in a small gathering how nice is has been to speak at interfaith meetings where people look at him as an authority on Islam rather than as an African American Muslim neophyte. The crisis recommitted the community to a deeper engagement with Qur'anic exegesis. Notably, Imam Khalil's *khutbahs* focus less on marriage and more on interfaith issues, including historical exegesis of Christianity, Judaism, and Islam.

Imam Khalil has passed the baton, so to speak, to several newer imams who were never in the Nation of Islam, and they continue to challenge any essentialist notions of race. In one *khutbah*, an imam focused on the Prophet Muhammad's last sermon in an attempt to explore in greater detail the kind of justice and tolerance envisioned by the Prophet. Another imam discussed the need for a greater sense of brotherhood within the community. None of the lectures or sermons overtly challenged the mainstream, but rather they attempted to instill in the congregation a sense of the beauty of the faith.

Perhaps one of the reasons for the shift in focus has to do with the decrease in community participation. In fact, most of the women I interviewed have retreated quite a bit from the community. While they still remain very faithful, they think the community needs better organization, but they do not feel that they can change the leadership. So the community, to me, seemed more decentralized than ever before, with the masjids playing less and less of a role in the lives of the women. Decline in masjid attendance is not, however, indicative of the size of the Muslim community. In fact, it is estimated that conversion is on the rise. What I think it indicates is that more and more women, in particular, are performing Islamic exegesis on their own and relying less on the leadership to interpret their faith.

Interestingly, along with this shift has come a decrease in the number of women who are wearing *hijab*. Nadia now only occasionally wears *hijab*, and Zipporah, who used to lecture on the importance of *hijab*, now rarely wears it to work. Zipporah said that she believes she used *hijab* to prove to herself the depth of her faith. Now that she feels more secure with her faith she does not feel she needs it. This has been a trajectory for many of the women in the community.

In terms of marriage, Afaf never married, but her mother, who has suffered several strokes, moved in and has lived with Afaf for more than six years. Hudah's marriage classes ended when she finally succumbed to the cancer she fought for years. Nadia has since divorced her Nigerian husband, but he remains a dear friend. Nadia told me that until now she had never lived alone, and she is finally getting to know herself. Nadia also has six grandchildren, who she adores, and after receiving a master's degree in counseling, Nadia now works with drug-addicted pregnant women and newborns.

Zipporah is still married to the husband she chose, and now that she is no longer running CARE, she and her husband find time to go to *Jumah* together and to jazz concerts. In addition, she creates training partnerships between the city and educational institutions, and so while the job has changed, she continues to put people to work. Imam Khalil's new wife is dynamic and committed and by all accounts is part of the reason the community is growing in terms of its sensitivity toward women's issues. Jamilah, I heard in an unconfirmed report, divorced her husband in the Sudan. Her mother, Hind, moved, and I have been unable to locate them. Safa is in a polygynous marriage again with an older man whose wife of thirty years could not have children. After waiting a number of years, Safa had another child and is also now a grandmother. By all accounts the family is doing very well. Aida and Maimouna continue to have fabulous careers, continue to be extremely well versed in their faith, and continue to wear *hijab* to work.

NOTES

CHAPTER 1: ENGAGED SURRENDER

1. "Masjid" is an Arabic word for mosque. I use "mosque" and "masjid" interchangeably.

2. *Hijab* is a covering—"a curtain"—in order to encourage modesty and lawful behavior in Muslim women. In different Muslim communities, customary forms of dress, or veiling, have been adopted, including the *burqa* in Afghanistan, and the *chador* in Iran. The extent of covering is, of course, contested and I discuss these debates in greater detail in chapter 3.

3. See Rosaldo and Lamphere, eds., *Woman, Culture and Society*; and Mohanty et al., *Third World Women and the Politics of Feminism*.

4. Visweswaran, "Histories of Feminist Ethnography," p. 594.

5. When reading critiques of pornography years ago I ran across this explanation. The judge's refusal to objectify his criteria for designating materials pornographic or not caught my attention, but while I remember the quote I do not remember its origins. His pronouncement, while honest, is problematic because it privileges his subjectivity. On the other hand, as an anthropologist, I appreciate the importance of situational ethics, which as a method for truth discovery is an inductive, rather than deductive, approach. The inductive approach is the mainstay of anthropological methods, but in order to temper the influence of one's own subjectivity most ethnographers inform their readers of the filters they use in their knowledge production. Just as a judge would identify him- or herself as a liberal or conservative during a nomination hearing, ethnographers

often lay bare their own subjectivity so that the reader can critically differentiate the objective from the subjective.

6. Suttee is the act of a Hindu widow throwing herself on her husband's funeral pyre. Foot binding is a practice now banned in China of wrapping little girl's feet in order for them to remain small. The practice caused horrible and painful foot disfigurement.

7. The categories of racism, sexism, and poverty already presuppose the reader's belief that these social phenomena are oppressive and should be eliminated. More importantly, I use these terms without fully defining them. I believe that the use of this tripartite division is problematic, but social science has yet to develop a language to articulate the varied way individuals experience these phenomena.

8. Muhammad, *Message to the Blackman in America*, p. 59.

9. Giddings, *When and Where I Enter*, pp.317–18.

10. Sizemore, "Sexism and the Black Male," p. 6.

11. Elijah Muhammad's message to control black women comes with an equally forceful message to respect black women, "My beloved brothers in America, you have lost the respect for your woman and therefore you have lost the respect for yourself. You won't protect her; therefore you can't protect yourself." See Muhammad, *Message to the Blackman in America*, p. 59. It is important to understand the discursive context in which Elijah Muhammad delivered his message. Importantly, his entire religious philosophy was a response to white supremacy. A core element of white supremacy was the idea that black men wanted to sleep with white women. In a letter sent by the Ku Klux Klan to a Muslim convention in Chicago in 1957, J. B. Stoner wrote, "Your desire for white women is an admission of your own racial inferiority. One reason why we whites will never accept you into our white society is because a nigger's chief ambition in life is to sleep with a white woman, thereby polluting her." Muhammad, *Message to a Blackman in America*, p. 332. For Elijah Muhammad, if black men had "thorough knowledge" of self, then they would not desire white women or assimilation into white America. If, in addition, black men respected black women and prospered economically, then women would not be tempted by "the streets," in which case men would have control over their women. In other words, "control over women" requires creating the conditions that would encourage women to want to cooperate with black men.

12. Clegg, *An Original Man*, p. 102.

13. My Sunni Muslim informants might be appalled that I collapse perceptions of women in the Nation with perceptions of Sunni Muslim women. I do so

only because most Americans lump all African American Muslims into one group, and in scholarly circles black nationalist movements of the 1960s and 1970s are often summarily dismissed as oppressive to women.

14. An anthropologist's entrée describes the steps taken in order to establish rapport with members of a community. The common wisdom is that one must be extremely careful positioning oneself in the field with respect to power. These initial encounters, it is believed, have tremendous repercussions in terms of how one is received by the community. If, for example, I acted inappropriately, people might refuse to talk with me; on the other hand, if I were too "appropriate," I might come across as an insider, which has another set of problems.

15. This identification I refer to is much less anchored in the kind of Afrocentrism espoused by Molefi Asante and Haki Madhubuti than in a kind of sisterhood that idealizes West African women as community and domestic leaders. See Asante, *Afrocentricity*; and Madhubuti, *Enemies*.

16. Most African American Muslim converts adopt Islamic names. All of the names in this book are pseudonyms without last names. Spelling for Arabic names reflects the transliteration most widely used within the African American Muslim community.

17. Worldwide Islam is not a minority faith. The number of adherents is well over one billion, making it the second most practiced faith after Christianity.

18. In a brilliant rereading of Gramsci, Stuart Hall finds that Gramsci is sensitive to the ways in which changing popular consent can manufacture changes in material structures. Hall describes how Gramsci is useful for understanding how race and ethnicity function to counter hegemony. Rather than simply being "false consciousness," Hall argues that alliances sensitive to issues of race and ethnicity are strategic in the context of race/ethnicity oppression. See Morley and Chen, eds., *Stuart Hall: Critical Dialogues*, pp. 411–40.

19. Omi and Winant say, "A racial project is simultaneously an interpretation, representation, or explanation of racial dynamics, and an effort to reorganize and redistribute resources along particular racial lines." Omi and Winant, *Racial Formation*, p. 56. The Sunni Muslim community is in no way a black nationalist or racial project, and does not use race as a means for determining community borders. The community does, however, appreciate that in the United States, race structures resource distribution. Therefore, while it does not essentialize race, it does respond to social inequalities based on race. A subtle, but important distinction.

20. The Prophet Muhammad says in his last sermon, "All Mankind is from Adam and Eve, an Arab has no superiority over a non-Arab nor does a non-Arab have any superiority over an Arab; also a white has no superiority over black nor

a black has any superiority over white except by piety and good action." There are numerous translations of the sermon on the Internet. I used the translation distributed by Precious International, Houston, Texas.

21. Population statistics for Muslims is the United States are only estimates. The Graduate Center of the City University of New York estimates 1.1 million adult Muslims as of 2001. Another report by the American Jewish Committee estimates 2.8 million Muslims. A Gallup poll estimates 1.9 million. Some polls have claimed as many as six million, but that high estimate is very doubtful. Of those estimates, the percentage who are converts to Islam could be as high as 40 percent or as low as 17 percent. In other words, the population of African American converts could be as low as 200,000 or as high as 1.1 million. Niebuhr, "Studies Suggest Lower Count." There are between ten thousand and one hundred thousand followers of the Nation of Islam, according to adherents.com, a service that compiles available demographic data.

22. Barbara Stowasser comments about the Qur'an: "Firstly the Arabic Qur'an is truly and literally God's Word as revealed verbatim and seriatim to God's Prophet Muhammad, Seal of the prophets, through a heavenly messenger, Gabriel. Secondly, the Qur'an Sacred Word of God is the faithful copy of a text contained in a preexistent heavenly tablet, God's heavenly Scripture. Thirdly, the Qur'an is God's final message to the world, a guidance for humankind. Fourthly, the Qur'an followed and confirmed other, earlier revelations that, likewise taken from God's heavenly Scripture, were sent to various peoples of history. These earlier revelations, however, were incomplete. In addition, the earlier monotheistic communities (mainly Jews and Christians) had corrupted their prophets' revelations (Torah and Evangel), so that the versions of scripture as preserved by their communities bore the traits of their falsifications. The Qur'an was sent down to correct all that had thus been corrupted, and also to complete God's message to the world. The Qur'an, then, is both God's original and eternal Scripture and also His last, perfect and unchangeable revelation to humankind." See Stowasser, *Women in the Qur'an*, p. 13. These distinctions took on great relevance for the African American Muslim community during "the transition" from the Nation of Islam to Sunni Islam.

23. Gramsci describes a "war of position" as a political struggle waged from within multiple institutional and ideological domains.

24. In Islam there are two *Eids: Eid al-Fitr* (the Festival of Fast-Breaking) and *Eid al-Adha* (the Festival of Sacrifice). The *Eid* where I met Imani was the *Eid al-Fitr* following Ramadan. The *Eid* is a festival marked by an early morning *salat* (prayer) and the exchange of gifts, charity, and food.

25. Lubiano, "Black Nationalism and Common Sense"; Giddings, *When and Where I Enter.*

26. For a discussion of some of the issues of race and homophobia, see Williams, "Living at the Crossroads."

27. Lubiano, "Black Nationalism and Black Common Sense," pp. 232–52.

28. Pierre Bourdieu describes the difference between official kinship and practical kinship in *Outline of a Theory of Practice.* The topic of official vs. practical with respect to gender, family, and Islam is explored in-depth in Ong and Peletz, *Bewitching Women, Pious Men.*

29. Jonathan Kozol has written extensively on how equality of opportunity does not exist in some of the poorest neighborhoods where educational facilities are severely underfunded. See Kozol, *Savage Inequalities.*

30. Ziba Mir-Hosseini, in a lecture given in March 2003 at Princeton, specifically argued against conceptualizing Islam as a blueprint. I recognize her concerns, given that a blueprint usually represents something fixed. I use blueprint not in the sense of a house design that is reproduced identically in multiple locations. Instead, I think that the structural designs authored by Islam are altered according to permutations in the ideological geography across time and across place.

31. Karl Marx in his early writings argues that it is not enough to understand the contradiction between ideals and material facts. The revolution he argues requires both becoming conscious of these divergences and then acting upon them; putting ideals into practice or "praxis." Therefore, I use praxis not in the Marxist sense of "true consciousness," but in the sense of marrying ideology and practice. For Muslims, the goal is for all social action to be preceded by consciousness. In other words, practice must be purposeful. I am arguing if, for example, community building is the goal, then ambivalence toward particular discourses or community practices can undermine this priority unless the ambivalence is handled in a manner that will not disrupt the first objective. Marx imagined that there was one noncontradictory social reality (communism), which means that there was one correct praxis. But I do not accept that there is a utopian ideal. Instead, I believe that there are many different types of praxis and that these must be negotiated. Muslims are ambivalent toward some, but certainly not all, of the community's agendas and discourses.

32. Giddens, *Capitalism and Modern Social Theory*, p. 8.

33. At the level of the everyday, women's religious exegesis has limited power because men continue to define the character of the masjids. However, leaders need followers. Therefore sensitivity to women's issues is required, at least at a discursive level, to hold the community together.

34. Lave and Wenger, *Situated Learning*.

35. The percentage of people who convert for these reasons is greater in the African American Muslim population than is represented in my study.

36. When I speak about embodiment I refer, in particular, to the work of Thomas Csordas and his study of Charismatic Christian healing rituals. In his seminal article, "Embodiment as a Paradigm for anthropology," Csordas quotes a religious participant who elaborates on a number of overt signs of demonic possession; a belch, a cough, and so on. For the participants, demons are understood to be external to the body, and in this respect they are cultural objects. Traditional understandings of perception identify self-awareness as the ability to identify self as an object among objects. Csordas argues that these classifications are simply "the manifestations . . . of an embodied process of self-objectification. The preobjective element of this process rests in the fact that participants, like the informant quoted, experience these manifestations as spontaneous and without preordained content. The manifestations are original acts of communication which nevertheless take a limited number of common forms because they emerge from a shared habitus." Csordas, "Embodiment as a Paradigm in Anthropology," p. 15. This "process," which differs from static "objectivity," is marked by a self-awareness that as Csordas says is "preobjective," meaning that it exists in the body at a level of signification and within a sensory modality that is often beyond our conscious control. For Charismatic Christians the self-awareness that something is not right, or that they have transgressed, precedes the casting of the behavior within a "conventional demonic idiom" p. 16. In other words, what we embody involves both what is objective, but also what is what Pierre Bourdieu describes as habitus and what Marcel Mauss calls techniques of the body. They are our acculturated practices for how we display our bodies and have come to know our bodies. They give shape to what we think of as "transgressive," well before we are given a language or a classification for describing it.

37. Moral fields is defined by Andre Simic as "an interactional sphere where those engaged behave towards each other with reference to ethically perceived imperatives (rules that are accepted as being typically 'good,' 'God-given,' 'natural,' 'proper,' and the like, and do not require instrumental or even logical explanation; they are accepted unreflectively as axiomatic). Moral fields usually encompass a group of people whose co-membership is determined by recruitment rules that effectively exclude others." See Simic, "The Ethnology of Traditional and Complex Societies," p. 49.

CHAPTER 2: A COMMUNITY OF WOMEN

1. Ramadan is a month where Muslims fast and abstain from drink, food, and sexual intercourse from dawn until sunset. It is the month in which the Qur'an was first revealed to the Prophet Muhammad.

2. This description of Alia's morning ritual comes from an interview during which she described in great detail everything from what she eats to how she prays.

3. John Esposito says, "Technically, *Sunnah* is divided into three categories: (1) *al-Sunnah al-qawliyah*, the Prophet's statements and sayings; (2) *al-Sunnah al-filiyah*, his deeds; and (3) *al-Sunnah al-taqririyah*, his silent or tacit approval of certain deeds which he had knowledge of. The record of the Prophetic words and deeds is to be found in the narrative reports or traditions *(hadith)* transmitted and finally collected and recorded in compendia. . . . These *hadiths* were evaluated through a painstaking attempt which produced a new Muslim science of *hadith* criticism *(mustalah al-hadith)*." Esposito, *Women in Muslim Family Law*, pp. 5–6.

4. *Lailat al-Qadr*, defined in the African American community as the "Night of Power" and by Maulana Muhammad Ali as the "night of grandeur or majesty," occurs on one of the last ten nights of Ramadan. It is the night, according to Ali, "in which the Qur'an was revealed, and it is further stated that it is the night on which angels and the Spirit descend," Muhammad Ali, *The Religion of Islam*, pp. 374–75.

5. *Sura* 46, *ayat* 15 states: "We have enjoined on man kindness to his parents: In pain did his mother bear him, and in pain did she give him birth. The carrying of the (child) to his weaning is (a period of) thirty months. At length, when he reaches the age of full strength and attains forty years, he says, "Oh my Lord! Grant me that I may be Grateful for Thy favour which Thou hast bestowed upon me, and upon both my parents, and that I may work righteousness such as Thou mayest approve."

6. *Dawah* is defined as "call to Islam," or propagating the faith through activities related to community development. Every Muslim in the African American community is encouraged to give some form of *dawah* that can be as simple as explaining Islam to a non-Muslim.

7. *Shirk* is defined as associating other gods with Allah. Idol worship is one form of *shirk*, as is nature worship, belief in the Trinity, and the doctrine of ascribing sons (for example Jesus) and daughters to Allah.

8. For this book I use a Qur'an translated by The Presidency of Islamic Researchers, IFTA, Call and Guidance. (Al-Madinah Al-Munawarah: King Fahd Holy Qur'an Printing Complex, 1405 A.H.). The Qur'an is divided into 114 *suras* defined by many scholars as "chapters" or "sections." Each *sura* is divided into *ayat*, defined as "signs" or "verses." When I quote from the Qur'an as I do above, I indicate the chapter and verse using the format (41:37); 41 is the chapter, and 37 is the verse.

9. See Cohen, "Ethnicity," for a discussion on identity diacritics.

CHAPTER 3: GENDER NEGOTIATIONS AND QUR'ANIC EXEGESIS

1. An Islamic greeting meaning "Peace be upon you."

2. Barbara Stowasser says, "On the one hand the semantic association of domestic segregation *(hijab)* with garments to be worn in public *(jilbab, khimar)* resulted in the use of the term *hijab* for concealing garments that women wore outside of their houses. This language is fully documented in medieval *hadith*. However, unlike female garments such as *jilbab, lihaf, milhafa, izar, dir'* (traditional garments for the body), *khimar, niqab, burqu'*, qina', miqna'a (traditional garments for the head and neck) . . . the medieval meaning of *hijab* remained conceptual and generic." Stowasser, *Women in the Qur'an*, p. 92.

3. Sallallahu alayhi wa sallam (sws): "This is an expression Muslims use whenever the name of Prophet Muhammad (sws) is mentioned or written. The meaning of it is: "May the Blessings and the Peace of Allah be upon Him." Muslims are informed that if they proclaim such a statement once, Allah will reward them ten times.

4. During the Prophet's lifetime revelations were memorized or written down, but it was not until Uthman ibn Affan ruled, the third caliph (644–56 C.E.), that the revelations were collected in the Qur'an. For this reason, some feminists like to emphasize that while the Qur'an is from Allah, it started as an oral document.

5. This *ayat* was revealed in the fifth year of the *hijra*, or 627 C.E. In 622, the growing Muslim community in Mecca relocated to Medina in order to avoid further persecution by the polytheistic Quraysh tribe. It was during the development of the Muslim community in Medina, and skirmishes with the Quraysh, that a significant portion of the Qur'an was revealed. Significantly, the beginning of *hijra* marks the beginning of the Muslim calendar.

6. Subhanahu wa taala means "Allah has no partners" and is used every time a Muslim says Allah.

7. Nadia [pseud.], interview by author, Los Angeles, September 1995.

8. Madyun, *Being Muslim*, p. 2.

9. Ibid.

10. "Peace Be Upon Him" (PBUH) is the same as *"sallallahu alayhi wa sallam"* (sws). Madyun uses the same proclamation for Jesus, who is considered a prophet in Islam.

11. Madyun, *Being Muslim*, pp. 2–3.

12. I refer in particular to Frantz Fanon, *The Wretched of the Earth;* Claude Steele, "A Threat in the Air: How Stereotypes Shape Intellectual Identity and Performance"; and Cornel West, *Race Matters.*

13. Nadia [pseud.], interview by author, Los Angeles, September 1995.

14. Madyun, *Being Muslim*, pp. 2–3.

15. Three years after these observations were made, Imam Khalil remarried.

16. Imam Khalil [pseud.], November 1994.

17. The Hanbali school, for instance, was founded by Ahmad ibn Hanbal, who died in 855 C.E.; the Maliki school was founded by Malik ibn Anas, who died in 796; the Shafi'i school by Muhammad al-Shafii, who died in 819; and the Hanifi school by Abu Hanifa, who died in 767.

18. Mujid, *An Introductory Note.*

19. *Purdah* is defined by Elizabeth Warnock Fernea as "an Indian term generally meaning the seclusion of women in separate quarters." Fernea, *Guests of the Sheik*, p. 336.

20. Engineer, *The Rights of Women in Islam*, p. 6.

21. References to slavery in the Qur'an can be found in *Sura* 2, *ayat* 177, 90:13, 9:60, and 4:92. Islam, like Christianity and Judaism, did not outlaw slavery. For a believer, emancipating a slave was an act of charity. In fact, the Prophet freed a dozen slaves (630 C.E.) and one of them, Abu Bakra, became his companion. Some Islamicists believe that certain oppressive traditions were ameliorated rather than being made unlawful because radical change was considered politically impractical. At the time, the Prophet was unifying warring tribes and establishing peaceful relations between Muslims, Jews, and Christians. One must remember that slavery was not like chattel slavery in the United States, and therefore did not present such clear moral imperatives. While the Prophet condemned slavery, he, much like the Muslim women in Los Angeles, had to prioritize political and legal reform.

22. Csordas argues that at the level of perception it is crucial to recognize

that "it is not legitimate to distinguish mind and body." He traces contemporary approaches to the study of perception to Descartes and Spinoza, who proposed a mind/body duality, or a split between cognitive/spiritual and the organic/corporeal. Csordas calls for a methodological approach to the study of culture that codes perception as the practice of both the mind and body; and by body he also means that which is beyond self-objectification. See Csordas. *The Sacred Self.*

23. Many women will simply dismiss sexist hadith, even "validated" hadith, but they cannot ignore pronouncements in the Qur'an. The Qur'an is from Allah and, therefore, generally thought to be beyond human corruption.

24. All Muslims are fundamentalists because the Qur'an is thought to be from Allah and revealed through the Angel Gabriel. Therefore, Muslims are supposed to follow both the spirit and the letter of the Qur'an.

25. I have used the word "curtain" in place of the word "screen." In my translation of the Qur'an, "screen" is used, but because Fatima Mernissi uses "curtain," I have decided to change the word to make the exegesis more understandable. See Mernissi, *The Veil and the Male Elite.* These seemingly minor changes in definition are in fact far from minor in some cases, again pointing to the myriad ways in which the Qur'an can be interpreted.

26. Mernissi, *The Veil and the Male Elite.*

27. Ibid., p. 93.

28. Zipporah [pseud.], lecture on *hijab*, tape recording, 1995, Los Angeles.

29. For an interesting discussion of the ways in which *hijab* was used as a post-colonial symbol of Malaysian unification, see Ong, "State Versus Islam: Malay Families, Women's Bodies, and the Body Politic in Malaysia."

30. Leila Ahmed, *Women and Gender in Islam,* p.130.

31. Sometimes, however, radical movements turn authorized discourse, once a tool for liberating transformation, into a tool for oppression. In Iran, where women willingly readopted the *chador* (public dress) as a symbol of antiimperialism, the government usurped the original meaning in order to reinstitute oppressive restraints on women. Mir-Hosseini, "Women and Politics in Post-Khomeini Iran."

32. Leila Ahmed, *Women and Gender in Islam;* Akbar Ahmed, *Islam Today.*

33. Bennigsen and Broxup, *Islamic Threat to the Soviet State.*

34. Zipporah [pseud.], lecture on *hijab.*

35. El-Guindi, "Veiling Infitah with Muslim Ethic."

36. Aida [pseud.], interview by author, Los Angeles, February 1993.

37. Kelley, *Yo' Mama's Disfunktional!* p. 8.

38. Zipporah [pseud.], lecture on *hijab.*

39. Afaf [pseud.], interview by author, Los Angeles, March 1994.

40. Mernissi, *Beyond the Veil,* p. 52.

41. Sunan of Abu Abd Allah Muhammad ibn Yazid ibn Maja Qazwini (9:50). See Muhammad Ali, *The Religion of Islam,* p. 448.

42. Taha, "Women in Al-Qur'aan," p. 69.

43. Ibid., p. 71.

44. Zipporah [pseud.], lecture on *hijab.*

45. While Chile has a high domestic abuse rate, I was not able to find any legal precedent in Chile or Argentina that asserts the right of a man to kill his wife or mistress. The veracity of the story is less important to me than how Aida uses it to rationalize the *ayat.*

46. Aida [pseud.], interview by author, Los Angeles, 2002.

47. For this translation, I used Amina Wahdud-Muhsin, *Qur'an and Woman* (1995), p. 68.

48. Sayyid Qutb was a famous writer and Islamicist who was hanged by Egypt's President Nasser in 1966. His writings inspire many contemporary Muslim "fundamentalists."

49. Wadud-Muhsin, *Qur'an and Women,* p. 14.

50. Esposito, *Islam: The Straight Path,* p. 80.

51. Quoted from a lecture on Islamic law and feminism given by anthropologist Ziba Mir-Hosseini at Princeton University, March 2003.

52. This hadith is from Sunan Abu-Dawud, Book 12, Number 2173, translated by Ahmad Hasan, and taken from the MSA-USC hadith search engine on the Internet.

53. Marx, *The Marx-Engels Reader,* p. 118.

CHAPTER 4: HISTORICAL DISCOURSES

1. *Purdah* is an Indian word meaning female seclusion. The African American community has adopted this term to describe women who wear both veil and *hijab.* The Prophet Muhammad's wives in the Qur'an are admonished to practice *purdah* by hiding themselves behind a screen at home when male guests are present and to hide their faces in public. (See also chapter 3.)

2. Field notes, Los Angeles, April 1991.

3. hooks, *Sisters of the Yam.*

4. Robert Dannin collected oral histories from members of African American

Sunni communities that have existed since the early twentieth century. Dannin, *Black Pilgrimage to Islam.*

5. Harding, *There is a River,* p. xii–xiii.

6. Wilmore, *Black Religion and Black Radicalism,* p. xiii.

7. Ibid., 146.

8. Garvey, *African American Political Thought, 1890–1930,* pp. 182–83; letter sent by Marcus Garvey to Booker T. Washington, February 29, 1916.

9. Ibid, p. 206.

10. Ibid., p. 176.

11. McCloud, *African American Islam,* p. 10.

12. Danin, *Black Pilgrimage to Islam.*

13. McCloud, *African American Islam,* p. 38.

14. Even the movement led by Louis Farrakhan is currently striving for "orthodoxy."

15. Dannin, *Black Pilgrimage to Islam,* p. 46.

16. Ibid., p. 47.

17. For a complete history of the Nation of Islam I highly recommend Clegg, *An Original Man;* and Evanzz, *The Messenger.* I could never do justice to the rich and complex history of the Nation and have chosen instead to highlight aspects important to the rise of Sunni Islam.

18. Haley, *The Autobiography of Malcolm X.*

19. Ibid.; Lincoln, *The Black Muslims in America;* Clegg, *An Original Man.*

20. Evanzz, *The Messenger,* pp. 49–51.

21. Lemann, *The Promised Land,* p. 63.

22. Evanzz, *The Messenger,* p. 55.

23. Lemann, *The Promised Land,* p. 65.

24. Frazier, *The Negro Family in Chicago,* p. 229.

25. Rawick, *From Sundown to Sunup,* p. 33.

26. Ibid.

27. Du Bois, *Dusk of Dawn,* pp. 311–13.

28. Higginbotham, *Righteous Discontent.*

29. Adam Green, letter to author, July 27, 2001. Green is the author of *Selling the Race: Culture and Community in Black Chicago, 1945–1955* (Chicago: University of Chicago Press).

30. Myrdal, *An American Dilemma.*

31. Maimouna [pseud.], interview by author, Los Angeles, February 1996.

32. Clearly the roots extend beyond the Nation and to communism, social-

ism, and even the Bible. However, the lineage is traceable much more directly to W. D. Mohammed and the ways in which he has refocused some of his father's teachings. The masjids have significant class and status integration, and the choice to live without material wealth is respected within the community, as is the choice to live outside mainstream society in an effort to devote oneself to Allah and the community.

33. Clegg, *An Original Man*, pp. 89–94.

34. Clegg, *An Original Man*, pp. 98–99; and Evanzz, *The Messenger*, p. 159.

35. Evanzz, *The Messenger*, p. 162

36. Clegg, *An Original Man*, p. 127.

37. Ibid., 222.

38. Evanzz, *The Messenger*, pp. 272–74.

39. Clegg, *An Original Man*, p. 217.

40. Clegg argues that Martin Luther King Jr.'s civil rights agenda was unsuccessful in the North, which is why King reached out to Elijah Muhammad. He also claims that the Nation of Islam remained strong even after the deaths of Malcolm X and Martin Luther King Jr. The tone of *Muhammad Speaks* changes from the late 1950s through the early 1970s. The paper focused more on the achievements within the community and less on defending the Nation's ideology. The reason could simply be that the organization had become more routinized. See Clegg, *An Original Man*.

41. Ibid.

42. Clifton Marsh provides more information on the transition from the perspective of the Nation of Islam. Marsh, *From Black Muslims to Muslims*.

43. Peller, *Critical Race Theory*, p. 151.

44. Peller, "Race Consciousness," p. 151.

45. Clegg, *An Original Man*, p. 277.

46. Tate, *Little X*.

47. Lubiano, "Black Nationalism and Black Common Sense," pp. 250–51.

48. Hall, "Gramsci's Relevance," pp. 435–36.

49. "The Prophet Muhammad's Last Sermon" can be found on the Internet. There are multiple sources and translations. This version was available at the masjid and is distributed by Precious International, Houston, Texas.

50. Maimouna [pseud.], interview by author, Los Angeles, February 1996.

51. Foucault, "The Eye of Power," in *Power/Knowledge*, pp. 146–65; and "Panopticism," in *Discipline and Punish*, pp. 195–208.

52. Scott, *Domination and the Arts of Resistance*, p. 81.

53. While many oppose affirmative action, some argue in favor of reparations in the form of free college or technical school education for descendants of Native Americans and African Americans until the year 2100.

54. Evanzz, *The Messenger.*

CHAPTER 5: SOUL FOOD

1. Haley, *Autobiography of Malcolm X*, p. 59.

2. Ibid.

3. The Ka'aba was built by the prophets Ishmael and Abraham and is considered God's sacred house. The Prophet Muhammad destroyed idols built on the same grounds as the Ka'aba, thus "purifying" it for the worship of God alone.

4. Witt, *Food and Politics*, p. 104.

5. See also Lubiano, "Black Nationalism and Black Common Sense"; and Sizemore, "Sexism and the Black Male."

6. Ortner, "Is Female to Male as Nature is to Culture?"

7. Collins, *Black Feminist Thought* and *Fighting Words: Black Women and the Search for Justice*; Mohanty, *Third World Women*; Moraga and Anzaldua, *This Bridge Called My Back.*

8. Claude Clegg describes how the members were required to buy a certain number of papers each week. If they did not sell the papers, they suffered the cost of each paper, not the Nation. I call the paper an "entrepreneurial venture," but perhaps that is too positive a term. Clegg, *The Original Man.*

9. Ibid, p. 51.

10. Muhammad, *How to Eat to Live* (1967), p. 6.

11. Valeri, *The Forest of Taboos.*

12. Durkheim, *Elementary*; and Douglas, *Purity and Danger.*

13. Radcliffe-Brown, *The Andaman Islanders.*

14. Valeri, *The Forest of Taboos.*

15. Muhammad, *How to Eat to Live* (1967), p. 14.

16. Collins, *Black Feminist Thought*; and Stack, *All Our Kin.*

17. This and the following quotations are from Afaf [pseud.], interview by author, Los Angeles, 1993.

18. Marsh, *From Black Muslims to Muslims.*

19. Geertz, *Islam Observed*, p. 2.

20. "Slave food" is defined as traditional black Southern cooking, including black-eyed peas, collards, pork, corn, chitlins, and other undesirable parts of the

animal. Elijah Muhammad also included foods like canned vegetables, bad meat, and some nuts.

21. Muhammad, "How to Eat to Live," p. 11.

22. Cartoon, *Muhammad Speaks*, 1975. Chicago: Muhammad Mosque of Islam No. 2.

23. In 1964 and 1965, in a number of articles in *Muhammad Speaks*, Malcolm X is referred to as a traitor or "Uncle Tom." After his assassination, a Pakistani Muslim wrote an article in tribute to Malcolm (March 5, 1965). Abdul Basit Naeem in "Demise of Malcolm," describes Malcolm as "the former 'Nation of Islam' member and one-time aide to the Honorable Elijah Muhammad," significantly reducing his role as the number-two man in the Nation. He describes Malcolm as one who had accepted Allah, but one who by separating with "our illustrious Prophet Muhammad," made a terrible mistake. Naeem is represented in this article as a follower of true Islam. He even mentions "hadith," but then has to define the word because most people reading the paper at the time would not have known what he was talking about. While he positions himself as an orthodox believer, Naeem accepts Elijah Muhammad as a Prophet of Allah. The article therefore accomplishes multiple goals of affirming the orthodoxy of the Nation of Islam, expressing condolences for Malcolm's demise, and finally asserting that "the peace-loving and law abiding Muslims" could not possibly have participated in the assassination. Naeem's article demonstrates how *Muhammad Speaks* repositioned the Nation within the *ummah* after the assassination of Malcolm X.

24. Geertz, *Islam Observed*, p. 3.

25. Wilson, *The Declining Significance of Race*.

26. This and the subsequent quotations are from Hudah [pseud.], interview by author, Los Angeles, October 1995.

CHAPTER 6: CONVERSION

1. The number twelve is based upon how I chose to count the masjids. I visited a masjid, for example, where a Muslim family had converted a room in their home in order to lead a group of Muslims in Friday prayers. I did not include this masjid in my count. Therefore, the number twelve represents only the most well-known of the masjids in Los Angeles County. Los Angeles County stretches from Pasadena to Lancaster to Malibu.

2. Carol Stone states that until the U.S. census includes questions about re-

ligion, the estimated number of Muslims in America will continue to be sketchy. Stone, "Estimates of Muslims Living in America," p. 34.

3. Zipporah [pseud.], interview by author, Los Angeles, August 1999.

4. hooks, *Sisters of the Yam*, pp. 65–68.

5. Aida [pseud.], interview by author, Los Angeles, February 1993.

6. Ibid.

7. Nadia [pseud.], interview by author, Los Angeles, September 1995.

8. Aida [pseud.], interview.

9. Nadia [pseud.], interview by author, Los Angeles, September 1995.

10. Maimouna [pseud.], interview by author, February 1996.

11. These definitions of religion are drawn from the works of Emile Durkheim, Sigmund Freud, and Bronislaw Malinowski.

12. Geertz, *The Interpretations of Cultures*, p. 90.

13. Edgerton, *Sick Societies*.

14. Richard Shweder, "The Astonishment of Anthropology," p. 16.

15. Ibid., 17.

16. Ibid., 18.

17. Giddings, *When and Where I Enter*.

18. Collins, *Fighting Words*.

19. Hamer, "It's in Your Hands."

20. Davis, *Women, Race, and Class*.

21. Beauvoir, *The Second Sex*; and Friedan, *The Feminist Mystique*.

22. Susan Faludi seems disturbed by challenges to the American feminist movement of the 1950s, 1960s, and 1970s. She even objects to the reappraisals of the feminist agenda by such feminist icons as Gloria Steinem and Betty Friedan. See Faludi, *Backlash*. A recent collection of essays addresses the diversity of "feminist" scholarship with several articles attempting to deconstruct the tension between "Western" feminists and "Third World" feminists. See Warhol and Herndl, *Feminisms*.

23. Nationalist movements include the Black Panther Party, the Nation of Islam, various Afrocentric educational movements, and liberation movements such as the Socialist and Communist Parties.

24. NOW responded poorly to multiple perspectives in their attempt to rally people to boycott a television interview with O. J. Simpson. NOW alienated many black women who had a different perspective on the murder investigation stemming primarily from a history of institutionalized racism throughout the U.S. justice system. Whether O. J. Simpson was guilty or not, NOW should have recognized the significance of promoting this unusual boycott when many mur-

der trials have questionable outcomes. NOW should have recognized the historical significance of trying to rally a community against a black man who allegedly violated a white woman. See Giddings, *When and Where I Enter*; Kennedy, *Race, Crime, and the Law.*

25. Moraga and Anzaldua, *This Bridge Called My Back.*

26. Chandra Mohanty, "Under Western Eyes," p. 52.

27. Moraga and Anzaldua, *This Bridge Called My Back.*

28. Collins, *Black Feminist Thought*, p. 222.

29. Barbara Smith believes that with the increase in black feminist scholarship she has seen an increase in black women claiming to be feminists. Smith, "The Truth That Never Hurts."

30. Thorne, *Rethinking the Family.*

31. *Al-Furqan* means "The Criterion." The Qur'an describes the *sura* as such, "This *sura* further develops the contrast between Light and Darkness, as symbolic of knowledge and ignorance, righteousness and sin, spiritual progress and degradation. It closes with a definition of the deeds by which the righteous are know in the environment of this world" (Introduction to *Sura* 25).

32. Hudah [pseud.], interview by author, Los Angeles, November 1995.

33. Collins, *Black Feminist Thought.*

34. Walker, *In Search of Our Mother's Gardens.*

35. Collins, *Black Feminist Thought*, p. 32.

36. Foucault, *Power/Knowledge*, p. 83.

37. Badran, *Feminists, Islam, and Nation*, p. 4.

38. hooks, *Talking Back*, p. 43.

39. Arebi, *Women and Words in Saudi Arabia*, pp. 289–91.

CHAPTER 7: PERFORMING GENDER

1. *al-Sahih al-Buhkari by al-Hafiz*, Abu Abd Allah Muhammad ibn Ismail al-Bukhari (67:1). In Muhammad Ali, *The Religion of Islam*, p. 446.

2. *al-Mishkat al-Masabih*, by Shaikh Wali al-Din Muhammad ibn Abd Allah. In Muhammad Ali, *The Religion of Islam*, p. 446.

3. Feminist scholarship that emerged in the United States during the 1960s and 1970s often referred to the universality of gender oppression, and to the universal association of women with the domestic sphere. For examples see Rosaldo and Lamphere, eds., *Woman, Culture and Society*; and Mohanty, Russo, and Torres, eds., *Third World Women and the Politics of Feminism.*

4. Muhammad Ali wrote, "The wife is bound to keep company with her husband, to preserve the husband's property from loss or waste, and to refrain from doing anything which should disturb the peace of the family. She is required not to admit any one into the house whom the husband does not like, and not to incur expenditure of which the husband disapproves. She is not bound to render personal service such as the cooking of food, but the respective duties of the husband and wife are such that each must always be ready to help the other. The wife must help the husband even in the field of labour if she can do it, and the husband must help the wife in the household duties. Of the Prophet himself, it is related that he used to help his wives in many small works of the household, such as the milking of the goats, patching his clothes, mending his shoes, cleansing the utensils, and so on." Ali, *The Religion of Islam*, p. 480.

5. As Fatima Mernissi notes, Khadija's age may not be historically accurate given that she conceived three sons and four daughters with Muhammad ibn Abdullah.

6. Although African American converts understand Khadija's position to be the result of Islam, Leila Ahmed and Fatima Mernissi argue that aspects of Khadija's marriage might have been typical in *jahiliya*, or pre-Islamic society. See Leila Ahmed, *Women and Gender in Islam*, p. 42. Ahmed's contentions are quite controversial; nevertheless, the type of autonomy and respect African American female converts demand as Muslims is represented in the Makkan period, or the early Qur'anic revelations (the first thirteen years of revelation). The later revelations of the Medinan period (622–30) are the ones interpreted (some would say misinterpreted) by conservative Islamic scholars as strictly regulating women's behavior. During the Medinan period, several *ayats* of the Qur'an regarding family organization were revealed. These *ayats* have been used by some religious scholars to justify men's superiority over women.

7. For further discussions of women's rights during *jahiliya*, see Mernissi, *Beyond the Veil*.

8. My estimate of the percentage of successful African American Muslim marriages is lower than the average in the United States. Estimating in this community, however, is very tricky because some converts divorced before entering the community, but after converting they have remained in one marriage. If I were to estimate the number of African American Muslims who have been divorced either before or after converting the number would be significantly higher, perhaps as high as 70 percent, if not higher. Another complication includes men who have been married to the same first wife, but have divorced more than one second wife.

9. Aida [pseud.], interview by author, Los Angeles, February 10, 1993.

10. Aida [pseud.], interview.

11. Aida [pseud.], interview by author, January 6, 1998.

12. For Aida's exegesis regarding *dharaba*, or to strike with a feather, please refer to chapter 3.

13. Aida [pseud.], interview by author, August 2002.

14. Zipporah's conversion story of her spiritual quest, and discovering the value of her own assertiveness, was discussed in chapter 6.

15. Zipporah [pseud.], interview, Los Angeles, August 1999.

16. Baudrillard, *For a Critique*, p. 60.

17. Macleod. *Accommodating Protest*.

18. Kondo, *About Face*.

19. Hutcheon, *A Poetics of Postmodernism*.

20. Wadud, *Qur'an and Woman*.

21. Maimouna [pseud.], interview by author, February 1996.

22. Afaf [pseud.], interview by author, March 1994.

CHAPTER 8: SEARCHING FOR ISLAMIC PURITY

1. Since my visit, Dar al Islam has changed its mission. According to their Website (www.daralislam.org), they have sold much of their land and have created an endowment in order to sponsor several yearly programs on Islam. Their stated mission reads: "Dar al Islam envisions an America whose people are honored by the presence of Muslims, and are aware of the values shared between Islam and those upon which America is founded. We envision an America whose institutions recognize and value the contributions that Islam and Muslims can make to its society." The Website also indicates that the North American Muslim Powwow is currently "dormant."

2. Maghrib prayer takes place just after sunset but before the last light fades.

3. Pro-Palestinian is wrongly collapsed with anti-Israeli, which is collapsed with anti-Jewish. Muslims who are overt about their faith allow themselves to be "read" by strangers and potential employers, who may, out of ignorance, be immediately hostile.

4. I know several Muslim women who either stopped wearing *hijab* because they were threatened following the attacks of September 11, 2001, or who have become hypervigilant in order to avoid being attacked.

5. Safa [pseud.], interview by author, Los Angeles, October 1996.

6. Douglas, *Purity and Danger*, p. 3.

7. Ibid.

8. Shweder and Much, "Determinations of Meaning" p. 187.

9. See Boas, *Race, Language, and Culture*; and Steward, "Evolution and Process."

10. Scott, *Weapons of the Weak*, pp. 304–50.

11. Willis, *Learning to Labor*, p. 175.

12. I actually believe that nothing exists firmly in the realm of *doxa*, or the undisputed. All ideology must continually be validated. For example, after the events of September 11, Americans were willing to accept limits on their liberties, and the liberties of others, that at other times would be considered anathema to "our democracy." See also Bourdieu, *Outline of a Theory of Practice*, pp. 164–71.

13. Hall, "What is this 'Black' in Black Popular Culture?" p. 28.

CHAPTER 9: CONCLUSION

1. Turner, *Dramas, Fields, and Metaphors*, p. 294.

2. Shweder, "Anthropology's Romantic Rebellion," p. 60.

3. Scott, *Weapons of the Weak*, p. 318.

4. Kondo, *About Face*; Strathern, *Reproducing the Future*.

5. In everyday life, structural/ideological limitations can be as innocuous as those imposed by having to obey a street sign, or the limitations can be as overwhelming as those imposed on a political candidate who believes in socialism but to say so would mean the end of her career. In order to be successful in shaping the opinions of people within our voluntary associations, we follow certain rules of engagement, but not to the exclusion of harboring a certain ambivalence to particular ideas. To voluntarily associate with the Muslim community implies an agreement at the level of faith, which becomes the platform from which people talk to one another.

6. Csordas, *The Sacred Self*.

GLOSSARY

ADHAN: call to prayer

ARHAM: mercy

ASABIYA: nation-building

AYAT: sign; Qur'anic verse

BARAQAT: prosperity and progress

BIDA: innovation of faith and practice; deviation from tradition

CHADOR: traditional *hijab* for women in Iran

DAWAH: call to Islam, propagating the faith, activities involving social welfare

DHARABA: to strike; as opposed to *darraba* – to strike intensely and repeatedly

DHIKR: remembrance of Allah, Sufi practice of repeating Allah's name in order to increase God consciousness, spiritual chanting

EID AL-ADHA: festival on the last day of the *hajj*

EID AL-FITRA: festival following Ramadan

FARD: obligatory

HADITH: narrative relating the deeds and words of the Prophet and his companions

HAJJ: pilgrimage to Mecca, one of the five pillars of the faith

HALAL: lawful, permissible

HAQQ: truth

HARAM: forbidden, prohibited, unlawful

HIJAB: veil, partition, curtain, separation, screen

HIJRA: migration of Muslims fleeing persecution from Mecca to Medina in 622 A.D.

IFTAR: breaking the fast after sunset during Ramadan

IJMA: consensus, community agreement, and a source of Islamic law

IJTIHAD: reinterpretation; in reference to Islamic modernization

IMAM: leader of prayers

ISLAH: reform

ISLAM: submission to God

KAFFIR: disbeliever

KHATWA: Islamic school

KHUTBAH: Friday sermon

JAHILIYA: the time of ignorance; pre-Islam Arabia

JANAZAH: cleansing ritual and preparation for the deceased

JANNAH: paradise

JIHAD: struggle for purity and in defense of the faith

JILBAB: traditional Middle Eastern robe/dress

JUMAH: Friday

LAILAT AL-QADR: Night of Power

MADRESSAH: school

MASJID: place for prayer and worship, mosque

MUHAJJABAH: women who wear *hijab*

MUSLIM: one who submits to God

MUSLIMA: Muslim woman

NAFS: common origin of all mankind, selves, soul

NIQAB: face veil

NISAA: woman

PURDAH: a South Asian word meaning the seclusion of women

QUIWAMAH: responsibility

RAKAH: prostrations for prayer

RAMADAN: month the Qur'an was revealed to the Prophet Muhammad and month for fasting

RAY: personal opinion in interpretation, judgment

RIJAL: man

SADAKA: charity

SALAT: daily prayer, one of the five pillars of the faith

SALATUL-ASR: late afternoon prayer

SALATUL-FAJR: early morning prayer

SALATUL-ISHA: night prayer

SALATUL-MAGHRIB: evening prayer

SALATUL-ZUHR: early afternoon prayer

SALAT-UT-TARAVIH: prayer during Ramadan

SANNATU-MUAKKADAH: prayers offered by the Prophet on occasion, not required but encouraged

SAWM: fasting, abstaining from food from sunup to sundown, particularly during Ramadan; one of the five pillars of the faith

SHAHADA: witness of faith spoken when one converts and during the daily call to prayer; one of the five pillars of the faith

SHAITAN: Satan

SHARIAH: Islamic jurisprudence

SHIRK: associating other gods and idols with Allah, polytheism

SHURA: consultation

SITR: curtain

SUHUR: predawn meal during Ramadan

SUNNAH: custom, practices of the Prophet Muhammad

SURA: chapter in the Qur'an; division of the faith

TAFSIR: religious interpretation

TAQWA: God consciousness, the desire to please Allah

TAWHID: the oneness of God, monotheism

UMMAH: community, nation

WAJID-UL-WITR: prayer during Ramadan

WALI: matchmaker

WUDU: ritual cleansing

ZAKAT: almsgiving, alms, 2.5 percent tithe levied on wealth, one of the five pillars of the faith

ZAWJ: mate, spouse

BIBLIOGRAPHY

Abu-Lughod, Lila. "The Romance of Resistance: Tracing Transformations of Power Through Bedouin Women." *American Ethnologist* 1, no. 18 (1990): 41–55.
———. *Veiled Sentiments: Honor and Poetry in a Bedouin Society.* Berkeley: University of California Press, 1986.

Adid, Rashad. *Elijah Muhammad and the Ideological Foundation of the Nation of Islam.* Newport, Va.: U.B. and U.S. Communication Systems, 1993.

Ahmed, Akbar. *Islam Today: A Short Introduction to the Muslim World.* New York: I. B. Tauris, 1999.

Ahmed, Leila. *Women and Gender in Islam.* New Haven: Yale University Press, 1992.

Arebi, Saddeka. *Women and Words in Saudi Arabia: The Politics of Literary Discourse.* New York: Columbia University Press, 1994.

Asante, Molefi Kete. *Afrocentricity.* Trenton, N.J.: Africa World, 1980.

Badran, Margot. *Feminists, Islam, and Nation:Gender and the Making of Modern Egypt.* Princeton: Princeton University Press, 1995.

Baudrillard, Jean. *For a Critique of the Political Economy of the Sign.* Ed. Charles Levin. St. Louis: Telos Press, 1981.

Baumeister, Roy, ed. *Self-Esteem: The Puzzle of Low Self-Regard.* New York: Plenum Press, 1993.

Beauvoir, Simone de. *The Second Sex.* New York: Modern Library, 1968.

Bell, Derrick. "Remembrances of Racism Past: Getting Past the Civil Rights Decline." In Herbert Hill and James E. Jones Jr., eds., *Race in America: The Struggle for Equality.* Madison: University of Wisconsin, 1993.

Bennigsen, Alexandre, and Marie Broxup. *Islamic Threat in the Soviet State.* New York: St. Martin's Press, 1983.

Boas, Franz. *Race, Language, and Culture.* New York: Macmillan, 1940.

Bourdieu, Pierre. *Outline of a Theory of Practice.* Trans. Richard Nice. Cambridge: Cambridge University Press, 1977.

Bulbeck, Chilla. *Re-Orienting Western Feminisms: Women's Diversity in the Postcolonial World.* Cambridge: Cambridge University Press, 1998.

Butler, Judith. *Bodies That Matter: On the Discursive Limits of "Sex."* New York: Routledge, 1993.

Claybourne, Carson. *In Struggle: SNCC and the Black Awakening of the 1960s.* Cambridge: Harvard University Press, 1981.

Clegg, Claude Andrew. *An Original Man: The Life and Times of Elijah Muhammad.* New York: St. Martin's Griffin, 1997.

Cohen, Ronald. "Ethnicity: Problem and Focus in Anthropology." *Annual Review of Anthropology* 7 (1978): 379–403.

Collins, Patricia Hill. *Black Feminist Thought: Knowledge, Consciousness, and the Politics of Empowerment.* Boston: Unwin Hyman, 1990.

———. *Fighting Words: Black Women and the Search for Justice.* Minneapolis: University of Minnesota Press, 1998.

Cruse, Harold. *The Crisis of the Negro Intellectual: From Its Origins to the Present.* New York: William Morrow and Company, Inc., 1967.

Csordas, Thomas. "Embodiment as a Paradigm for Anthropology." *Ethos* 18, no. 1 (1990): 5–47.

———. *The Sacred Self: A Cultural Phenomenology of Charismatic Healing.* Berkeley: University of California Press, 1994.

Dannin, Robert. *Black Pilgrimage to Islam.* New York: Oxford University Press, 2002.

Davis, Angela Y. *Women, Race, and Class.* New York: Vintage Books, 1983.

Douglas, Mary. *Purity and Danger: An Analysis of the Concepts of Pollution and Taboo.* London: Routledge, 1966.

Du Bois, W. E. B. *Dusk of Dawn.* New York: Harcourt, Brace and Company, 1940.

Durkheim, Emile. *The Elementary Forms of the Religious Life.* Trans. Joseph Ward Swain. New York: The Free Press, 1915.

Edgerton, Robert B. *Sick Societies: Challenging the Myth of Primitive Harmony.* New York: The Free Press, 1992.

El-Guindi, Fadwa. "Veiling Infitah with Muslim Ethic: Egypt's Contemporary Islamic Movement." *Social Problems* 28, no. 4 (1981).

El-Solh, Camilia Fawzi, and Judy Mabro. *Muslim Women's Choices: Religious Belief and Social Reality.* Providence, R.I.: Berg, 1995.

Engineer, Ashgar Ali. *The Rights of Women in Islam.* New York: St. Martin's Press, 1992.

Esposito, John L. *Islam: The Straight Path.* New York: Oxford University Press, 1998.

———. *Women in Muslim Family Law.* Syracuse: Syracuse University Press, 1962.

Evanzz, Karl. *The Messenger: The Rise and Fall of Elijah Muhammad.* New York: Pantheon Books, 1999.

Faludi, Susan. *Backlash: The Undeclared War Against American Women.* New York: Crown Publishers, Inc., 1991.

Fanon, Frantz. *The Wretched of the Earth.* New York: Grove Press, 1963.

Farb, Peter, and George Armelagos. *Consuming Passions: The Anthropology of Eating.* Boston: Houghton Mifflin, 1980.

Fernea, Elizabeth Warnock. *Guests of the Sheik: An Ethnography of an Iraqi Village.* New York: Anchor Books, 1965.

Foucault, Michel. *Discipline and Punish: The Birth of the Prison.* Trans. Alan Sheridan. New York: Vintage Books, 1977.

———. *The History of Sexuality: An Introduction, Volume I.* Trans. Robert Hurley. New York: Vintage Books, 1990.

———. *Power/Knowledge: Selected Interviews and Other Writings, 1972–77.* Ed. Colin Gordon. New York: Pantheon Books, 1980.

Frazer, James. *The Golden Bough: A Study in Magic and Religion.* New York: Macmillan, 1929.

Frazier, E. Franklin. *The Negro Family in Chicago.* Chicago: Chicago University Press, 1932.

Friedan, Betty. *The Feminine Mystique.* New York: Dell, 1963.

Geertz, Clifford. *The Interpretations of Cultures.* New York: Basic Books, 1973.

———. *Islam Observed: Religious Development in Morocco and Indonesia.* New Haven: Yale University Press, 1968.

Giddens, Anthony. *Capitalism and Modern Social Theory: An Analysis of the Writings of Marx, Durkheim, and Max Weber.* Cambridge: Cambridge University Press, 1971.

Giddings, Paula. *When and Where I Enter: The Impact of Black Women on Race and Sex in America.* New York: Bantam Books, 1984.

Gramsci, Antonio. *Selections from the Prison Notebooks.* Ed. Quinton Hoare and Geoffrey Nowell Smith. New York: International Publishers, 1971.

Haddad, Yvonne Yazbeck. *Contemporary Islam and the Challenge of History.* Albany: State University of New York, 1982.

———. *The Muslims of America*. Oxford: Oxford University Press, 1991.

Haleh, Afshar, ed.. *Women and Politics in the Third World*. London: Routledge, 1996.

Haley, Alex. *The Autobiography of Malcolm X*. New York: Grove Press, 1966.

Hall, Stuart. "Gramsci's Relevance for the Study of Race and Ethnicity." In *Critical Dialogues in Cultural Studies*, 411–440. New York: Routledge, 1996.

———. "What is this 'Black' in Black Popular Culture?" In *Black Popular Culture*, 20–33. Seattle: Bay Press, 1992.

Hamer, Fannie Lou. "It's in Your Hands." In *Black Women in White America: A Documentary History*, 609–14. New York: Vintage, 1992.

Haneef, Suzanne. *What Everyone Should Know About Islam and Muslims*. Des Plaines, Ill.: Library of Islam, 1985.

Harding, Vincent. *There is a River: The Black Struggle for Freedom in America*. New York: Vintage Books, 1983.

Higginbotham, Evelyn. *Righteous Discontent: The Women's Movement in the Black Baptist Church, 1880–1920*. Cambridge: Harvard University Press, 1993.

The Holy Qur'an. Ed. The Presidency of Islamic Researches, IFTA. Al-Madinah Al-Munawarah: King Fahd Holy Qur'an Printing Complex, 1405 A.H.

Homans, Margaret. " 'Women of Color': Writers and Feminist Theory." In *Feminisms: An Anthology of Literary Theory and Criticism*. New Brunswick, N.J.: Rutgers University Press, 1997.

hooks, bell. *Feminist Theory: From Margin to Center*. Boston: South End Press, 1984.

———. *Sisters of the Yam: Black Women and Self-Recovery*. Boston: South End Press, 1993.

———. *Talking Back: Thinking Feminist, Thinking Black*. Boston: South End Press, 1989.

Hutcheon, Linda. *A Poetics of Postmodernism: History, Theory, Fiction*. New York: Routledge, 1988.

Kelley, Robin D. G. *Yo' Mama's Disfunktional! Fighting the Culture Wars in Urban America*. Boston: Beacon Press, 1997.

Kennedy, Randall. *Race, Crime, and the Law*. New York: Vintage Books, 1997.

Kondo, Dorinne. *About Face: Performing Race in Fashion and Theater*. New York: Routledge, 1997.

Kozol, Jonathan. *Savage Inequalities: Children in America's Schools*. New York: Crown Publishers, 1991.

Kristeva, Julia. *Powers of Horror: An Essay on Abjection.* New York: Columbia University Press, 1983.

Lave, Jean, and Etienne Wenger. *Situated Learning: Legitimate Peripheral Participation.* Cambridge: Cambridge University Press, 1991.

Lemann, Nicholas. *The Promised Land: The Great Black Migration and How It Changed America.* New York: Alfred A. Knopf, 1991.

Lincoln, C. Eric. *The Black Muslims in America.* Boston: Beacon Press, 1961.

Lubiano, Wahneema. "Black Nationalism and Black Common Sense: Policing Ourselves and Others." In Wahneema Lubiano, ed., *The House That Race Built.* New York: Vintage Books, 1998.

Macleod, Arlene Elowe. *Accomodating Protest: Working Women, the New Veiling, and Change in Cairo.* New York: Columbia University Press, 1991.

Madhubuti, Haki. *Enemies: The Clash of Races.* Chicago: Third World Press, 1978.

Madyun, Gail. *Being Muslim: A Rites of Passage Manual for Girls.* Los Angeles: Gail Madyun, 1993.

Mahmood, Saba. "Rehearsed Spontaneity and the Conventionality of Ritual: Disciplines of *Salat.*" *American Ethnologist* 28, no. 4 (2001): 827–53.

Malcolm X. *February 1965: The Final Speeches of Malcolm X.* New York: Pathfinder, 1992.

Marsh, Clifton. *From Black Muslims to Muslims: The Resurrection, Transformation, and Change of the Lost-Found Nation of Islam in American, 1930–1995.* Lanham, Md.: Scarecrow Press, 1996.

Marx, Karl. *The Marx-Engels Reader.* Ed. Robert C. Tucker. New York: W. W. Norton and Co., 1978.

Mauss, Marcel. *Sociology and Psychology: Essays.* London: Routledge and Kegan Paul, 1979.

McCloud, Aminah Beverly. *African American Islam.* New York: Routledge, 1995.

Mernissi, Fatima. *Beyond the Veil: Male-Female Dynamics in Modern Muslim Society.* Bloomington: Indiana University Press, 1987.

——. *The Veil and the Male Elite: A Feminist Interpretation of Women's Rights in Islam.* Trans. Mary Jo Lakeland. Reading, Mass.: Addison-Wesley Publishing Co., 1987.

Mintz, Sidney. *Sweetness and Power: The Place of Sugar in Modern History.* New York: Viking, 1985.

——. *Tasting Food, Tasting Freedom: Excursions into Eating, Culture, and the Past.* Boston: Beacon Press, 1996.

Mir-Hosseini, Ziba. "Women and Politics in Post-Khomeini Iran: Divorce, Veiling, and Emerging Feminist Voice." InHaleh Afshar, ed., *Women and Politics in the Third World*. London: Routledge, 1996.

Mohanty, Chandra Talpade. "Under Western Eyes: Feminist Scholarship and Colonial Discourses." In Chandra Talpade Mohanty, Ann Russo, and Lourdes Torres, eds., *Third World Women and the Politics of Feminism*. Bloomington: Indiana University Press, 1991.

Mohanty, Chandra Talpade, Ann Russo, and Lourdes Torres, eds. *Third World Women and the Politics of Feminism*. Bloomington: Indiana University Press, 1991.

Moore, Henrietta L. *Feminism and Anthropology*. Minneapolis: University of Minnesota Press, 1988.

Moraga, Cherrie, and Gloria Anzaldua. *This Bridge Called My Back: Writings by Radical Women of Color*. New York: Kitchen Table; Women of Color Press, 1983.

Morley, David, and Kuan-Hsing Chen, eds. *Stuart Hall: Critical Dialogues in Cultural Studies*. New York: Routledge, 1996.

Muhammad, Elijah. *How to Eat to Live*. Chicago: Muhammad's Temple of Islam No. 2, 1972.

———. *How to Eat to Live*. Chicago: Muhammad's Mosque of Islam No. 2, 1967.

———. "How to Eat to Live." *Muhammad Speaks* (1965).

———. *Message to the Blackman in America*. Chicago: Muhammad's Mosque of Islam No. 2, 1965.

Muhammad Ali, Maulana. *The Religion of Islam*. Columbus, Ohio: Ahmadiyya Anjuman Ishaat Islam, 1990.

Mujid, Muhammad. *An Introductory Note to Change in Muslim Personal Law*. New Delhi: 1982.

Myrdal, Gunnar. *An American Dilemma: The Negro Problem and Modern Democracy*. New York: Harper and Brothers, 1944.

Nelson, C., and V. Olesen. "Veil of Illusion: A Critique of the Concept of 'Equality' in Western Feminist Studies." *Catalyst* (1977): 8–36.

Niebuhr, Gustav. "Studies Suggest Lower Count for Number of U.S. Muslims." *New York Times*, 25 October 2001.

Omi, Michael, and Howard Winant. *Racial Formation in the United States from the 1960s to the 1990s*. New York: Routledge, 1994.

Ong, Aihwa, and Michael G. Peletz, eds. *Bewitching Women, Pious Men*. Berkeley: University of California Press, 1995.

Ortner, Sherry B. "Is Female to Male as Nature Is to Culture?" In *Woman, Culture and Society*. Stanford: Stanford University Press, 1974.

Peller, Gary. "Race Consciousness." In Kimberle Crenshaw, Neil Gotanda, Gary Peller, and Kendell Thomas, eds., *Critical Race Theory: The Key Writings that Formed the Movement*, 127–58. New York: The New Press, 1995

Rawick, George. *From Sundown to Sunup: The Making of a Black Community*. Westport, Conn.: Greenwood Publishing Company, 1972.

Rosaldo, Michelle Z., and Louise Lamphere. *Woman, Culture and Society*. Stanford: Stanford University Press, 1974.

Scott, James C. *Domination and the Arts of Resistance*. New Haven: Yale University Press, 1990.

———. *Weapons of the Weak: Everyday Forms of Peasant Resistance*. New Haven: Yale University Press, 1985.

Shweder, Richard A. "Anthropology's Romantic Rebellion Against the Enlightenment, or There's More to Thinking Than Reason and Evidence." In Richard Shweder and Robert LeVine, eds., *Culture Theory: Essays on Mind, Self, and Emotion*, 27–66. Cambridge: Cambridge University Press, 1984.

———. "The Astonishment of Anthropology." In Richard Shweder, ed., *Thinking Through Cultures: Expeditions in Cultural Psychology*. Cambridge: Harvard University Press, 1991.

Shweder, Richard A., and Nancy Much. "Determinations of Meaning: Discourse and Moral Socialization." In Richard Shweder, ed., *Thinking Through Cultures: Expeditions in Cultural Psychology*, 186–240. Cambridge: Harvard University Press, 1991.

Simic, Andre. "The Ethnology of Traditional and Complex Societies." Paper presented at the annual meeting of the American Association for the Advancement of Science. Washington, D.C., 1975.

Sizemore, Barbara. "Sexism and the Black Male." *Black Scholar* (March–April 1973).

Smith, Barbara. "The Truth that Never Hurts: Black Lesbians in Fiction in the 1980s." In Chandra Mohanty, Ann Russo, and Lourdes Torres, ed., *Third World Women and the Politics of Feminism*. Bloomington: Indiana University Press, 1991.

Stacey, Judith. *Brave New Families: Stories of Domestic Upheaval in Late-Twentieth-Century America*. Berkeley: University of California Press, 1990.

Stack, Carol. *All Our Kin*. New York: Basic Books, 1974.

Steele, Claude. "A Threat in the Air: How Stereotypes Shape Intellectual Identity and Performance." In Jennifer L. Eberhardt and Susan T. Fiske, eds., *Confronting Racism: The Problem and the Response*. Thousand Oaks, Calif.: Sage Publications, 1998.

Steward, Julian. "Evolution and Process." In *Anthropology Today*. Chicago: University of Chicago, 1953, 313–326.

Stone, Carol. "Estimates of Muslims Living in America." In Yvonne Yazbeck Haddad, ed., *The Muslims in America*. Oxford: Oxford University Press, 1991.

Stowasser, Barbara Freyer. *The Islamic Impulse*. London: Croom Helm, 1987.

———. *Women in the Qur'an, Traditions, and Interpretation*. Oxford: Oxford University Press, 1994.

Strathern, Marilyn. *Reproducing the Future: Anthropology, Kinship, and the New Reproductive Technologies*. New York: Routledge, 1992.

Taha, Daa'iyah Muhammad. *Women in Al-Qur'aan*. Oakland, Calif.: American Islamic Life, 1993.

Tate, Sonsyrea. *Little X: Growing Up in the Nation of Islam*. San Francisco: Harper, 1997.

Taussig, Michael T. *The Devil and Commodity Fetishism in South America*. Chapel Hill: University of North Carolina Press, 1980.

Thorne, Barrie, and Marilyn Yalom, eds. *Rethinking the Family: Some Feminist Questions*. Boston: Northeastern University Press, 1992.

Turner, Victor. *Dramas, Fields, and Metaphors: Symbolic Action in Human Society*. Ithaca: Cornell University Press, 1994.

Valeri, Valeria. *The Forest of Taboos: Morality, Hunting and Identity among the Huaulu of the Moluccas*. Madison: University of Wisconsin Press, 2000.

Visweswaran, Kamala. "Histories of Feminist Ethnography." Annual Reviews of Anthropology 26 (1977): 591–621.

Wadud, Amina. *Qur'an and Woman: Rereading the Sacred Text from a Woman's Perspective*. New York: Oxford University Press, 1999.

Wadud-Muhsin, Amina. *Qur'an and Woman*. Kuala Lumpur: Penerbit Fajar Bakti Snd. Bhd., 1995.

Walker, Alice. *In Search of Our Mother's Gardens: Womanist Prose*. San Diego: Harcourt, Brace, Jovanovich, 1983.

Warhol, Robyn R., and Diane Price Herndl. *Feminisms: An Anthology of Literary Theory and Criticism*. New Brunswick, N.J.: Rutgers University Press, 1997.

Weber, Max. *The Sociology of Religion*. Boston: Beacon Press, 1963.

West, Cornel. *Race Matters*. Boston: Beacon Press, 1993.

Williams, Rhonda M. "Living at the Crossroads: Explorations in Race, Nationality, Sexuality, and Gender." In Wahneema Lubiano, ed., *The House That Race Built*, 136–56. New York: Vintage Books, 1998.

Willis, Paul. *Learning to Labor: How Working Class Kids Get Working Class Jobs*. New York: Columbia University Press, 1977.

Wilmore, Gayraud S. *Black Religion and Black Radicalism: An Interpretation of the Religious History of Afro-American People.* New York: Orbis Books, 1984.

Wing, Adrien Katherine. *Critical Race Feminism: A Reader.* New York: New York University Press, 1997.

Wintz, Cary D., ed.. *African American Political Thought, 1890–1930: Washington, Du Bois, Garvey, and Randolph.* Armonk, N.Y.: M. E. Sharpe, 1996.

Witt, Doris. *Black Hunger: Food and the Politics of U.S. Identity.* Oxford: Oxford University Press, 1999.

INDEX

234–35n32. *See also* financial responsibility; wealth
materialism, 143, 202–3
Mauss, Marcel, 228n36
McCloud, Amina Beverly, 5, 86
Mecca, 10, 11, 61, 107
Medina, 38, 61, 69
mercy. *See arham*
meritocracy, 186
Mernissi, Fatima, 61–62, 70, 232n24, 240nn5,6
Message to the Blackman in America (Elijah Muhammad), 5
"metaphors of anti-structure," 211
Middle East, 50, 96
Middle Eastern cuisine, 109
migration, black, 83, 88–89
milhafa, 230n2
millenarian beliefs, 84, 104
Million Man March, 32, 100
miqna', 230n2
Mir-Hosseini, Ziba, 77, 227n30, 233n51
Miriam, 7–8
modesty, 25, 60–61, 64
Mohammed, Warith Deen: on food, 118, 124–25; *Muslim Journal* and, 21; Nation of Islam and, 96, 99, 234–35n32; Sunni Muslim movement and, 96, 102–3, 125, 234–35n32; WCIW and, 97–98
Mohanty, Chandra, 2, 144
monotheism. *See tawhid*
Moorish Science Temple, 85, 86
moral codes, 58–59
moral fields, 23, 228n37
moral truths, 186
moral worlds, 18, 204
moral yardsticks, 89–92
morning ritual, 24–25, 229n2
mosques. *See* Masjid al-Mustaqim; Masjid Ummah; masjids
Much, Nancy, 184–85
muhajjabah, 8, 11, 244

Muhammad, Abdul, 189
Muhammad, Akbar, 96
Muhammad Ali, 240n4
Muhammad Ali, Maulana, 21, 229n4
Muhammad al-Shafi'i, 231n17
Muhammad, Clara, 13, 88, 94
Muhammad, Elijah: on dress codes, 66; on food taboos, 109–11, 115–18, 123, 124–25; on gender roles, 4–5, 224n11; Malcolm X and, 95–97; Martin Luther King, Jr., and, 97, 235n40; Nation of Islam and, 87–88, 94–99, 102, 115; on self-hatred, 42
Muhammad Speaks, 1, 97, 109, 117, 235n40, 236–37nn8,23
Muhammad, Wallace. *See* Mohammed, Warith Deen
Mujid, Muhammad, 58
Muslim calendar, 230n5
Muslim feminists, 151, 170
Muslim Journal, 1, 21, 125
Muslim Mosque, Inc. (Harlem), 97
Muslim population growth, 127–28, 226n21, 237–38n2
Muslim Prayer Book, The, 121
Mustafa, 181
mustalah al-hadith, 229n3
Myrdal, Gunnar, 92

NAACP (National Association for the Advancement of Colored People), 90, 99
Nadia: on Christianity, 40–41, 231n7; on conversion, 136–37, 238nn7,9; on divorce, 220–21; on gender roles, 53–55; Nation of Islam and, 32; on self-worth, 43; Sister-to-Sister meetings and, 37; *tafsir bil ray* and, 57
Naeem, Abdul Basit, 237n23
nafs, 46, 244
nail polish, 31, 35
narrative praxis, 135–38
narrative therapy, 133–35

Compositor:	Binghamton Valley Composition
Text:	10/15 Janson
Display:	Janson
Printer and Binder:	Maple-Vail Manufacturing Group